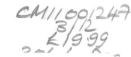

Jame
of rel
argui   es
shoul   nt
of ne   re
of the

This   er
of rel   1g
a sig   ne
is mc   is
affec   1y
of the   1s
that l   .y.
The   re
all in   re
listed   )n
to so

Eilee   ol
of Ec   2d
into 2   1d
the a   0-
edite   er
and (es
that

The Centrality of Religion in Social Life

Essays in Honour of James A. Beckford

Edited by

EILEEN BARKER
London School of Economics, UK

ASHGATE

Published by
Ashgate Publishing Limited
Wey Court East
Union Road
Farnham
Surrey, GU9 7PT
England

Ashgate Publishing Company
Suite 420
101 Cherry Street
Burlington
VT 05401-4405
USA

www.ashgate.com

British Library Cataloguing in Publication Data
The centrality of religion in social life : essays in honour of James A. Beckford
    1. Religion and sociology I. Beckford, James A. II. Barker, Eileen, 1938–
    306.6

Library of Congress Cataloging-in-Publication Data
Barker, Eileen, 1938–
    The centrality of religion in social life : essays in honour of James A. Beckford / Eileen Barker.
        p. cm.
    Includes bibliographical references and index.
    ISBN 978-0-7546-6515-1 (hardcover : alk. paper) 1. Religion and sociology. I. Beckford, James A. II. Title.

    BL60.B27 2008
    306.6—dc22

                                                                        2008009559

ISBN 9780754665151 (hbk)
ISBN 9781409403432 (pbk)

Mixed Sources
Product group from well-managed forests and other controlled sources
www.fsc.org Cert no. SGS-COC-2482
© 1996 Forest Stewardship Council
FSC

Printed and bound in Great Britain by
TJ International Ltd, Padstow, Cornwall

Contents

List of Contributors

Véronique Altglas holds an ESRC fellowship at the faculty of Social and Political Sciences, at the University of Cambridge, where she is teaching in the Department of Sociology. She has a PhD from l'Ecole Pratique des Hautes Etudes (Paris). Her research interests include the globalization of religion, transformations of religiosity in modern societies, and cross-national comparisons of the responses to religious diversity. She has conducted research on the diffusion of neo-Hindu movements in the West, on the management of minority religions in France and Britain, and on anti-Semitism in France. She is currently conducting a study of Rav Berg's Kabbalah movement. Recent publications include: *Le Nouvel Hindouisme Occidental.* Paris: Éditions du CNRS, 2005.

Eileen Barker, OBE, FBA, is Professor Emeritus of Sociology with Special Reference to the Study of Religion at the London School of Economics. Her main research interest is new religious movements, and the social reactions to which they give rise; but since 1989 she has also been studying the religious situation in post-communist countries. Over 250 publications (in 27 languages) include the award-winning *The Making of a Moonie: Brainwashing or Choice?* and *New Religious Movements: A Practical Introduction.* In 1988, with support from the Government and mainstream Churches, she founded INFORM, a charity based at the LSE, providing information about minority religions. She is a past President of the *Society for the Scientific Study of Religion* and the *Association for the Sociology of Religion*, Honorary Life President of *ISORECEA*, and a recipient of the *American Academy of Religion's* Martin E. Marty Award for the Public Understanding of Religion.

Grace Davie has a personal Chair in the Sociology of Religion in the University of Exeter. She is a past-president of the American *Association for the Sociology of Religion* (2003) and of the Research Committee 22 (Sociology of Religion) of the *International Sociological Association* (2002–2006). In 2000–2001 she was the Kerstin-Hesselgren Professor in the University of Uppsala, where she returned for the 2006–2007 academic session. In 2005 she spent a semester at Hartford Seminary, CT. In addition to numerous chapters and articles, she is the author of *Religion in Britain since 1945* (Blackwell 1994), *Religion in Modern Europe: a Memory Mutates* (OUP 2000), *Europe: the Exceptional Case* (DLT 2002), *The Sociology of Religion* (Sage 2007), co-author of *Religious America, Secular Europe? A Theme and Variations* (Ashgate 2008), and co-editor of *Predicting Religion* (Ashgate 2003).

Jay Demerath is the Emile Durkheim Distinguished Professor of Sociology Emeritus at the University of Massachusetts, Amherst, where he arrived as Chair in 1972 following a Harvard A.B., a University of California, Berkeley PhD, ten years at the University of Wisconsin, Madison, and two years as Executive Officer of the

American Sociological Association. He is a past-President of the Society for the Scientific Study of Religion, the Association for the Sociology of Religion, and the Eastern Sociological Society. A specialist in religion and politics at home and abroad, his three most recent books are *Crossing the Gods: World Religions and Worldly Politics* (Rutgers 2001); *Sacred Circles and Public Squares: The Multicentering of American Religion* (Indiana 2004 with A. Farnsley); and *The Sage Handbook for the Sociology of Religion* (Sage, 2007, co-edited with James Beckford).

Karel Dobbelaere is Emeritus Professor of the Catholic University of Leuven (Louvain, Belgium) and of the University of Antwerp (Belgium) where he taught sociology, sociology of religion and sociological research. He is member of the *Royal Flemish Academy of Belgium for Sciences and Fine Arts* (Section of Human Sciences), and of the *Academia Europaea* (Section of Human Sciences). He was a visiting fellow of All Souls College (Oxford University, 1977, 1990 and 1991), the Nanzan Institute for Religion and Culture (Nagoya, Japan, 1984), Sofia University (Tokyo, 1984), and the *Institut de Recherche sur les Sociétés Contemporaines* (CNRS, Paris,1994), and a visiting professor at Kent State University (Ohio, USA, 1969 and 1989). He has more than 200 publications, including 20 books. His main fields of interest are: religious and church involvement, pillarization, new religious and sectarian movements, and secularization.

Sophie Gilliat-Ray is a Senior Lecturer in the School of Religious & Theological Studies at Cardiff University, and Director of the Centre for the Study of Islam in the UK, established in 2005. She has authored and co-authored a number of academic books and scholarly journal articles, as well as contributing to edited volumes. With James Beckford, she co-authored *Religion in Prison: Equal Rites in a Multi-Faith Society* (Cambridge University Press 1998). She is Chair of the Advisory Board at the Centre for Research in Ethnic Relations (CRER) at the University of Warwick, and on the editorial board of the journal *Fieldwork in Religion*. From 1997–2000 she was the Convenor of the *British Sociological Association Sociology of Religion Study Group*.

Danièle Hervieu-Léger was born in 1947. She holds academic degrees in political science, law and sociology, including Docteur d'Etat en Lettres et Sciences Humaines (Paris Sorbonne). She is currently Professor at l'Ecole des Hautes Etudes en Sciences Sociales (Paris). In 2004 she was elected President of the *EHESS*. Her 17 books, translated into several languages, include: *La religion pour mémoire* (Paris: Cerf 1993; translated into English as *Religion as a Chain of Memory* (Cambridge: Polity Press 2000); *Les identités religieuses en Europe* (edited with G. Davie, Paris: La Découverte 1996); *Le Pèlerin et le convert: La religion en mouvement* (Paris: Flammarion 1999); *Sociologies et religion: Approches classiques en sciences sociales des religions* (with J.P.Willaime, Paris: PUF, 2001); *La religion en miettes ou la question des sectes* (Paris: Calmann-Lévy 2001); and *Catholicisme français: La fin d'un monde* (Paris: Bayard 2003).

Thomas Luckmann is Professor Emeritus at the University of Constance, Germany. He studied at the Universities of Vienna and Innsbruck and at the New School for Social Research in New York. His work has ranged over such areas as the sociology of religion, the sociology of knowledge, the sociology of communication and the philosophy of science. In 1966 he wrote, with Peter Berger, *The Social Construction of Reality: A Treatise in the Sociology of Knowledge*. Other publications include *The Invisible Religion: The Problem of Religion in Modern Society* (1967), *The Sociology of Language* (1975), and *Life World and Social Realities* (1983), and, with Alfred Schütz, *The Structures of the Life-World* (volume 1, 1973; volume 2, 1983). In 1978, he edited the Penguin reader, *Phenomenology and Sociology*, and in 1989 he edited (with James Beckford) *The Changing Face of Religion* (Sage). He holds honorary doctorates from the Universities of Linköping (Sweden), Ljubljana (Slovenia), Trondheim (Norway) and Trier (Germany), and was a Fellow at the Center for Advanced Studies in Behavioral Science at Stanford.

David Martin, OBE, is Emeritus Professor of Sociology at the London School of Economics and Adjunct Professor at Liverpool Hope University. He is author of some twenty books and three hundred articles concerned in particular with secularisation, the relation of religion and politics, religion and war, and the growth of Pentecostalism. His main titles include *A General Theory of Secularisation* (1978); *Tongues of Fire* (1990), *Does Christianity Cause War?* (1993); *Pentecostalism: The World Their Parish* (2002); and *On Secularization* (2005).

Meredith McGuire (PhD, New School for Social Research) is Professor of Sociology and Anthropology at Trinity University, San Antonio, Texas. She is past-President of both the *Society for the Scientific Study of Religion* and the *Association for the Sociology of Religion*, as well as an active member of other national and international associations in sociology and anthropology. Her books on religion include: *Lived Religion: Faith and Practice in Everyday Life* (Oxford University Press 2008), *Religion: The Social Context* (5th edn. 2002), *Ritual Healing in Suburban America* (1988), and *Pentecostal Catholics* (1982). She is also co-editor of *Personal Knowledge and Beyond: Reframing the Ethnography of Religion* (2002). Her current research examines everyday religious practices and spirituality in an historical and cross-cultural context.

Enzo Pace is Full Professor of Sociology and Sociology of Religion at Padova University, Italy. Visiting Professor at l'Ecole des Hautes Etudes en Sciences Sociales in 1995 and 2000, and President of the *International Society for the Sociology of Religion (ISSR)*. His membership of Scientific Committees includes: the *Observatoire de Sociologie de la Religion de la Suisse de l'Université de Lausanne*; *ISORECEA (International Association of Sociology of Religion in Eastern and Central Europe)*; and the *Social Scientists of Religion Association of the Cono Sur* (Latin America). His main research areas are: secularization and de-secularization; new religious movements; fundamentalism; sociology of Islam; Pentecostalism and new ethnic Churches in Europe. Recent publications include: *Sociologia dell'Islam* (2004); *Perché le religioni scendono in guerra?* (2005); *Los fundamentalismos* (2006);

'Salvation Goods, the Gift Economy and Charismatic Concern', *Social Compass* 2006 (47); *Introduzione alla sociologia delle religioni*, (Roma: Carocci, 2007) and *Raccontare Dio. La religione come comunicazione*, (Bologna, Il Mulino, 2008).

James T. Richardson, JD, PhD, is Director of the Grant Sawyer Center for Justice Studies at the University of Nevada, Reno, where he also directs the Judicial Studies graduate degree program for trial judges and other justice related programs. He earned his PhD in Sociology from Washington State University and his JD degree from Nevada School of Law, Old College. His research interests include the intersection of law and religion, especially the use of the legal system to exert control over new religions and other minority faiths. He also specializes in social and behavioural science evidence, a course he teaches in the Judicial Studies program. His numerous publications include the edited volume *Regulating Religion* (2004).

Susumu Shimazono is Professor in the Department of Religious Studies of the University of Tokyo, and has published widely on modern and contemporary religious movements as well as on modern Japanese religions in general. Although focussing mainly on empirical and historical research on religions in Japan, he has always been interested in comparisons with the West and various parts of Asia. His publications in English include *From Salvation to Spirituality: Popular Religious Movements in Modern Japan* (2004) and, with Mark Mullins and Paul Swanson (eds), *Religion and Society in Modern Japan* (1993). Recent Japanese publications include *A Genealogy of Healing Knowledge* (2003). His work on Aum Shinrikyo (*Gendai Shukyo no Kanousei* 1997) has been widely cited in Japan and the West. He has taught at the University of Chicago, l'Ecole des Hautes Etudes en Science Sociales, and Eberhardt Karls Univesitaet Tuebingen. Most recently he has been working on the interface between religion and medicine, including bioethics and the new interdisciplinary area of the death and life studies.

Jennifer Shoemaker is a doctoral student in the Social Psychology PhD program at the University of Nevada, Reno, working under the direction of James Richardson, and is a research assistant at the Grant Sawyer Center for Justice Studies. She holds an M.A. in Professional Counselling from the Illinois School of Professional Psychology. Her research interests include religious motivation, growth and management of religious-based non-profits, and cultures of world religions, including a recent presentation regarding Western attitudes toward individuals of perceived Middle Eastern religions at the 2007 *Society for the Scientific Study of Religion* conference in Tampa, FL. She also has done research on the Religious Freedom Restoration Act and on the European Court of Human Rights.

David Voas is Simon Professor of Population Studies in the Institute for Social Change at the University of Manchester. After studying at the London School of Economics and Cambridge he spent many years outside academic life prior to returning to a university post. During the past six years he has been principal investigator on ten projects funded by UK research councils. He is particularly interested in the social mechanisms of secularization, the fertility transition, cross-national comparisons of intergenerational change and related topics. He has recently started work on creating an online centre for British data on religion, funded by the AHRC/ESRC Religion and Society research programme. His work has been published in *Sociology*, the *British Journal of Sociology*, *American Sociological Review*, *Population and Development Review* and elsewhere.

Margit Warburg, Dr Phil. is a sociologist of religion and Professor, at the University of Copenhagen. She is a member of the advisory board of the Ministry of Ecclesiastical Affairs concerning religions outside the Danish Lutheran Church. She is also co-chair of the *Research Network on New Religions (RENNER)*, and of the priority area of the University of Copenhagen's *Religion in the 21st Century*. She has published widely on the Baha'i religion and has also written about East European Jewry and civil religion. Her research interests are recruitment and conversion, religion and demography, and religion, migration and globalisation. Among her publications are *New Religions and New Religiosity* (Aarhus University Press 1998, edited with Eileen Barker), *Baha'i*, (Signature Books 2003); *Religion and Cyberspace* (Routledge 2005, edited with Morten T. Højsgaard) and *Citizens of the World. A History and Sociology of the Baha'is from a Globalisation Perspective* (Brill, 2006).

Jean-Paul Willaime, born in 1947, has been Director of Research at l'Ecole Pratique des Hautes Etudes, Department of Religious Studies, Sorbonne, Paris since 1992. He is also Director of the European Institute of Religious Studies and President of the *International Society for the Sociology of Religion (ISSR/SISR)*. He studied Protestant theology, philosophy and sociology at the Universities of Strasbourg, Lausanne and Groningen, with Doctorates in Religious Studies (1975) and Sociology (1984) from Strasbourg University, where he taught from 1975 to 1992. His research covers mainline and evangelical Protestantism; the sociology of ecumenism; religions and school education; Europe and religions; history and theories in the sociology of religion. His publications include: *Profession: pasteur. Sociologie de la condition du clerc à la fin du XXe siècle* (1986); *La précarité protestante* (1992); *Sociologie des Religions* (3ème éd. 2004); *Sociologies et religion: Approches classiques* (with D. Hervieu-Léger 2001); *Le religieux dans la commune* (ed. with F. Frégosi 2001); *Europe et religion: Les enjeux du XXIe siècle* (2004); *Sociologie du protestantisme* (2005) and *Des maîtres et des dieux* (ed. with S. Mathieu 2005). English publications include 'Religion in Ultramodernity', in *Theorizing Religion: Classical and Contemporary Debates*, J. A. Beckford and J. Walliss (2006), *Religion and Education in Europe: Developments, Contexts and Debates* (eds with R. Jackson, S. Miedema, W. Weisse 2007).

Introduction

Eileen Barker and James T. Richardson

James A. Beckford: Sociologist

James Arthur Beckford is one of the foremost sociologists of religion in the world today. His writings have been influential throughout the world, not merely in academia, but also in informing policy in a number of practical fields ranging from new religious movements to the prison service. On first acquaintance, Jim Beckford might seem rather quiet and unassuming – as, indeed, he is. One does not, however, have to spend all that much time with him before recognising his unusual strengths and his depth of character. He has gained the widespread respect and affection of both students and colleagues throughout the globe both as a visiting scholar and as a frequent participant, speaking and serving as an officer at international conferences. Although quintessentially British, Jim is completely at home in France and in French; he can read scholarly works in several other languages – and has recently been adding Japanese to his linguistic accomplishments.

Having begun his academic life by obtaining a First Class Honours degree in French Studies from the University of Reading in 1965, Beckford decided to move into sociology and turned his attention to a doctoral study of the British Watch Tower movement. He was determined to combine both theoretical analysis and empirical investigation from the outset. As well as conducting extensive interviews and distributing numerous questionnaires, he spent four years observing Jehovah's Witnesses in their homes, in congregations, in large assemblies and in public evangelism. In this endeavour he was greatly helped and influenced by Dr Bryan R. Wilson of All Souls College, Oxford, whose sociological perspective on the study of sectarian organisations was to remain with him throughout his career. In 1972 Beckford was awarded a PhD from the University of Reading, and his thesis was published three years later as the now-classic monograph, *The Trumpet of Prophecy: A Sociological Study of Jehovah's Witnesses*.

Beckford's teaching career started while he was still pursuing his doctorate – from 1966 to 1973 he taught as a Lecturer in Sociology at Reading. He then took a similar post at Durham University, being promoted to Senior Lecturer in 1978. Ten years later he left Durham for an appointment as Professor of Sociology at Loyola University in Chicago, returning to England in 1989 to take up a Chair as Professor of Sociology at the University of Warwick, where he remained until his retirement in 2007. Around the world there are literally thousands of men and women – be they professors, researchers, politicians, journalists, business men, housewives or nuns – who owe an enormous debt to Jim for all he taught them and the concern he showed for their welfare while they were students. They, like all who know him, will remember his reliable scholarship, his enthusiasm for the subject, and his quiet, but truly delightful, sense of humour.

Beckford's international career had begun with an invitation to be a Visiting Associate Professor at Carleton University in Ottawa in 1974. Since then, he has been a Visiting Scholar at Tsukuba University in Japan (1978), a Fulbright Senior Visiting Fellow at the University of California, Berkeley and the Graduate Theological Union (1982–83). He has also lectured at numerous universities and other institutions around the world, particularly enjoying the time he has spent in Paris at the *Ecole des Hautes Etudes en Sciences Sociales* (2001) and the *Ecole Pratique des Hautes Etudes* (2004).

Beckford's honours and achievements include his being awarded a D.Litt. in 1985 by the University of Reading and, in 2004, his election as a Fellow of the British Academy. He was the founder and first convenor of the British Sociology Association's Study Group for the Sociology of Religion in 1975 and its Chairman from 1978 to 1983. He has held various offices in the International Society for the Sociology of Religion (SISR), serving as Vice-President from 1995–99, and President from 1999–2003. He also has served in several posts with the Association for the Sociology of Religion (ASR), and was President from 1988–89. For someone to have served as President of both the SISR and the ASR, one centred in Europe and the other in North America, is an indication of the esteem in which Beckford is held by his colleagues around the world. He has, furthermore, been active in the International Sociological Association, being a delegate to its Research Council from 1982–86, editor of the Programme for the 1986 World Congress of Sociology in New Delhi, and a Vice-President from 1994–98. He was also President of the ISA's Research Committee (RC22) for the Sociology of Religion from 1982 to 1986. Advisory posts that he has held in other countries include membership of the Irish Research Council's Assessment Board and of the *Conseil Scientifique* of the *Observatoire des Religions* in Switzerland. More recently his ground-breaking research on religion in prisons has led to his being a member of the Race and Diversity Training Advisory Group of the Prison Service of England and Wales, and a member of the scientific council of the national research programme on *Enjeux sociologiques de la pluralisation religieuse dans les prisons suisses*, funded by the Swiss National Research Council.

The quantity of editorial work that Beckford has done over the years for his profession is prodigious. He edited *Current Sociology*, the journal of the International Sociological Association from 1980–87, and has been a member of the Editorial Board for *Sage Studies in International Sociology*, chaired the Editorial Committee of the SISR, and served as an associate editor for *Sociological Analysis*, *Review of Religious Research*, and *International Sociology*. He has also served on the editorial boards of numerous other scholarly endeavours, including *Religion, Identity and Culture*, *The Journal of Contemporary Religion*, the *Encyclopedia of Politics and Religion*, *Arxius*, *The British Journal of Sociology*, and *Religion – Staat – Gesellschaft*. He has, moreover, been a member of the Steering Committee of the *Dictionnaire des Faits religieux* since 2004.

Beckford has also been in considerable demand as an external examiner for both Bachelor and higher degrees, mainly in Sociology but also in Religious Studies and related fields. He has served in such a capacity in well over a dozen British and numerous overseas universities, including the National University of Singapore, the University of California, Berkeley, Loyola of Chicago, Paris, Florence, Copenhagen, Århus and Florence.

The international flavour of Beckford's work is once again evident in the research funding that he has received over the years. Apart from several UK grants from such bodies as the Nuffield Foundation, the Leverhulme Trust, the Social Science Research Council, the Church of England and the Office of the Deputy Prime Minister, he has received funding from the European Centre for Social Welfare Training and Research, the United States-United Kingdom Educational Commission, UNESCO's Division of Human Rights and Peace, UNESCO's Division of International Development of the Social Sciences, the Agnelli Foundation, and the Japan Society for the Promotion of Science.

The list of Beckford's publications is impressive by any standard. He has five single-authored books to his credit, all of which demonstrate his intellectual prowess and research abilities. These are his classic study of the Jehovah's Witnesses, *The Trumpet of Prophecy* (1975), *Religious Organization* (1975), the much-cited *Cult Controversies: Societal Responses to New Religious Movements* (1985), *Religion and Advanced Industrial Society* (1989), and *Social Theory and Religion* (2003). He has also co-authored two books: *Religion in Prison: Equal Rites in a Multi-Faith Society* (with Sophie Gilliat, 1998) and *Muslims in Prison: Challenge and Change in Britain and France* (with Danièle Joly and Farhad Khosrokhavar, 2005), the 1989, 2003 and 2005 volumes having been translated, respectively, into Italian, Polish and French. Add to these a number of edited and co-edited volumes and special issues of journals, including *New Religions and Rapid Social Change* (1986), *The Changing Face of Religion* (1989) with Thomas Luckmann; *Secularization, Rationalism and Sectarianism* (1993) with Eileen Barker and Karel Dobbelaere, *Challenging Religion: Essays in Honour of Eileen Barker* (2003) with James Richardson, *Theorizing Religion: Classical and Contemporary Debates* (2006) with John Wallis, and, most recently, with Jay Demerath, the impressive 746-page *Sage Handbook of the Sociology of Religion* (2007).

We shall not attempt to discuss the nearly 150 journal articles and chapters in edited works that Beckford has produced over his long career, starting in 1972 with his first publication in *A Sociological Yearbook of Religion in Britain*. However, a selection of these is included at the end of this volume as an appendix to which we would refer readers. We shall, however, now try to illustrate just a few of the major themes running through his work, especially those that are taken up by the contributors to this volume.

Major Themes in Beckford's Work

James A. Beckford can be described as both a sociologist of religion and as a social theorist. He has, in fact, stated on more than one occasion that his life's work has been an attempt to draw those too often distinct fields of study together, and to integrate the sociology of religion more fully into the corpus of sociology with its many subdisciplines. He laments that sociology of religion scholarship is so often devoid of any ties with other areas of sociological study and with classical sociological theory, and that developments in these other areas seldom refer to that ubiquitous area of human experience, religion. In most, if not all, of his publications, he has warned that sociologists ignore religion at their peril, and that a comprehensive understanding of contemporary society cannot be acquired without an understanding of the complexities of religious expression in today's world. His introduction to *Religion and Advanced Industrial Society* opens with the following statement.

> The modern sociology of religion is remarkably self-contained. It has its own concepts, theories and general problematics .... But its links with other fields of sociology are, at best, tenuous. As a result, it is rare for studies of religion to be based on, or to influence, broad ideas about the dynamics and problems of today's societies. The main aim of this book is to show how the estrangement between sociology of religion and other fields of sociology has taken place and what its consequences are for sociological studies of religion.
>
> .... modern religion presents sociologists with *theoretical* problems. It challenges many taken-for-granted assumptions about their models of modernity. (1989: xi, his emphasis)

This theme is reiterated fourteen years later in the opening words of *Social Theory and Religion*:

> This book begins at a point where my *Religion and Advanced Industrial Societies* (1989) ended. My main argument there was that religion had been at the very centre of the first generation of sociological and anthropological classics, but that, over the course of the twentieth century, it had moved into a marginal position ... [of] insulation against, and isolation from, the principal currents of social scientific thinking. (2003: 1)

In this major book Beckford adopts a social constructionist approach to examining modern-day religion, and presents us with a series of chapters deconstructing concepts, such as secularization, pluralism, and globalization, that are central to the sociology of religion. In these chapters he is understandably critical of the many definitions used sometimes too casually by scholars. He takes issue with the major thrust of traditional secularization theory, and describes in considerable detail the evidence that counters any notion that religion is losing a role in human affairs, arguing that '... debates about secularization are a dialogue of the deaf. The antagonists talk past each other and cannot agree on ways to resolve their differences.'(ibid: 68)

The 'vagaries of pluralism' are also subjected to Beckford's critical assessment. He examines some simplistic uses of the term 'pluralism' that refer to various types of religious diversity, and urges that the focus should be on levels of acceptance of the diversity that exist in most modern societies. He argues that pluralism should be considered from a normative perspective – in short, pluralism should be a value sought in the diversity of contemporary societies. His treatment of the term globalization is notable primarily for its severe critique of most globalization theorists for ignoring the obviously important role played by religion in the modern world. He also offers a convincing discussion of how certain types of religion have profited from and promoted certain aspects of globalization.

But, as already intimated, Beckford's work embraces empirical studies as well as theoretical commentary. Through his exploration of societal reactions to new religious movements (NRMs) in the United States, Britain, France and Germany, he demonstrates comparative sociology at its best. The basic conclusion he reaches in his influential and frequently cited *Cult Controversies* is that the controversies reveal more about the societies in which they are occurring than they do about the movements themselves:

> ... today's NRMs are significant mainly for being indicative of several tendencies emerging in contemporary western societies. The movements may be relatively unimportant in themselves, but their limited success and modes of operation can throw light on the social conditions which facilitated them. At the same time, however, it is essential to keep in mind that ... the *opposition* to NRMs is in itself no less indicative of prevailing social and cultural conditions. 'Cult controversies' are very revealing about taken-for-granted notions of normality. And anti-cult campaigns in particular have brought to light some interesting cross-national differences in ideas about the nature of perceived threats to the social, moral, and religious fabric of western societies. (1985: 282, his emphasis)

More recently, Beckford's research has been concerned with ground-breaking scholarship on the place of religion in prisons. The work has resulted in his being involved in significant ways in policy-making in both the United Kingdom and France. The first such book, *Religion in Prison* (1998), is a careful study of the way that the religious experiences of prisoners in the UK are handled in a society that is becoming ever more religiously diverse. The domination of the Church of England in the Prison Chaplaincy Service is examined, and the Church's role in 'brokering' the access of other religious representatives is criticized as being out of step with the changing social context. Again, there is a strong comparative emphasis in the research, comparisons being made in particular with how growing religious diversity is dealt with in the United States.

The second and more recent book on the subject, *Muslims in Prison* (2005), compares how the disproportionately growing numbers of Muslim prisoners are treated in French and British prisons. Despite, or perhaps because of France's *laïcité*, Muslim inmates find themselves discriminated against – because all are officially treated equally as part of a single, indivisible culture, they are unable to receive halal food and have few opportunities for collective worship. Britain, however, has tended to favour the integration of religious and ethnic minorities into a 'community of communities', fostering diversity as a basis for social cohesion. As a result, British prisons are more likely to facilitate and, to some extent thereby, control the practice of Islam, while, by attempting to discourage the practice, French prisons can sow the seeds of extremism.

The significant differences between the two nations found by Beckford and his co-authors have given rise to fresh insights and further reflection about what Western societies can do to deal with this escalating problem. The volume, simultaneously published in French and English, is having an impact not only in France and Britain, but elsewhere throughout Europe and North America. It promises to be another classic that will provide a major reference for understanding not only the dynamics of prison life for Muslims, but also for providing insight into the much wider issues related to the challenges of multi-religious societies.

The policy implications of Beckford's work are evident, but his contributions to 'making a difference' in society are not confined to the ivory tower of academia. For almost twenty years he has served as the BSA's Sociology of Religion Study Group's representative on the Board of Governors of Inform, an NGO supported by the British government and mainstream Churches, which provides information about minority religions that is as objective and up-to-date as possible.[1] He is also one of Inform's Vice-Chairs and the Chairman of its Management Committee, a responsibility that involves frequent (often daily) contact with other members of the Committee and the office staff. His work for Inform exhibits just one example of both his dependability and his generosity in being prepared to give time and consideration to ensuring the results of research based on social science methodology can be utilised to the best advantage – particularly in preventing unnecessary suffering through actions arising out of ignorance and/or misinformation.

Off Duty

Despite the prodigious amount of work Jim has undertaken throughout his career, it would be a great mistake to think of him as the 'dull boy' of all work and no play. While he may be internationally known in academic circles as a scholar of renown, he is also known to his friends as an enthusiastic grower of leeks, an impressive runner, and a voracious tourist, whose delight in discovering the hot tub in California can be matched by the awe he experienced on seeing the carvings in Khajuraho and his pride at having observed a black mamba at perilously close quarters while on safari in the Kruger National Park. And, like most proud grandparents, Jim requires little encouragement to produce the latest photograph and relate the miraculous achievements of his young grandchildren – and some may be surprised to learn that one of his more challenging retirement preoccupations is mastery of the skills of unicycling.

In an environment that is frequently charged with rivalries, resentments and backstabbing, Jim's popularity is exceptional and unquestionable. It would not have been difficult to have invited twice the number of scholars to join this venture. The sixteen (drawn from eight different countries) who have contributed are all internationally acclaimed academics, and all of them know Jim both as a colleague and as a friend – all have enjoyed both intellectual exchanges and the occasional cup of coffee, glass of wine and/or tot of Glenturret with him in some foreign clime. They were asked to provide a chapter that would add to our understanding of the centrality of religion in contemporary society, which, as we have seen, is a subject that Jim has forcefully and repeatedly insisted needs far more attention within social science than it has received. Exactly how the contributors interpreted this challenge

---

1   For further information about Inform (Information Network on Religious Movements), see www.Inform.ac.

was left for them to decide, and each of them has responded in his or her own way to Jim's *cri de coeur*.

The French Connection

Grace Davie took on the task at a personal level, explaining how Jim's work has affected and, indeed, provided a point of reference for her own research and teaching. She combines the point that Beckford made so clearly over twenty years ago in *Cult Controversies* that an understanding of the place of new religious movements in any society depends as much on the society as it does on the new religions themselves, with his point that one needs to understand both its religious history and its current situation to recognise the way any particular society functions. Sharing with Beckford an interest in the situation in France, Davie takes that country to illustrate the point, comparing it to Britain and other countries and drawing on the conceptual clarity offered by Beckford in his analysis of the different meanings of pluralism, she directs us to the apparent paradox that while France is both constitutionally and institutionally a more democratic society than Britain, Britain is a more tolerant one than France.

Davie's chapter is followed by three French scholars who provide us with further insights into the French situation. Danièle Hervieu-Léger sketches an intellectual history of European religiosities, demonstrating the interconnected developments of two conflicting notions – a close God and a distant God. It is, she concludes, necessary to study the diverse configurations of the relationship between modernity and spirituality over the past four centuries if we wish to refine our understanding of the 'new religions', which, it can be shown, do not embody completely new ways of being individual, but emerge as a logical consequence of 'the incorporation of the spiritual quest in a psychological modernity characterised by the individual concern for self-fulfilment'.

Jean-Paul Willaime addresses the tensions that underlie *laïcité*, a concept that has long confused many a non-French scholar – and can also present a challenge for the French. In institutional and legal terms, *laïcité* stands for a separation between church and state that respectfully protects the freedom of the religious and the non-religious alike. It has, however, been manifest in certain times and places as a secularist suspicion of religions, the new religious movements and Islam being, in recent years, a particular focus of tension. Having traced the historical grounds of French *laïcité*, Willaime guides us through the ways in which the religious diversity increasingly found in contemporary France has engendered both secular tensions and, more recently, a more broad-minded regulation in the form of 'a benevolent neutrality' toward religious belief. A generation after Beckford's *Cult Controversies*, Véronique Altglas provides further empirical illustration for Willaime's analysis of the 'paradox of *laïcité*' by presenting an account of the controversies surrounding what are now referred to as *les dérives sectaires* or 'sectarian deviations'. Starting with the murders and suicides perpetrated by the Order of the Solar Temple in the mid-1990s, and the French parliamentary Report with its notorious list of 172 'dangerous' movements, Altglas guides us through the intricacies of French law and the organisations set up by the French government to combat sectarian deviations – and some of the tensions within the government arising in response to these organisations. Concurrently, we learn about the activities of the French 'anti-cult movement' and, as yet another part of the ongoing controversies, the emergence of an 'anti-anti-cult movement'.

The next chapter is written by the Belgian scholar, Karel Dobbelaere, who compares the *laïcité* found in Belgium with that in France. Dobbelaere starts from the stance that, while Protestant countries tended to undergo a process of 'latent secularization', when religion and internally related social sub-systems occurred simultaneously, in Catholic European countries there was a process of 'manifest secularization' with conflict and tensions arising between the Church and the institutions over which it had wielded authority – this being as a result of the conscious and intended process of functional differentiation. However, although the term *laïcité* can be applied equally to both France and Belgium, in France the term refers as a constitutional and legal principle to the nation-state, the *République Laïque*, while in Belgium it refers to a particular group, the *culte laïque*, which, alongside the Catholic Church and other recognized religions, offers the public services such as education and health.

Religious Insertions in Society

In *Cult Controversies*, Beckford suggests that a useful way of approaching new religious movements is to ask how they are inserted into their societies. In this section, we start with an examination of how an older religion that is new to a particular society adjusts to the new society *without* controversies. Enzo Pace asks how it is that Sikh immigrants manage to be so successful in adapting to European society, and reaches the conclusion that the inner-worldly mysticism of the Sikh conception of religion and ethics has an 'elective affinity' with 'the spirit of adaptation to the social and economic order of this world'. Sikh inner-worldly mysticism, while mobilizing the individual to act in *this* world, links the meaning of such action to a transcendental, yet immanent, purpose. Because worship involves working in the world, Sikhs can uproot themselves from their original environment and adapt to the rules and regulations of the host society.

There is a sense in which the next chapter turns the theme of the previous one on its head. For Jay Demerath, 'a movement without a crisis is a movement with a crisis'. Not all crises are functional for a movement, but, he persuasively argues, some undoubtedly are. Movements and organisations sometimes exploit and often depend on crises both as a source of their basic missions and as aids in pursuing these missions. Crises can, Demerath suggests, be conceptualised into four main types, depending on whether they are external or internal on the one hand, and cultural or structural on the other. His argument that movements sometimes require enemies more than friends sheds an interesting light on the earlier discussions about the controversies in France and elsewhere, and on the conclusions of the following chapter by James T. Richardson and Jennifer Shoemaker, who focus on decisions concerning minority religions in the European Court of Human Rights (ECHR), which they see as the most important court of human rights in the world and, since the *Kokkinakis* case in 1993, a major constructor of religious freedom in contemporary society. Richardson and Shoemaker take us through a number of recent ECHR cases relating in particular to France and to Russia, using the comparison to re-examine an earlier hypothesis posited by Richardson and Garay concerning a possible double standard in the Court's decisions, with Russia being dealt with 'in an almost perfunctory manner' compared to France, an original member of the Council of Europe. Their conclusion is that although France has now received some negative decisions, they remain undecided as to whether these are of the same 'weight' as those found against Russia. In other words, they consider that the jury is still out on exactly what messages the ECHR is sending to societies with minority religions inserted in their midst.

David Voas examines the relative lack of success that Jehovah's Witnesses (JWs) have experienced since the early 1980s in inserting their religion into Europe and the Americas. His analysis of the statistical data leads him to question the 'supply-related' propositions proffered by Stark and Iannaccone, offering instead a demand-related explanation. He suggests that each society has a particular niche but, once this has reached a saturation point, there will be no more 'customers' to which the 'religious product' is likely to appeal. Of interest in the light of Demerath's chapter is an exchange between Voas and Beckford, the issue here being the extent to which the relative failure that JWs experience in their missionising efforts can be given a positive spin. How far, they debate, might failure be interpreted as a sign that the end time really is imminent, and how far does it lead to discouragement? And to what extent could 'a modest dose of martyrdom … help to build solidarity'?

Margit Warburg's chapter also considers processes involved in joining a minority religion, but from a micro rather than a macro perspective. Having reviewed a number of sociological approaches to conversion, she points to the usefulness of Beckford's depiction of JWs' 'conversion accounts' as constructions (which can, nonetheless, give us valuable information), and of George W. Brown's distinction between 'situational causality' and 'distal causality'. Warburg then illustrates how the researcher might analyse conversion accounts, providing examples from her own study of conversion among the Baha'is of Denmark, and finally suggests that a useful comparison can be made between conversion and conversion accounts on the one hand and the process of falling in love and the construction of courtship stories on the other hand.

The chapter by Sophie Gilliat-Ray takes us back to the macro level with its concern about ways in which a minority religion may be inserted into particular institutions of a society. She starts off from the research that she conducted with Beckford for the report on the Church of England and other faiths in Britain and their book *Religion in Prison*. She traces the somewhat intricate and sometimes challenging processes whereby a minority religion (in this case, Islam) moved from a situation in which it was allowed to have 'visiting ministers' on an individual and *ad hoc* basis in prisons and hospitals, to one in which it became part of the institutionalised structure of the prison service and the National Health Service, with a state-supported and increasingly professionalized chaplaincy, together with a growing awareness of the rights of Muslims as British citizens and their role in the public life of British society.

Religion, Power and Politics

The topic of David Martin's chapter is that of the confrontation between the Christian transcendent vision of peace on earth on the one hand and the secularity of politics, power and violence on the other hand. Drawing on a rich assortment of sociological, historical, literary and theological sources, Martin weaves a tapestry of intertwined and interacting themes and counter-themes, tracing the fortunes of voluntary groups and 'the social sacred', whilst confronting the rationality of religion in the public square.

Some of his themes can be found also in the chapter by Thomas Luckmann, although Luckmann is telling a significantly different story. Luckmann describes how, while power and powerlessness are universal elements of the human condition, these are experienced in very different ways according to time and place. In archaic society, human beings were helpless in the face of God and the Church, and power, law and economy were 'fused' as part of an all-embracing kinship system; in contemporary Western society, functionally 'rational' economic and political norms have increasingly replaced religious norms – 'first went the fear of the Inquisition, and then the fear of hell.' The close control over the individual is anonymous and discontinuous, but with a space of solitary freedom within the interstices of the social structure.

The Spiritual and/or the Religious?

The chapter by Eileen Barker starts with a quotation from Beckford in which he states that one aspect of the sacred that is currently undergoing re-location is the relationship between conceptions of religion and spirituality. This is a theme that is taken up by three of the contributors, each from a different continent. Barker's contribution attempts to locate spirituality among the other kinds of worldviews on offer in contemporary society, contrasting it in some ways with secularisms on one hand and conservative religiosities on the other. She then draws an ideal-typical distinction between the two poles of spirituality and religiosity and, having described briefly some of the ways spirituality is conceptualised, draws on some survey material to test the kinds of meanings that being a spiritual person may have for respondents. One possibly unexpected discovery is that those who define themselves as spiritual-*and*-religious are likely to be closer to the ideal-typical religious pole than those who define themselves as religious-but-not-spiritual.

Moving to a country that, like France, has long fascinated Beckford's intellectual curiosity, the next chapter comes from the Japanese sociologist of religion, Susumu Shimazono who uses his concept of the 'New Spiritual Movements and Culture' (NSMC) – a concept somewhat akin to the New Age in the West – to explore a trend towards resacralization in contemporary Japan. Those participating in the NSMC tend to think of themselves as being spiritual rather than religious; they believe they are espousing a new worldview that has overcome the defects of both traditional religion and modern science, and that while they are aiming for a personal 'self-transformation', this can result in a global transformation. Shimazono illustrates the ways in which the NSMC has entered into such institutional spheres as the medical and welfare services, education and national ritual. He concludes a process of resacralization can be observed as the NSMC spreads throughout an increasing number of spheres in the Japanese national consciousness.

The following chapter is also concerned with ways in which a sociological analysis of 'spirituality' reveals important features of both the private and the public aspects of religion in contemporary society. In her contribution too, Meredith McGuire discusses the possibility of being spiritual but not religious, and in the process of drawing an historical comparison between understandings of spirituality and religiosity, points to four key elements shared by contemporary and earlier forms of popular spirituality: religious eclecticism; materiality and attention to the human body (which can be associated with sensual ways of being spiritual); pragmatic concerns (which may range from finding ways that 'work' to obtain health, a new job or a new washing machine); and, finally, a blurring of boundaries between the sacred and the profane. McGuire's conclusion is that by using the term spirituality, she wants to convey a sense of an individual 'condition in process'. In contrast to 'religiosity', she argues, 'spirituality' might be used to refer to patterns of spiritual practices and experiences that comprise individual 'religion-as-lived'.

The incorporation of the concept of spirituality into the sociology of religion does not, of course, diminish the need for the social sciences to recognise the centrality of religion in society, far less does it diminish the need for sociologists of religion to look beyond their sub-discipline. On the contrary, it stresses the importance of Beckford's argument by expanding traditional conceptualisations of religion and promoting an increasing awareness of the centrality of religion in all its changing contemporary forms at all levels of contemporary social life.

As always, thanks must be expressed to those who helped produce this volume. Sarah Lloyd and her colleagues at Ashgate were consistently cheerful and helpful. Inform's Research Officer, Sarah Harvey, edited the bibliographies and painstakingly searched for inconsistencies in the citations, and Peter Barker judiciously scanned the text for infelicities and typos and brewed copious cups of coffee. But finally, and most importantly, all of us thank Jim for everything he has given to us, and to many others, over the years by way of challenging ideas, scholarly inspiration, unstinting support and an enduring friendship. With gratitude, respect and affection we wish him a deservedly long and happy retirement.

PART I
The French Connection

CHAPTER 1

Thinking Sociologically about Religion:
Contexts, Concepts and Clarifications

Grace Davie

There are some publications which become touchstones of debate – they are also points of reference for individual scholars. James (Jim) Beckford's writing has provided many such, for the profession as whole, but also for me personally. In this contribution I will exemplify what I mean with three rather different illustrations, all of which have helped me to 'think sociologically' about religion. Not only this: all three have contributed extensively to my teaching in this field. All three, finally, reveal the centrality of religion to social life.

The first takes as its starting point Beckford's knowledge of France – an interest that I have shared from the outset of my career. More precisely, I have gleaned from Beckford's writing in this field a more developed awareness of the importance of context in framing the debate about religion in any given country. I will explore this with reference to the work on new religious movements, first in France and then elsewhere – paying particular attention to the post-communist countries of central and East Europe. My second illustration is rather different and derives from Beckford's insistence that the sociology of religion should take more notice of the sociological mainstream and vice versa. In stressing this point, Beckford has proved himself unusually prescient – anticipating by a decade or two the significance of religion in the public sphere. For obvious reasons, mainstream sociologists are now expressing an interest in religion; conversely at least some in the sub-discipline are beginning to engage the debates in the mainstream. From both points of view, the recent writing of Jose Casanova (1994; 2006) and Jürgen Habermas (2005; 2006) offer particularly telling comments in that they interrogate the philosophical underpinnings of this shift.

None of these 'conversations' will prosper, however, without proper conceptual clarity. Learning both to understand and to apply effectively the conceptual infrastructure of the discipline is central to Beckford's work. In this chapter, I have taken the example of religious pluralism to illustrate this approach, an idea which reflects once again Beckford's interest in new religious movements – keeping in mind that debates about the latter can be seen as a precursor to the work on larger minorities now present in almost all European societies, most notably Islam. Grasping the implications of Islam for the future of Europe has become a crucially important feature of political debate, in which Beckford is a key player. More specifically, his insights into the care of prisoners from the minority faiths have attracted the attention of policy-makers as well as social scientists. Effective policies, moreover, depend for their success on the clarity of thought that lies behind them.

One more introductory remark is necessary before continuing. Some five years ago, Jim Beckford, together with Jim Richardson, edited a festschrift for Eileen Barker (Beckford and Richardson 2003). Now a similar volume is being produced for Jim Beckford. I have been privileged to be a contributor to both books, but have discovered that I need in one or two places to use somewhat similar passages of text in my argument – the reason being precisely that the writing of both scholars has been formative in the sub-discipline. I hope that Jim and Eileen will be happy to 'share' these sections of my, or perhaps more accurately their, thinking. Jim Richardson's meticulous editing of a long text on *Regulating Religion* (Richardson 2004), which includes a number of essays on France, completes the trio.

Cult Controversies: a Formative Text in the Sociology of Religion

Beckford's contribution to our understanding of sects and new religious movements is indisputable, not least the reminder to his readers that while the numbers involved in these movements are tiny, the issues that they raise are considerable. *Cult Controversies: The Societal Response to New Religious Movements* (1985) is now more than twenty years old. It remains, however, a text that I habitually recommend to students, in that it explains more clearly than any other the following – crucial – point: that a full understanding of the place of new religious movements in any given society, depends as much on the society in question as it does on the religious movements themselves, and nowhere more so than in France. Nearly two decades later, it is interesting to reflect on a contribution whose importance is now self-evident. Such self-evidence, however, is more clearly seen in retrospect than it was at the time, given the somewhat different emphases in the sub-discipline that prevailed in the 1980s.

In the mid post-war decades the debate about new religious movements – though intense – was largely an Anglo-Saxon industry. This is easily explained in the sense that the discussion fitted well with American denominationalism, and reasonably well with the more moderate pluralism (in both a descriptive and normative sense) of Britain. In Latin Europe, sociological work in the period had a rather different emphasis; it too was concerned with non-standard beliefs and practices, but in the form of popular religion – more precisely of popular Catholicism. Interesting regional studies were central to this endeavour (Hervieu-Léger 1986). Some thirty years later, the situation has changed dramatically. New religious movements remain a crucial aspect of the sociological agenda, but in different parts of the world – most notably in France and in the post-communist countries of Europe.[1] The reasons are clear enough and endorse a point already made: that such movements are important, not so much for themselves, but for what they reveal about the societies of which they are part. The questions they raise, moreover, go to the core of the sociological debate, in which the careful conceptualizations of Beckford resonate at every stage.

---

1   That is not to say that work in this field has disappeared in Britain and the United States, but it has certainly diminished relatively speaking.

Each of these statements requires expansion. The starting point, however, is clear enough: it lies in an increase in religious diversity in practically all modern societies, within which new religious movements form a significant element. But even a cursory glance at the data reveals both that new religious movements take root more easily in some places than in others, and that they are treated in very different ways. By and large, societies which have been religiously plural from the start or which have learnt over time to accommodate diversity – the Anglo-Saxon variant – simply extend this to new forms of religious life (albeit more easily to some than to others). Conversely, societies which once enjoyed a religious monopoly, or quasi monopoly, react rather differently; here the resistance to new religious movements raises important issues of religious freedom. Normative questions can no longer be avoided – indeed in many parts of Europe, they dominate the debate. The French case is not the only European society where this occurs, but has become something of a *cause célèbre*.

A first, and very crucial, step in understanding the specificity of the French situation was taken by Beckford himself in 1985. This essay, the penultimate chapter in *Cult Controversies*, draws directly on David Martin's analysis of secularization (Martin 1978), but uses this in innovative ways. It is this step that I find intriguing. Just as the historic churches form different 'patterns' across Europe in terms of their modes of secularization, so too do the minority groups, including new religious movements – and for exactly the same reasons. Particular features can be identified which have predictable effects both for the process of secularization and for the management of innovative forms of religious life. One such feature is the state. In France the state assumes a moral quality, becoming itself an actor in the religious field; no other European society exhibits this tendency to quite the same degree. The particular difficulties facing new religious movements in France derive very largely from this situation. In effect they are hemmed in on two sides, by a monopoly church (historically speaking) and a monopoly state – they are victims of a classic 'double whammy'. The reasons, as ever, can be found in the past.

A full account of the historical process can be found in Davie (1999). Here the story will begin in 1905, the culmination of a notably acrimonious separation of church and state. The 1905 law has iconic status in France;[2] it symbolizes the moment when 'church' finally gave way to 'state' as the dominant institution in French society. Two parallel organizations emerged, one Catholic and one secular, each with its own set of beliefs, institutions and personnel. Even more important, however, are the default positions set in place in the course of this process: what did and what did not count as religion in the French context? The system that was worked out at the beginning of the twentieth century was predicated on a particular understanding of religion, one which could encompass the Catholic Church, the historic forms of Protestantism and Judaism, but not much else.[3]

---

2   Hence, the elaborate commemorations – including significant publications – in 2005 (see for example Baubérot 2005).

3   Recognition of these minorities came gradually in France. Centuries of persecution predated gradual acceptance during the eighteenth century, which was formalized at the time of the Revolution.

The situation at the beginning of the twenty-first century, examined in some detail by Hervieu-Léger (2001a; 2001b), is markedly different. Innovative forms of religious belief, including new religious movements,[4] have exploded in France just as they have everywhere else, causing immense strain on the system. More precisely, the checks and balances so carefully worked out in 1905 are thrown into disarray. A model that has served France well for the best part of a century cannot cope, either conceptually or institutionally, with the forms of religion that are presenting themselves at the start of the new millennium. Hervieu-Léger puts this as follows:

> ... the system topples when the mesh of the confessional net is strained by the multiplication of groups and movements claiming religious status and demanding the benefits of a freedom taken for granted in democratic societies. In reaction to the anarchic proliferation of self-proclaimed and extradenominational religious groups, *laïcité's* deep-rooted suspicion that religious alienation poses a constant threat to freedom is tending to resurface. (Hervieu-Léger 2001b: 254)

A whole range of factors come together in these sentences: the frameworks (both legal and conceptual) set in place in 1905, the quintessentially French notion of *laïcité* (itself related to French understandings of the Enlightenment), the transformation of the religious scene in the late twentieth century, and the clearly normative reactions of French officialdom and the French public to these changes. These reactions reveal the fundamental points: first, the definitional issue – what can and cannot count as religion and who should decide; and second, a persistent and at times worrying reflex – a widespread and very French belief that religion as such might be a threat to freedom. The size of the questions are, it seems, inversely related to the size of the movements in question.

Interestingly, very similar debates are now happening in other parts of Europe, not least those that were under communist domination in the post-war decades. Here the historic forms of religion had been pushed to the margins, never mind the minorities. Post 1989, the structures and ideologies of communism imploded, releasing spaces for religion that had not existed for several generations. In most places the mainstream churches have re-emerged to fill the gaps, some more successfully than others, but new forms of religion have also flooded in through open borders. The questions that follow are by now becoming familiar: which forms of religion are to be welcomed and which are not, and who is to decide? The debate has repeated itself in one country after another in the search not only for democratic institutions, but also for the philosophies that underpin these. Just as in France, it is the rapid deregulation of the religious field that has prompted the discussion; the catalyst is the same in each case.

The place of the mainstream churches within these debates is interesting. Paradoxically, or perhaps not, in those parts of Europe where the mainstream churches themselves were victims of pressure or worse, there is in many places a marked resistance to new forms of religious life. The historic churches, having reclaimed the centre, are reluctant to share their hard won freedoms with a multitude of competing denominations. Instead these essentially territorial institutions conspire to 'protect' both the physical spaces of which they are part and the populations who live therein.

---

4   New religious movements are still known as 'sects' in the French case.

Attempts to manage these encounters are fraught with difficulty. They involve, amongst other things, the writing of constitutions and the administration of finance and property, the details of which impinge on many vested interests, calling into question centuries-old assumptions about local as well as national power. A detailed discussion of these issues cannot be pursued here, except to remark that Beckford's conceptual clarity (see below) is not always as present in these discussions as it ought to be.[5] Given the tumultuous circumstances in which such arrangements were worked out, this is hardly surprising; at times, however, the attempts to find solutions to these very difficult issues create almost as many problems as they solve – debates that will continue well into the twenty-first century.

This section has moved some way from its origins in the French case. It was, however, in this connection that I learnt two things from Beckford's work: one general (the need to take context seriously) and one specific (the detail of the French situation). Some thirty to forty years ago, I applied the latter knowledge to my own doctoral project which concerned the Protestant community in France. At the time Jim Beckford taught sociology at the University of Reading, where I was linked with a group of graduate students, though formally registered elsewhere. More recently, I have used this knowledge in rather different ways: not only to further my understanding of France itself but to create a more effective comparative perspective. Both will re-emerge in the course of this chapter.

Religion and the Sociological Mainstream

For the best part of two decades, the 'insulation' and 'isolation' of the sociology of religion from the principal currents of sociological thinking has formed a dominant theme in Beckford's writing. Two important volumes epitomize this way of working: *Religion and Advanced Industrial Society* published in 1989 and, a decade and a half later, *Religion and Social Theory* (2003). Bearing both books in mind, the following section explores selectively the reasons for the 'problem' and its partial, and continuing, resolution.

Over several decades, mainstream sociologists – indeed social scientists in general – have ignored the significance of religion. Why is this so? The question is all the more significant given the centrality of religion to the founding fathers of the discipline. It is also much discussed. A full account of the gradual exclusion of religion from the sociological canon, together with the repercussion for the sub-discipline, cannot be engaged in this chapter,[6] which will focus on one point in particular: that is the relationship between the European roots of social scientific thinking and a *particular* rather than general process of modernization. Such an approach, moreover, provides an obvious link between this section and the previous one, in that the discussion will underline the significance of the context – economic, social and cultural – for the development of social scientific reflection, just as its

---

5   See in particular the case studies brought together in Richardson (2004).
6   Quite apart from Beckford's own work, Davie (2007) covers this point in some detail.

predecessor did for the development of religious institutions, whether large or small. The specificity of the French case forms part of the same conversation.

The key to the argument lies in recognizing that secularization – as a theory as well as a process – emerged initially to explain a set of changes in the religious situation of modern Europe. Exactly when this process began, and for what reasons, constitutes a core debate in social science. The contributions are many and varied. All of them, however, recognize that a critical moment occurred as Europe began bit by bit to industrialize, and at the same time to urbanize. Both industrialization and urbanization were problematic for the historic churches of Europe for the following reasons. These were churches that were rooted in territory: that is to say they were organized on a territorial (parochial) model, and – precisely because of this – they were deeply embedded in a primarily rural, pre-industrial model of society. Unsurprisingly, this essentially static model was unable to adapt quickly enough to the very different forms of society that were beginning to emerge – hence the crisis from which they have never fully recovered. Of course the process took place differently in different parts of the continent, but take place it did – inexorably. The parish churches of Europe were literally 'left behind', increasingly out of touch with the cities in which their 'people' now resided.

Equally important to this story are the philosophical shifts that underpin the changes taking place. Modern scholarship is torn between commonality and difference in its accounts of the Enlightenment.[7] By and large, however, the European Enlightenment – especially in its French forms – becomes not only an intellectual revolution that permitted the various innovations central to the industrial revolution, but a movement opposed to religion. It becomes, in fact, a means of achieving a *freedom from* (religious) belief and from the institutions that sustained not only the belief systems themselves but also the patterns of behaviour that went with these. Voltaire's famous cry '*écrasez l'infâme*' (meaning the Catholic Church) epitomizes this way of thinking; it is not a neutral discourse. And, taken to its logical conclusions, there is only one outcome: religion is not only irrelevant to modern living, but inimical to modernity itself. The final step is a small one. If religion is inimical to modernity, so too is the social scientific study of it.

What emerges in fact is a downward spiral in which the gradual disintegration of the European churches, at least in their traditional forms, is exacerbated by the philosophical changes taking place which offer an alternative way of thinking – itself associated with the birth of modern social science. It is hardly surprising, therefore, that the thinking of social science with respect to religion took the form that it did, concentrating on decline rather than growth, and seeking explanations for the former rather than the latter. That is straightforward enough. The next step in the argument, however, is much more difficult. The empirical connections present in Europe gradually – but inexorably – turned into theoretical assumptions, with the strong implication that secularization would necessarily accompany modernization whenever and wherever the latter occurred. More than this: Europe became the case against which all other cases were measured and, it is often implied, found

---

7   See for example, Himmelfarb (2004).

wanting. The connections between modern and secular became not only empirical, but normative and deeply embedded in social scientific thinking.

How then can this process be reversed? There are several possibilities in this respect, of which three will be engaged here. The first is to recognize that something very different has happened in other parts of the world, leading not only to a different empirical situation, but to different modes of theorizing. The second is to grasp that, even in Europe, things are changing and with them the assumptions that are made with respect both to religion itself and to the social scientific study of this. The third is to invite a qualitatively different approach: that is, to embrace the fact that for most people in most parts of the world, to be religious is an integral *part of* their modernity, not a reaction to this. Taken seriously, the latter would transform the social scientific agenda – an exciting if somewhat daunting prospect.

The first point is most easily exemplified by the American case. Here can be found an upward rather than a downward spiral within which religion – in a myriad of different forms, almost none of which were embedded in territory – moved easily into the growing cities of the United States. Religious organizations grew rapidly alongside the developing economy, and both contributed to the building of a new nation. Each of these processes, moreover, was enhanced by an understanding of the Enlightenment as a freedom to believe, rather than a freedom from belief – a very significant mutation. Almost everything, in fact, is different, including the sociological theories that emerge to explain the situation. Realizing that secularization theory was not appropriate to the transatlantic case, American theorists have created something different. The details of rational choice theory (RCT) need not concern us here, except to remark that one of the hallmarks of this way of thinking is the premise that religious thinking and religious behaviour should be considered part and parcel of human behaviour as a whole: religious choices, in effect, are no different from (say) political choices, and religious institutions work in very similar ways to secular ones in their need to attract both members and money (Young 1996). It follows that religion should be approached with the same analytic tools as its secular counterparts.

There are signs of change in Europe also, and for two rather different reasons. On the one hand, religion is beginning to reassert its presence in public as well as private debate, a point to be developed further in the following section. On the other, at least some European intellectuals are beginning to pay attention to religion. Either way, there are signs that the so-called 'secular neutrality' of both European approaches to religion, and the policies which emerge from these, have increasingly been called into question. Two European social scientists – Jose Casanova and Jürgen Habermas – provide interesting illustrations of this shift.

Casanova is best known as a critic of the cruder versions of secularization theory (Casanova 1994). More precisely, Casanova resists the idea that in modern societies, religion is necessarily a private matter, illustrating this point with a wide range of case studies. In his more recent writing, often focused specifically on Europe, Casanova approaches this topic in a rather different way. He begins by articulating the following (secularist) paradox: 'that in the name of freedom, individual autonomy, tolerance, and cultural pluralism, religious people – Christian, Jewish, and Muslim – are being asked to keep their religious beliefs, identities and norms 'private' so that they do not disturb the project of a modern, secular, enlightened Europe' (2006:

66–7). Differently put, Casanova argues that the secularist assumptions of many (if not all) social and political commentators have had the effect of turning the public expressions of religion into a problem, thus precluding – almost by definition – the resolution of religion-related challenges in a balanced and pragmatic manner.

A second, even more provocative, theme runs parallel: that is to suggest that the process of secularization in Europe might effectively be a self-fulfilling prophecy. In other words, it has more to do with the triumph of the knowledge regime of secularism than with structural processes of socio-economic development (2006: 84). Not everyone, including myself, would accept this conclusion in its entirety – the socio-economic situation remains a significant element in this story.[8] All of us, however, should ponder the following – politically urgent – statement: if we are to guarantee equal access to the European public sphere and undistorted communication about religious issues, 'the European Union would need to become not only post-Christian but also post-secular' (2006: 82). Only then can the essential confusion be unravelled – namely that the problem lies not so much in religion itself as in the secularist assumptions about this. Thinking clearly about these issues is essential for constructive policy-making concerning religious issues in modern Europe, but that in turn requires a similar shift in the social scientific agenda – which must once again embrace the scientific study of religion.

Habermas, perhaps the most distinguished philosopher working in modern Europe, pursues a broadly similar argument. An initial version of his thinking constitutes the dominant theme in a lecture delivered following the award of the Holberg prize in 2005 – a year later it was expanded into a longer article. The core of the lecture resides in the following claim: secular citizens – Habermas insists – must learn to live in a post-secular society. In so doing, they will be following the example of religious citizens, who have already come to terms with the ethical expectations of democratic citizenship, in the sense that they have adopted appropriate epistemic attitudes toward their secular environment. So far, secular citizens have not been expected to make a similar effort – a situation which leads to the current 'asymmetric distribution of cognitive burdens', an imbalance which needs to be rectified sooner rather than later (Habermas 2005).

The expanded version of this essay develops the argument further. Taking as his starting point the increasing significance of religious traditions and communities in much of the modern world (Berger 1999, Jenkins 2002), Habermas addresses the debate in terms of John Rawls' celebrated concept, the 'public use of reason', using this to challenge secular citizens, including Europeans, about their underlying assumptions. Specifically, they are invited to take part in 'a self-reflective transcending of the secularist self-understanding of Modernity' (2006: 15) – an attitude that quite clearly goes beyond 'mere tolerance' in that it necessarily engenders feelings of respect for the worldview of the religious person. Hence the need, not only for a growing reciprocity in the debate (see above), but for an additional question. Are religious issues simply to be regarded as relics of a pre-modern era, or is it the duty of the more secular citizen to overcome his or her narrowly secularist consciousness

---

8   Not least for the reasons already set out in the section concerning the modernization process in Europe and its implications for the historic territorially-embedded European churches.

in order to engage with religion in terms of '*reasonably expected disagreement*' (2006: 15), assuming in other words a degree of rationality on both sides? The latter appears to be the case. Habermas' argument is challenging in every sense of the term and merits very careful reflection; it constitutes an interesting response to a changing *global* environment – one moreover in which the relative secularity of Europe is increasingly seen as an exceptional, rather than prototypical case.

More precisely, in the initial pages of Habermas' article, two closely linked ideas are introduced: on the one hand, the increasing isolation of Europe from the rest of the world in terms of its religious configurations, and, on the other, the notion of 'multiple modernities'. It was exactly this combination that that was developed in some detail in *Europe: The Exceptional Case* (Davie 2002). The starting point lies in reversing the 'normal' question: instead of asking what Europe *is* in terms of its religious existence, it asks what Europe *is not*. It is *not* (yet) a vibrant religious market such as that found in the United States; it is *not* a part of the world where Christianity is growing exponentially, very often in Pentecostal forms, as in the case in the Southern hemisphere (Latin America, Sub-Saharan Africa and the Pacific Rim); it is *not* a part of the world dominated by faiths other than Christian, but is increasingly penetrated by these; and it is *not* for the most part subject to the violence often associated with religion and religious difference in other parts of the globe – the more so if either becomes entangled in political conflict. Hence the inevitable, if at times disturbing conclusion: that the patterns of religion in modern Europe, notably its relative secularity, might be an exceptional case in global terms.

Here, moreover, is a principal reason for the growing interest in religion in the modern world, even among mainstream sociologists – indeed it becomes increasingly difficult to avoid. All too often however, such approaches concentrate on the forms of religion that appear on first sight to resist the modernization process. The growing number of studies concerned with fundamentalism illustrate the point perfectly. An excellent example can be found in Zygmunt Baumann's insightful essay on 'Postmodern Religion'. Baumann pays considerable and direct attention to the attitudes (including religious ones) of postmodern people, recognizing their innate diversity. Within such a framework, fundamentalism is identified as a specifically postmodern form of religion – exposing by its very nature the anxieties and premonitions integral to the postmodern condition, which itself undermines the certainties that fundamentalism seeks to replace. Given the impossibility of a permanent solution to an essentially circular problem, Baumann argues that the fundamentalist is 'saved', not only from sin, but also from the agonies of perpetual choice (Baumann 1998: 73–4).

Such an argument is clearly helpful and symptomatic of a change in the sociological climate – religion is most certainly taken seriously. That said, a consistent thread unites even the most positive of thinkers in this respect. For the great majority, religion is still conceptualized first and foremost as a way of coping with the vicissitudes of late or post-modern life, but not – or not yet – as *a way of being modern*. To embrace the fact that for most people in most parts of the world, to be religious is an integral part of their modernity, not a reaction to this, constitutes the final 'leap of faith', that – if taken to its logical conclusion – would transform much of modern sociology. Both the insulation and the isolation of religion would disappear at a stroke.

One place to look for this transformation lies, perhaps, in the growing number of publications on Pentecostalism, the fastest-growing form of Christianity in the modern world – one, moreover, which combines a distinctively modern vision with a visible, and often very practical, means of support for the believer and his or her immediate circle. In the fragile economies of the developing world, this has proved a winning combination. Progress, however, is slow. Indeed, for most of the post-war period, neither Pentecostalism itself, nor the social-scientific study of it, pleased the academy, who had considerable difficulty grasping that these rapidly-growing forms of religion had become a central and effective part of the modernization process for growing numbers of late twentieth-century individuals. The fact that they consciously incorporated emotional (i.e. non-rational) expressions of faith simply made the whole thing more difficult. So much so that, in the short term at least, it was easier to ignore the facts than to dismantle the paradigms – a story poignantly told by David Martin in an essay published in 2000. A decade or so later, the situation is easier, but there is more, much more, to be done if the transformation is to be complete.

Conceptual Clarity: the Different Meanings of Religious Pluralism

Beckford presents himself as an advocate of constructivism in a sociological account. How then does he apply this approach to religious pluralism? In the chapter devoted to this question in *Social Theory and Religion*, he goes straight to the heart of the matter: in public as well as sociological discourse several ideas have been conflated in one term. Not only is the term 'pluralism' used to describe markedly different things (diverse religious organizations, the multitude of individuals associated with these, distinctive faith traditions, innovative combinations of religious beliefs, and/ or the fragmentation of existing creeds), it is also used to evoke the moral or political values associated with religious diversity. The inference is clear enough: there is a persistent confusion between what is and what ought to be, and until we get this straight, there are bound to be misunderstandings in public as well as sociological debate. Some of these have already been evoked.

Equally diverse are the ways in which different societies accommodate religious diversity. Legal or constitutional arrangements provide the starting point – analyses that call on a range of different disciplines, including a knowledge of law. Rather more penetrating, however, are Beckford's remarks concerning the 'normal' or 'taken for granted' in any given society's acceptance or regulation of religion. The examples from France outlined above exemplify this point; they also reveal the importance of paying careful attention to the chain of events through which the 'default positions' have been – consciously or unconsciously – put in place. An inevitable question follows from this: can they be changed and if so, by whom? Who, in other words, has the right to recognize or to reject the parameters of religious life in any given society? This is becoming an increasingly important question, in which definitional issues constitute a crucial thread.

'Tolerance' opens another Pandora's box. Like pluralism, it means different things to different people – along a continuum which runs from a tacit acceptance of a restricted list of religious activities to a positive affirmation of forms of religion very different from the norm. Tolerance, moreover, operates at different levels: individuals who are tolerant of religious differences may exist in societies that have difficulty with the idea, and vice versa. Nor is there any direct correlation between pluralism (in its various forms) and toleration, though it is at least likely that those who affirm that religious diversity is beneficial rather than harmful are more likely to be tolerant of forms of religion that allow for more than one version of 'truth'. They will be less happy with forms of religion that aspire to monopoly status. The converse is equally true.

The discussion could continue. Enough has been said, however, to alert the reader to the pitfalls. How then do these ideas work out in practice? The following comparison is used both to illustrate this point and to conclude this chapter. In order to do this, it returns once again to the French case – comparing it this time with its British (and more especially English) equivalent in terms of their respective approaches to religious pluralism. The facts and figures are straightforward enough. France now houses the largest Muslim community in Western Europe (a population that comes largely from North Africa). Britain contains a much more diverse religious population, many of whom have come from the sub-continent (for example Muslims, Hindus and Sikhs) alongside a significant influx of Christians from English-speaking Africa and the Caribbean. Here, in other words, are the increasingly significant religious minorities of modern Europe, for which the debates concerning new religious movements were, in many respects, the precursor.

Examining the French and British cases in light of Beckford's conceptual clarifications constitutes an interesting exercise, from which the following – somewhat surprising – paradox emerges. Both constitutionally and institutionally France is undoubtedly a more democratic society than Britain, but Britain is more tolerant than France, if by tolerance is meant the acceptance of group as well as individual differences, and the right to display symbols of that group membership in public as well as private life. One further point is important: that is to appreciate the relative flexibility of the state church (in the English case) if this is compared with the ideological rigour of the secular state across the Channel.

France, for example, is markedly more democratic than Britain on almost all institutional or constitutional measures. Here – as we have seen already – is a secular Republic, with two elected chambers, no privileged church (in the sense of connections to the state), and a school system in which religious symbols are proscribed by law. There is a correspondingly strong stress on the equality of all citizens whatever their ethnic or religious identity. As a result, France follows a strongly assimilationist policy towards incomers, with the express intention of eradicating difference – individuals who arrive in France are welcome to maintain their religious belief and practices, provided these are relegated to the private sphere. They are actively discouraged from developing any kind of group identity. Exactly the same point can be put as follows: any loyalty (religious or otherwise) that comes between the citizen and the state is regarded in negative terms. In France, it follows, *communautarisme* is a pejorative word, implying a less than full commitment to the nation embodied in the French state.

Britain is very different. On a strict measure of democracy, Britain fares less well than France – with no written constitution, a monarchy, a half-reformed and so far unelected House of Lords, and an established church. More positively, Britain has a more developed tradition of accommodating group identities (including religious ones) within the framework of British society, a feature that owes a good deal to the relatively greater degree of religious pluralism that has existed in Britain for centuries rather than decades. Hence a markedly different policy towards newcomers: the goal becomes the accommodation of difference rather than its eradication. Rather more provocative, however, are the conclusions that emerge if you look carefully at who, precisely, in British society is advocating religious as opposed to ethnic toleration. Very frequently it turns out to be those in society who do *not* depend on an electoral mandate: the royal family and significant spokespersons in the House of Lords (where the larger other-faith communities are well represented by appointment, not by election).

Both the Monarchy and the House of Lords are, of course, intimately connected to the Church of England, a significant player in its own right. Here the crucial point lies precisely in appreciating the difference between an historically strong state church and its modern, somewhat weaker equivalent. The former almost by definition becomes excluding and exclusive; the latter cannot. A weakened church can, however, use its still considerable influence to include rather than to exclude, to acknowledge rather than to ignore, and to welcome rather than to despise. Even more positive are its capacities to create and to sustain a space within society in which faith is taken seriously – doing so *by means of* its connections with the state. If these things are done well, it would be hard to argue that a state or established church has no part to play in an increasingly plural society.

The situation in Britain is by no means perfect; it can, however, be made to work effectively for the benefit of religious minorities as well as the mainstream. Working out exactly how this happens, and how it might be improved, has formed a central plank in Jim Beckford's work. The most apt illustration in this case is his commitment to understanding better the place of religious minorities in the prison systems of both Britain and France (Beckford and Gilliat 1998; Beckford *et al.* 2005) – an aspect of his work developed more fully in Chapter 11, below. In *this* chapter, it is the following point that requires attention. In the first of these volumes, Beckford and Gilliat recognize the brokering role of the Anglican chaplain (the local representative of the established church) in prison chaplaincy. Such a system is fine when it works well, but may not be viable in the longer term given the increasingly diverse nature of the prison population and a growing insistence on religious rather than ethnic identities – a situation that calls for innovative thinking. In the second book, however, the advantages of the British system become clearer. Three years of systematic research by an international team reveal that British prisons are more likely to facilitate and control the practice of Islam within the institution (albeit more effectively in some places than others), whereas French prisons actively oppose this – encouraging thereby the seeds of extremism. The policy implications of these findings are examined in considerable detail – a task of immense importance in twenty-first century Europe. Interestingly, they return us once again to the starting point of this chapter: that is, the crucial importance of context (economic, social, historical and cultural) in understanding the place of religion in the institutions of any given society.

What then can be said in conclusion? The range of Beckford's work is deeply impressive. It includes a detailed knowledge of a wide range of national situations (both in Europe and beyond), an appreciation of the wider sociological canon and the place of religion in this, clear conceptualization at all levels, and the following through of this thinking into effective policy-making. May Beckford's 'retirement' from the minutiae of university life permit increased activity in all these fields: his insights are sorely needed.

References

Baubérot, J. (2005) *Histoire de la laïcité en France*, Paris: Presses Universitaires de France.

Baumann, Z. (1998) 'Postmodern religion?', in P. Heelas, with D. Martin and P. Morris (eds), *Religion, Modernity and Postmodernity*, Oxford: Blackwell, pp. 55–78.

Beckford, J. (1985) *Cult Controversies: The Societal Response to New Religious Movements*, London: Tavistock.

—— (1989) *Religion and Advanced Industrial Society*, London: Routledge.

—— (2003) *Social Theory and Religion*, Cambridge: Cambridge University Press.

Beckford, J. and Gilliat, S. (1998) *Religion in Prison. Equal Rites in a Multi-Faith Society*, Cambridge: Cambridge University Press.

Beckford, J. and Richardson, J. (eds) (2003) *Challenging Religion: Essays in Honour of Eileen Barker*, London: Routledge.

Beckford, J., Joly, D. and Khosrokhavar, K. (2005) *Muslims in Prison: Challenge and Change in Britain and France*, Basingstoke: Palgrave Macmillan.

Berger, P. (ed.) (1999) *The Desecularization of the World: Resurgent Religion and World Politics*, Grand Rapids, MI.: Eerdmans Publishing Co.

Casanova, J. (1994) *Public Religions in the Modern World*, Chicago: Chicago University Press.

—— (2006) 'Religion, European secular identities, and European integration', in T. Byrnes and P. Katzenstein (eds) *Religion in an Expanding Europe*, Cambridge: Cambridge University Press, pp. 65–92.

Davie, G. (1999) 'Religion and laïcité', in M. Cook and G. Davie (eds) *Modern France: Society in Transition*, London: Routledge, pp. 195–215.

—— (2002) *Europe: The Exceptional Case. Parameters of Faith in the Modern World*, London: Darton, Longman and Todd.

—— (2007) *The Sociology of Religion*, London: Sage.

Habermas, J. (2005) 'Religion in the Public Sphere', a lecture presented at the Holberg Prize Seminar, 28 November 2005.

—— (2006) 'Religion in the Public Sphere', *European Journal of Philosophy*, 14: 1–25.

Hervieu-Léger, D. (1986) *Vers un nouveau christianisme: Introduction à la sociologie du christianisme occidental*, Paris: Cerf.

—— (2001a) *La Religion en miettes ou la question des sectes*, Paris: Calmann-Lévy.

—— (2001b) France's obsession with the 'sectarian threat', *Nova Religio*, 4: 249–58.

Himmelfarb, G. (2004) *The Roads to Modernity: The British, French and American Enlightenments*, New York: Alfred Kopf.

Jenkins, P. (2002) *The Next Christendom: The Coming of Global Christianity*, New York, Oxford: Oxford University Press.

Martin, D. (1978) *A General Theory of Secularization*, Oxford: Blackwell.

—— (2000) 'Personal reflections in the mirror of Halévy and Weber', in R. Fenn (ed.) *The Blackwell Companion to the Sociology of Religion*, Oxford: Blackwell, pp. 23–38.

Richardson, J. (ed.) (2004) *Regulating Religion. Case Studies from around the Globe*, New York: Kluwer Academic/Plenum Publishers.

Young, L. (ed.) (1996) *Rational Choice Theory and Religion: Summary and Assessment*, London: Routledge.

CHAPTER 2

Religious Individualism, Modern Individualism and Self-fulfilment:
A few Reflections on the Origins of Contemporary Religious Individualism[1]

Danièle Hervieu-Léger
Translated by Deborah Furet

The Rise of the Religious Subject: Between Pre-Modernity and Modernity

Sociological descriptions of the religious landscape of Western societies in the last twenty-five or thirty years all share a focus on the irresistible progression of individualism and a subjectivization of beliefs and practices which have altered, from top to bottom, modes of religiosity and the role of institutions. 'Religious modernity is individualism': this proposition – which has assumed an infinite variety of forms based upon observations drawn from all the Western societies – thus constitutes the *leitmotif* of theoretical reflection upon the contemporary evolution of religion. This phrase, however, is not without ambiguity, for it would seem to suggest that religious individualism necessarily coexists, like an unprecedented phenomenon, with modernity. We can, however, speak of religious individualization as soon as we see a differentiation between a ritual religion (wherein meticulous observation of prescribed practices is required only of the faithful) and a religion of interiority that implies, in a mystical or ethical way, a personal and permanent adoption of religious verities by each believer. In all the great religious traditions, this differentiation became apparent under various forms, long before the emergence of modernity. From this point of view, the history of Christian mysticism can be seen entirely as the history of the construction of the religious subject.

The search for union with God, from a mystical perspective, is achieved through the work of self-renouncement. We must seek to rid ourselves of passions, interests, thoughts, sentiments and ideas which carry within them the singularity of the individual. But this renouncement, this severing of the individual from the particular determining factors of his or her life, paradoxically constitutes, for those who go down this road, a more intimate pathway to their innermost self. It leads to the highest possible consciousness of the self: that which proceeds from the experience of union

---

1   This approach to modern religious individualism is presented and developed in D. Hervieu-Léger, *Le pélerin et le converti. La religion en mouvement*. Paris, Flammarion, 1999 (Translations in Italian, Spanish, German and Portuguese.)

with the One. From the third century on, Plotinus, whose experience, impregnated as it was with neo-Platonist influences, decisively oriented the entire Christian spiritual tradition, clearly expressed the movement of the 'negative affirmation' of the believing subject: 'Often,' he wrote, 'I wake to myself by escaping from my body, a stranger to everything; in my own intimacy, I see a Beauty that is as marvellous as possible. I am above all convinced that I have a superior destiny; my activity is the highest degree of life; I am united with a divine being.' Thus we see that, on the one hand, the mystical way, stretching out over centuries of Christian history, constitutes an extreme path to the individualization of religious experience, reserved, in fact, to a small number of virtuosos, bearers, as Max Weber would say, of a 'charisma of a mystic sort'. On the other hand, it is through the leading of a 'rational and methodical life' that the individual is transformed into a believing subject by the ethical way (Weber 1958: 267–301). In Christianity, it was Calvinism that pushed this ethical logic of religious individualization the furthest, by developing the idea that all individuals must confirm their personal predestination for salvation in all aspects of their daily life in the world and more particularly, in their professional life. In the absence of any mediation between themselves and God, believers thus find themselves confronted by the question of their own salvation in a radically individual way.

What is the relationship between mystical or ethical religious individualism and modernity? There is no point in dwelling on the classic Weberian thesis which highlighted the elective bond forged between the individualistic and intra-worldly code of ethics of Calvinist Puritanism and the nascent spirit of economic, capitalistic modernity. But it would be a mistake to draw the conclusion from this that the Christian trajectory of religious individualization, which found its most radical form with Calvin, anticipated the emergence of modern individualism in a perfectly continuous and linear fashion. To posit a seamless continuity between religious individualism of a mystical or ethical sort and the modern conception of the individual is as absurd as the opposite point of view, which would cast religious individualism as a fresh conquest of modernity. Religious individualism is in fact divergent from modern individualism – which originated in the recognition of the autonomy of the subject – in at least two ways: first, it constitutes individuals in the very movement that they relinquish themselves to give themselves over to God; and, secondly, it absolutely rejects the mundane realities that impede such a union with the divine.

This twofold aspect characterizes not only an extra-worldly conception of what is mystical and ethical, as was developed by the Catholic tradition. It can also be discerned in the intra-worldly code of ethics put forward by the Reformation. This is why the German theologian and sociologist Ernst Troeltsch reacted with criticism to the hackneyed idea that the religious individualism of an intra-worldly sort that issued from the Reformation would have directly prepared and foretold the emergence of the modern conception of the individual, thus opening the way for the rise of democracy. Troeltsch did indeed insist upon the fact that the Lutheran regard for work in the world facilitated the development of a functional religious ethic in relation to the development of capitalism. But at the same time, he emphasized that this ethic is itself in contradiction with a modern ethic that recognizes and magnifies the autonomy of mundane realities. Luther still places himself in the neo-Platonic perspective of a deprecation of worldly realities. In an even more decisive fashion, Troeltsch challenged the idea that by developing his doctrine of predestination and by pushing the logic of the *gratia sola* to its end, Calvin had paved the way for the modern process of individualization. For Calvin, the elected creature is not esteemed as such: saved by pure grace, its life only had meaning in the service of the Kingdom. If the believer is intensely engaged in worldly tasks, he does so exclusively for the glory of God and because this world was itself willed by God. But this activity is in itself insignificant. It does not allow individuals a guarantee of their salvation or to draw any value from the personal fulfilment it offers them. Calvinist individualism denies the autonomy of the individual and remains, from this point of view, in contradiction with the rationalistic and positivistic individualism of the Enlightenment. 'Calvin,' wrote Troeltsch in his *Soziallehren*

> does not acknowledge man's liberty. It is excluded from his theological system and from his social system. The reign of God is not subject to the free acceptance of man; it is established by persuasion without doubt, but also by the repression of any rebellion, by constraint .... For him, the honour of God is maintained when man is bent before His Law in an attitude of submission, free or forced. (Troeltsch 1912: 635)

This Calvinist insistence on obedience is fundamentally opposed to the modern conception of the autonomous individual. It also distinguishes Calvinism from the Puritan sects to the extent that these last require their members to be free and voluntary members of the community. In fact, if there is indeed a 'Protestant modernity', Troeltsch would mainly locate it within the Pietist and Puritan neo-Calvinist movements. For the most part, it resulted from the political conflicts that brought these communities to call for liberty of conscience, to promote a community organization founded upon the free will of each, and to affirm their independence by spreading the practice of electing pastors. In reaction to the stewardship of the churches and their ritual formalism, these communities radicalized the Lutheran problem of the ethical internalization of the relation to God. Simultaneously, they developed a separatism with the world that had, *de facto*, recognized their autonomy. The sectarian spirituality of the radical Reformation maintained, from this point of view, positive, elective affinities with modern individualism. But Protestant spirituality – Lutheran and Calvinist – essentially remained part of the logical order of negative affirmation of the individual that was characteristic of pre-modern religious individualism.

Religious individualism was no more responsible for modernity than was modernity for the invention of religious individualism. What characterizes the contemporary religious scene is not religious individualism as such; it is the absorption of religious individualism first by modern individualism, and then by its progressive incorporation in the ultra-modern quest for self-realization which, during most recent times, has overrun common notions about the autonomy of the subject.

The Ultra-Modern Mutation of Religious Individualism: the Case of the 'Mystical-Esoteric Nebula'

This ultra-modern transfiguration of religious individualism is nowhere more evident than among the composite ensemble of spiritual groups and networks that constitute the 'mystical-esoteric nebula'. What unifies this ensemble is a religiosity entirely centred on the individual and his or her personal fulfilment (Champion 1993).

This form of religiosity is first and foremost characterized by the primacy attributed to the personal experience that each undergoes in his or her own way. The aim is not to discover and embrace a truth that exists beyond oneself: it is to find – each for oneself – one's own truth. No authority can, in spiritual matters, define any orthodoxy or orthopraxis to be imposed upon the individual from without. The objective pursued is the perfection of the self, a perfection not of the moral fulfilment of the individual but of his or her access to a superior state of being. This self-perfection is attainable by psycho-corporal practices which may be drawn from the whole range of techniques elaborated by the great spiritual and mystical traditions. But recourse to these techniques belongs to a definitively optimistic vision of the capacity of human beings to achieve the complete realization of themselves according to the particular path they choose in a completely responsible way.

The salvation sought by this work of self-perfection exclusively concerns life in the here and now. The goal is to reach, by oneself, in the most complete way possible, the objectives that modern society offers as a promise for all: health, well-being, vitality, beauty. This strictly intra-worldly notion of salvation belongs to a monistic conception of the world: it rejects all dualism (human/divine, natural/supernatural, amongst others). At the same time, it brings into question the fragmentation of knowledge and practices which were responsible for the failure of the modern aspiration for individual and collective progress. Any such prospect of a spiritual reunification of individual and collective life should guarantee the reign of an 'ethics of love' which manifests the convergence of the paths of truth explored by individuals. It also implies a new alliance with modern science. The objective of wielding power over nature thus pursued in fact meets up with the objective of getting the most potential out of the physical and psychic capacities of the individual that guide the spiritual quest. This is why so many of these groups attribute so much importance to 'non-ordinary realities' (out-of-body experiences, trips to past lives, communication with spirits and aliens, amongst others). The fact that individuals can reach these realities by personally developing their specifically spiritual capacities is not in contradiction with the scientific project. On the contrary, it completes it, for it constitutes a way for the individual to enter into the project of knowledge and power over the world which is being developed by modern science using other means.

If the groups and networks of the mystical-esoteric nebula constitute, in spite of the relatively confidential character of their development, at least in France, an instrument for the analysis of contemporary religious reality, it is because they push to the limit tendencies that were also present in the revival movements at work in historical religions: the search for personal authenticity, the importance accorded to experience, the rejection of ready-made systems of belief, the intra-worldly conception of a salvation conceived as individual self-perfection, and so on. These different tendencies illustrate very exactly the phenomenon of the absorption of religious individualism by modern individualism under the sign of an appreciation of the world on the one hand and the affirmation of the believing subject on the other. 'Religious modernity' is fundamentally a product of this operation. The moment of ultra-modernity corresponds to the most recent instalment of this modern individualism: that of an invasion by the theme of personal realization of the subject, an episode that Jean Baudrillard would designate in the early 1980s, as the time of 'psychological modernity'.

Near to God, Far From God: the Two Poles of the Mutation

It is obvious that the question we must pose is what were the historical stages of this change? One might think that it began when, in society, politics and culture, modernity, defined by itself as the realization of the reign of reason, imposed itself, opening up the way to a quest for the methodical conquest of nature while establishing autonomy for individuals capable of a collective exercise of their political sovereignty. The cultural and political turning-point of the eighteenth century inaugurated, in this twofold way, the potential for a re-composition of religious individualism within modern individualism. This re-composition is even a logical outcome of that re-composition to the extent that the coming of modernity does not attenuate –far from it – all the metaphysical and spiritual questions of a humanity confronted with incertitude and the finitude of its condition. An exhaustive historical study would clearly be necessary to support this idea in a convincing way. To do it properly, one would have to pay particular attention to a study of the spiritual movements that preceded and accompanied the development of the Enlightenment. In the present context, I will limit myself to a few remarks.

Contemporary religious individualism is characterized, as we have seen above, by its emphasis on the personal accomplishment of the individual, but also by the recognition it accords to the realities of the world in which that individual develops in an autonomous fashion. One could put forward the hypothesis that if pre-modern religious individualism of a Christian sort accomplished its transformation in modern individualism, it is because it had already chosen these two paths: first, it had placed God within reach of human beings, and second, it had radically distanced God from the sphere of human activities. The first movement shifted the quest for the renouncement of the self with a view to divine union toward affective experience of the divine presence within. The second, by reducing the plausibility of divine intervention in the world, liberated the autonomous potential of the individual.

Thus formulated, this hypothesis is a bit succinct. It must certainly be handled with caution. But various pieces of evidence allow us to measure its significance. One might also suggest that the invention of the personal guardian angel at the end of the fifteenth century – an invention whose importance in the history of Catholic spirituality was brought to our attention by J. Delumeau (1989) – offers a first and evocative representation of the affectionate attention that God pays to human needs, an attention that would become increasingly important. More generally, one may observe that the seventeenth century is characterized, in regard to Protestants as well as Catholics, by the rise of movements that developed a highly emotional piety, more sensitive to the affective proximity of the divine than to the distance from a God whom the faithful can reach only at the cost of a renouncement requiring merciless ascetic work on themselves. Does this not explain the popularity among a large lay public of what we have become accustomed to call, since *l'Histoire littéraire du sentiment religieux d'Henri Brémond* came out in 1925, the 'French School of Spirituality'? The fact is that this movement, most notably related to the 'humanisme dévôt' (devotional humanism) inspired by Saint François de Sales, contributed to the spread of a gentler and more humane spirituality than did the heroic mysticism of the great Spanish mystics from whom they drew their inspiration: a spirituality, in any case, that defined a member of the faithful not by his losing battle to rid himself of the conditioning of his existence, but by the peaceful contemplation of Christ 'in each of the "states" of his humanity'. In general, the different currents of spirituality that proliferated in seventeenth-century France sought not to abolish the individual in God but to open the way, through meditation and chanting, to the simple sentiment of the divine presence. This tranquilized form of contemplation requires an inner availability, a 'loving meditation', a 'loving, simple and permanent attention to the divine'; it does not, however, necessarily imply a frenzied ascetic effort. By offering a spiritual path centred on the peaceful and fulfilling inner presence of God, French mystics opened the gates – at least potentially – to a greater number of faithful. All one had to do was simply to stand before God, and 'enjoy and accustom oneself to His divine company, speaking humbly and lovingly conversing with Him at all times, at every moment, without rule or measure' (Jossua 1997: 9–12).[2] This orientation is not reserved to virtuosos of exceptional vocation. It thus describes – even if it remains within the confines of the mystical problem of an annihilation in God that occurs through renouncing desire and fear – a potential way to an 'easy',[3] accessible, positive spirituality in which the individual can find a personal path to fulfilment. It heralds a friendly God, a God 'close to the heart', concerned with the needs of men and women and available for intimate communication with them. This figure would take on diverse forms later on in the nineteenth and twentieth centuries.

The emphasis of seventeenth-century Catholic spirituality upon the perceptible presence of God and upon the believer's potential affective experience of it suggests a parallel with the revival of the emotional experience as a living source of faith pursued by the Pietist movement among the German Protestants of the seventeenth century. Rejecting both the formalism of dogmatic constructions and the coldness of a Christian practice that had become routinized, the movement began with the creation of 'communities of saints' and the publication by Jacob Spener of his *Pia Desideria, or the Heartfelt Desire for God-pleasing Reform* in 1675. Spener brought

---

2   The remarkable synthesis written by J.P. Jossua (1997) sheds particular light on this path. The quotations from Saint François de Sales and from the lay Carmelite brother Laurent of the Resurrection (like the quote from Plotin above) are taken from him.

3   This 'ease' drew the violent hostility of opponents of 'Quietism' since it appeared to encourage the passive abandonment to divine will and an equally entirely passive notion of prayer. The quietist controversy would culminate in 1689 with the putting of Jeanne Guyon's book, *Le moyen court et très facile de faire oraison* on the Index.

inner piety to the forefront and powerfully highlighted the affective dimension of the personal spiritual experience. This orientation would dominate European and North American Protestant theology until the middle of the eighteenth century and gave rise not only to a profound revival of church life, but also to a multiplication of Protestant initiatives in the medical, pedagogic, social, and artistic domains (Schrader 1995: 1156). The *rapprochement* with seventeenth-century French spirituality seemed all the more justified because Pietism was also characterized by a concern for the vitalization of the faith of the Christian people and not merely by the exploration of a path of religious virtuosity reserved for the few. In a more general way, one might ask if the spiritual effervescence of the seventeenth and eighteenth centuries could not be related, at least in an indirect fashion, to the first appearance of a modern individualism which emphasized the psychological realization of the subject. In some ways, this question is justified by certain identifiable links between the spiritual problem of the repose and unification of the self in God and reflections upon the nature of happiness offered to men and women on earth that flourished in the eighteenth century (Mauzi 1994). The 'happy apathy' that results, according to Marmontel, from the silencing of passions, from equilibrium and rest, or from the Rousseauian idea of happiness as a *'rapprochement de soi'* (ibid.: 120) (a closer relationship to oneself) which coexist, for the author of the *Rêveries*, with the search for an intensity and exaltation associated with an extreme acuity of consciousness, would also suggest such a connection. Does not Jean-Jacques Rousseau, in *La profession de foi du vicaire savoyard*, invoke a God who is 'sensitive to the heart'? The literature that, in the eighteenth century, made the heart and the sentiments the means to accede to truth (and simultaneously to the realization of the self) echo, in some ways, the spiritual currents that cast affective experience as the moment *par excellence* of the encounter with the divine. The central place attributed by Pietism to individuals and their feelings, the importance given to introspection – as manifest in the great volume of letters and private journals – left, moreover, a profound mark on German pre-Romantic and Romantic literary inspiration. Although we must watch carefully how we manipulate these connections and influences, we may at least ask if a diversified set of questions about personal spiritual fulfilment did not seek its path among these various currents, beyond the pre-modern mystical problem of the annihilation of the individual in God.

When compared to the movement which envisions a God who is close and friendly and who intimately manifests His presence in our hearts, the culture of the Enlightenment seems to be marked by the completely opposite tendency to push God out of the way into a distant heaven and leave Him there. This spirituality of divine distance reached its greatest development, in the most explicit way, in the various forms of Deism. Born on the other side of the Channel, in the heart of the Anglican Church and the Nonconformist Protestant churches, it had no better apostle in France than Voltaire, whose role in promoting a religion without a church, capable of superseding the limited particularity of the different credos, was admirably brought to light by Alphonse Dupront (1996b). This was a religion rooted in natural religion, that universal religion of humanity. This true religion, according to Voltaire, is 'the adoration of the Supreme Being, without any metaphysical dogma.' God is the power of unity and eternity of the universe, a God who reigns by the general laws that govern nature, a surveyor God 'who has arranged everything with order, weight, and measure', but who in no way intervenes in the life of men and women. Voltaire accepts the idea of God the Creator and the Father. On the other hand, he rejects the idea of an incarnated God, who interacts with human beings and with whom one might have a personal relationship. According to Voltaire, God is present in our lives only to the extent that He is, according to Dupront, the foundation for a collective affectivity: a community of brothers in a universal fraternity. 'What I mean by natural religion,' wrote Voltaire, '[is] the moral principles common to mankind.' This phrase sums up, once more according to Dupront, 'the movement that, through the universal, reduces the natural to the moral.' This is a laic avowal of religious de-sanctification 'where Deism, if not a laic morality, is the religiosity of a necessary collective code of ethics.' If it is worthwhile to consider Voltaire's ideas about religion from the viewpoint of the relationship between modernity and spirituality, it is because they lend the most explicit form to a much more general movement that would develop after his time. Eighteenth-century Deism carried within it a radical critique of clerical Christianity which was taken to task not only for maintaining a mythical sacredness – source of 'prejudices' and 'superstitions' – but also for ignoring, by rendering absolute the revelation to which it referred, the existence of a religion that was universal across space and time, a religion shared by all men and women and which existed through the diversity of historical religions.[4] English Deism, the intellectual mysticism of Spinoza, the Masonic notion of the Great Architect of the Universe which spread during the eighteenth century all over enlightened Europe: all of these movements, each in its own way, developed this theme. The Deist movement of the Enlightenment originated in a critique of traditional religion, but it retained the reference to God and sought, during the entire century, to establish itself as a positive religion. It is especially important to note that in Deism, God is present, but He does not communicate with man. This is the last instalment, according to Dupront, of a religious evolution composed of three parts (1996: 210–11).

1) In the medieval religion of the Christian world, the supernatural and the natural are co-participants in God, and any theodicy of salvation is a common salvation; the paths of communication are at once natural and eschatological.
2) With the crisis of the Reformation, God became separated from men or at least became increasingly distinct; communication became individual; that is the religion of *Deus solus*.
3) The third period is our own: between two worlds, between God and man, is a silent coexistence.

Thus Deism takes its place in the religious experiences of the modern West, as the 'proof' of the exhaustion of a traditional religion of common salvation and of the fear on the part of society to admit to all the consequences of a religion exclusively

---

4   Voltaire's ideas about Deism are inseparable from his interest in the history of religions, wherein he found evidence of a common religious fund at the source of the diversity of historic religions.

based on individual salvation (Dupront 1996b: 210–11). In other words, it marks the transition between the universe of traditional religion and that of religious modernity.

To recapitulate: the spirituality of the Enlightenment was established between two poles which we can define using ideal types. The first pole is the discovery of the intimate and friendly proximity of people to a God who could be known by the heart, the second is the establishment of an indifferent coexistence between human beings and God, a coexistence that allows men and women the possibility of affirming their autonomy. The first pole gave rise to the Christian spiritual currents of the seventeenth century, but also to Jewish Hassidism, born in Poland in the eighteenth century, and which prospered by countering the intellectualist chilliness of rabbinical Judaism with an emotional, joyous and enthusiastic piety which bore the stamp of Cabbalist influences. Deism, in its various forms, is very close to the second pole. On one side, God is near, on the other, God is distant. The proximity to a God with whom communication is possible, easy, and emotionally gratifying gradually transformed Him into an agent for the personal development of the individual. The distancing of a God Whom we adore from afar and Whom we do not expect to intervene in our lives insures full earthly autonomy for human affairs. These two spiritual configurations arise in the junction between the traditional religious world governed by the heteronomous authority of the Revelation and the modern world where the autonomy of the individual is the rule. As the split between these two worlds grew, the density of the spiritual content carried by each pole tended progressively to recede: Deism, confronted with the rationality of modern scientific thought, was rapidly exhausted; Catholic mysticism as well as Pietism would decline during the eighteenth century in contrast to the spiritual effervescence of the preceding century.

During their entire courses, both movements, although in appearance contradictory, revealed themselves to be inseparable from one another and mutually reinforcing. The emotional internalization of the divine presence in oneself allowed one to confront the experience of a world in which God was no longer active while sharpening the painful experience of emptiness that marks the beginning of modernity.[5] The two conflicting notions – a close God versus a distant God – *together* constitute the transitional figure from which religious individualism managed to come to terms with modern individualism which, at the time, was beginning to dominate Western culture. If the movement that brought closer relations to God is pushed to its logical end, it allows, in fact, nothing to survive aside from a purely inner, subjective and private piety, less and less apt to express itself in a shared, communitarian faith, and which thus precludes any vision of an active presence of God in the reality of the world. In this scenario, the closest God is also the most distant God. The spiritual value placed upon the emotional proximity of the divine allows a theological justification for God's withdrawal from a definitively secular world. The recognition

---

5   The history of Jansenism in the eighteenth century, as described in detail by C. Maire (1997), in a way constitutes, through the convulsive explosions brought on by popular appropriations of the figuristic theological constructions, an exacerbated form of the crisis that came from this social absence of a God who henceforth acted only through taking possession of the bodies of individuals.

of this absence henceforth constitutes a legitimate attitude of belief. This perspective would be developed in the thought of the Italian philosopher G. Vattimo, for whom the incarnation of Christ is the foundation of a 'friendly Christianity' ('I no longer call you servants, but friends') which evacuates, in principle, all the transcendent, incomprehensible, and mysterious attributes of natural sacredness. According to Vattimo (1998), God's intimacy with man constitutes the very vector for the secularization brought about by Christianity. This 'friendly Christianity' implies and gives rise to the modern revolution that is the affirmation of believing subjects, capable of conceiving of themselves as equal partners in this relationship between friends; capable as well of moving in an autonomous fashion in a world rid of the alienating presence of the sacred. A new figure of religious individualism is thus inaugurated: that of *modern religious individualism*, which is exacerbated by the most contemporary forms of religiosity.

Modern Religiosity and the Search for Power: the Search for a New Alliance with Science

The picture of spiritual effervescence that immediately preceded and framed the turning point of the Enlightenment brings to mind, in still other ways, the characteristic features of this contemporary religiosity, distinguished in particular by the multiform currents of the mystical-esoteric nebula. To complete this survey, we must take stock of a third element that is very directly prolonged by these currents. That element is the mystical esotericism that in many ways testifies to the search for an individual spiritual practice that will grant access to a knowledge of and a new approach to the world. This practice must also be capable of endowing individuals with a mastery of the forces at work in all aspects of natural, social and psychological reality, which would permit them to realize, by this path, their aspiration to a better and more authentically human society. In the eighteenth century, the spiritual currents that developed such a will to demiurgic power were sustained by many different sources. The Jewish Cabbala, whose diffusion all across Europe was carried out by the Christian Cabbalists of the Renaissance and their successors in the various schools of Theosophy, offered them inexhaustible resources (Mopsik 1997: 235 ff). The fecundity of this vein among a multiplicity of groups in search of a primordial wisdom that encompassed all learning and traditions is not the least of the threads that demonstrate the continuity, over two centuries, between the spiritual effervescence of the century of the Enlightenment and the new contemporary spiritual culture. The city of Lyons prior to the Revolution gives us an idea of this fertile ground (Dupront 1996: 88–136). The search for the power associated with the development of new knowledge permeates, for example, the *martinésisme* of Martinès de Pasqually, whose *Traité de la réintégration des êtres* (*Treaty on the Reintegration of Beings*) combines a Theosophical reading of the universe with the doctrine of 'Emanation': in the beginning, the divine unity contained all things; it grew unceasingly through the emanation (emancipation by the Creator) of 'emanated' beings whom he furnished with wills of their own, that is, liberty and autonomy. The doctrine of Villermoz, which came from the theories of Pasqually, present themselves as a Masonic crypto-Catholicism with the accent placed on the union of Churches, the search for communication with the spiritual world, and the call for moral purity. Martinès de Pasqually's other disciple, Claude de Saint-Martin, founder of the great mystical movement called *Martinism*, bore witness to the full universality of the revelation – all the peoples without exception received the divine word – and defined religious life as an individual search for communication. His 1782 work, called *Tableau naturel des rapports qui existent entre Dieu, l'homme et l'univers* [*A Natural Tableau of the relations between God, Man, and the Universe*], develops an individualistic spiritual theology, likely to satisfy both the Enlightenment spirit and the pre-Romantic urges that appeared at that time. The development of these movements (we could cite many others) which proliferated in France on the eve of the Revolution reflected a search for an alliance – and even a melding – of the spiritual quest and the project of scientific knowledge and the technical mastery of the world that we often identify as a specific feature of the most contemporary religious currents. The spiritual experience as a means and expression of the power that individuals can exercise over the world and over themselves, outside of any commitment to a particular church, is one of the essential aspects of the refurbishing of religious individualism brought about by its absorption by modernity.

We must pursue the study of the diverse configurations of the relationship between modernity and spirituality since the seventeenth and eighteenth centuries in order to refine our perspective on the contemporary development of 'new religious movements' whose novelty tends to be exaggerated by sociologists of religion. The specificity of these movements comes not from their completely new way of bearing witness to the 'triumph of the individual' but rather from their pushing to its logical consequences the incorporation of the spiritual quest in a psychological modernity characterized by the individual concern for self-fulfilment.

References

Champion, F. (1993) 'Religieux flottant, éclectisme et syncrétismes', in J. Delumeau (ed.) *Le fait religieux*, Paris: Fayard, pp. 741–72.

Delumeau, J. (1989) *Rassurer et protéger. Le sentiment de sécurité dans l'Occident d'autrefois*, Paris: Fayard.

Dupront, A. (1996a) 'Province et Lumières: l'exemple de Lyon' in A. Dupront *Qu'est-ce-que les Lumières?* Paris: Folio, pp. 88–136.

—— (1996b) 'Lumières et religion: la religion de Voltaire' in A. Dupront *Qu'est-ce-que les Lumières?* Paris: Folio, pp. 137–230.

Hervieu-Léger, D. (1999) *Le pélerin et le converti. La religion en mouvement*, Paris: Flammarion.

Jossua, J.P. (1997) *Seul avec Dieu. L'aventure mystique*, Paris: Gallimard.

Maire, C. (1997) *De la cause de Dieu à la cause de la Nation. Le jansénisme au XVIIIe siècle*, Paris: Gallimard.

Mauzi, R. (1994) *L'Idée du bonheur dans la littérature et la pensée françaises au XVIIIe siècle*, Paris: Albin Michel (1st edn 1979, Armand Colin).

Mopsik, C. (1997) *Cabale et cabalistes*, Paris: Bayard.

Schrader, H.J. (1995) 'Piétisme', in *Encyclopédie du Protestantisme*, Cerf/Labor et Fides.

Troeltsch, E. (1976) *The Social Teachings of the Christian Churches* (2 vols), Chicago: University of Chicago Press (1st German edition 1912, Tübingen: Mohr).

Vattimo, G. (1998) *Espérer croire*, Paris: Seuil.

Weber, M. (1958) *Essays in Sociology*, Oxford: Oxford University Press.

CHAPTER 3

The Paradoxes of *Laïcité* in France

Jean-Paul Willaime
Translated by Allyn Hardyck

Talking about French *laïcité* in other countries leads to translation issues. For example, translating the French word *laïcité* with *secularism* in English or with *Laïzismus* in German already implies a biased interpretation of French *laïcité*, as secularism and laicism both represent an ideology with antireligious connotations that does not acknowledge what French *laïcité* is in institutional and legal terms: a separation between church and state that protects the freedom of religion and of non-religion, whose intention is to avoid any discrimination against people on the basis of their religious affiliation or lack thereof. But seeing French *laïcité* in terms of secularism and laicism, and therefore in terms of a 'neutral attitude' regarding religions that in reality is rather negatively inclined toward them, is in some respects understandable. Indeed, French *laïcité*, throughout its history and in the current context, conveys in different degrees and with differing consequences, a profound suspicion of religion that regularly engenders a somewhat tense attitude where religion is concerned. This suspicion and this tension are kept alive by critical perceptions of religion as expressed by intellectuals and supported by militant groups (the antireligious left and the teaching community for example) and by Masonic organisations (such as the *Grand Orient de France*).

In other words, *laïcité* is not free of secularism and there is a power struggle at work between two tendencies: on the one hand, the advocates of a kind of *laïcité* that is open-minded and respectful of the existence of religion, a tendency that has no problem integrating itself into the legal structures of European democracies; and on the other hand, the advocates of a hard-line *laïcité* that has not abandoned its intent to disqualify all public relevance of religious systems and to reduce their influence as much as possible. The first tendency is a management-minded *laïcité* that corresponds for the most part with the actual practices of relations between religions and public authorities in France on both the national and community levels. The second tendency, which is seen more in words than in actions, is much more ideological and corresponds to an often polemical rhetoric – as with the issue of Muslim headscarves in the school – which captivates intellectuals and public opinion and which demonstrates that *laïcité* remains a French passion (Baubérot 2004). Is the process that had brought French *laïcité* to the point where it could manage religious practices in a peaceable and dispassionate manner within the framework of fundamental human rights, the process which marked the end of the war between Catholic and secular France, under threat today? In other words, faced with the question of cults and new religious movements on the one hand, and with that of Islam on the other, are we witnessing in France today the awakening of a hard-line *laïcité* and the reactivation of the concept's secularist aspects? My answer to this question, though affirmative, will nonetheless be measured and qualified. Indeed, French *laïcité*, despite the traces of antireligious criticism that may linger in it, is effectively evolving toward a broad-minded regulation of religious diversity in tune with the rest of Europe.

Let me start by quoting the way in which the so-called 'Stasi Commission' (the report of the 'advisory commission on the application of the principle of *laïcité* in the Republic', submitted to the then President, Jacques Chirac, on 11 December 2003) defines *laïcité*:

> The State neither imposes nor compels; no creed is either required or prohibited. *Laïcité* implies the State's neutrality: it must not favour any spiritual or religious belief. Basing its actions on the principle of equality, the secular State does not grant public privileges to any religion, and its relations with religions are characterised by its separation from them from a legal perspective. Freedom of religion allows all religions freedom of expression and association and the shared pursuit of spiritual goals. Seen in this way, this freedom must exclude any anti-religious approach. The secular State does not promote atheistic or agnostic convictions any more than it defends a religious dogma of any kind. Similarly, spiritual and religious systems must refrain from seeking influence upon the State and give up their political dimensions. *Laïcité* is incompatible with any idea of religion that wishes to regulate social or political systems on the basis of its supposed principles.
>
> In the secular framework, spiritual or religious choices are a matter of individual freedom. However, this does not mean that these questions are limited to the depths of one's conscience, 'privatising' them so to speak, and that the social dimension of religious beliefs or the possibility of expressing them in public is denied. *Laïcité* distinguishes between the free expression of spiritual or religious beliefs in the public sphere – which is legitimate in and essential to democratic debate – and influence by religion on the public sphere, which is not legitimate. In this capacity, the representatives of different spiritual alternatives are justified in taking part in public debate, as is any other constituent element of society. (Stasi 2004: 30–31)

According to this approach, *laïcité* is neither an agnostic counterculture, nor the implementation of a complete privatisation of religion. It is rather a means of social pacification that allows for the regulation of religious diversity in society, while guaranteeing the religious neutrality of the State. In reality, things are not as simple as this and the French handling of religious beliefs remains marked by a profound suspicion by public authorities of religion and the threat that it could pose to individual liberties and freedom of thought. The Stasi report itself does not hesitate to remind the State of its duty in the areas of education, 'helping to create a sense of personal autonomy and freedom of judgment'; 'the defence of the freedom of individual conscience against all proselytising'; and 'critical awareness of religions'. The report is not exempt from quite biased representations of religion, as shown by the following quote, which seems amazed that a religion could have universal aims and be as interested in the material world as the hereafter: 'When a religion has universal aims, encompassing the hereafter as well as the material world, it finds it hard to accept separating one from the other' (ibid.: 37).

We shall develop our analysis in three parts. The first part will cover the historical grounds of the construction of *laïcité* in France. The second part will present the current reactivation of certain secular tensions concerning religion. The third part will discuss the underlying tendency at work in France as in other European countries: an evolution toward a broad-minded regulation of religious diversity.

The Historical Grounds of French *Laïcité*

Article 1 of the Fifth Constitution of the French Republic (1958) declares: 'France shall be an indivisible, *secular* [our emphasis], democratic and social Republic. It shall ensure the equality of all citizens before the law, without distinction of origin, race or religion. It shall respect all beliefs.' It is a secular republic that, according to Article 2 of the law of 9 December 1905 separating Church and State, 'neither recognises nor funds any religion', while ensuring 'freedom of conscience' and guaranteeing 'the free exercise of religion' (1st Article of the law of 1905). All religions are put on an equal footing: as none are 'recognised', there is no particular legal status accorded to the majority religion (Catholicism). It therefore goes without saying that no special provisions are granted to minority religions either. This *laïcité* recognises the internal organisation of each religion: the Catholic Church, having refused the status of a 'religious association' granted in the 1905 law because it did not take into account the church's hierarchical structure and the authority of bishops, was offered the status of a 'diocesan association' in 1923, which it accepted. The fact remains that *laïcité* has established itself in a confrontational context: the much talked-about 'war of the two Frances', secular and Catholic. French *laïcité* cannot be understood without taking into account the fight against clericalism; that is, against the power of the Church over society and individuals, in particular in the area of education.

In the case of France, the process by which religious systems were rendered secular accompanied another process by which political systems were made sacred, where the State was invested with the mission of regenerating the individual and reforming society, thus a truly ethical mission. This came about as a result of the French Revolution, whose hidden goal 'was to found a new religion, a civic theocracy whose vocation was none other than to replace the traditional frameworks of belief' (Deloye and Ihl 2000: 142). Tocqueville (1988: 106) had correctly observed that the French Revolution was a political revolution which 'acted like and began to look like a religious revolution'. In the same way, Jack A. Goldstone (1989: 405), an American sociologist doing a comparative study of various revolutions, points out that what distinguishes the French Revolution is a 'cultural framework' where, 'for the first time, the eschatological framework of the Christian era, the belief in the destruction of the past and the creation of a new age of virtue, appears completely secularised and transformed into a belief in man's power to create a superior world with his own hands'. In the very name of the equality of all individuals before the law, in other words in the name of the principle of non-discrimination and the universality of the citizen-individual, 'the notion of the minority as a group is unknown to French law' (Lochak 1989: 111). Minority voices are acceptable, but not minority groups. As

Pierre Birnbaum states regarding the emancipation of the Jews carried out by the French Revolution, it is a matter of 'a specific mode of entry into modernity via a 'liberating state universalism, one which however is not very favourably disposed toward maintaining distinctive identities' (Birnbaum 1989: 497–510).

In France, much more than in other countries, the construction of democracy and the institutionalisation of a republican system therefore took place in a context of frontal opposition to religion, in this case an open conflict with the Catholic Church which, since 1790, found itself cast among the counter-revolutionary groups. The impact that this conflict had in the institutionalisation of the Republic was such that the State often took the form of a counter-system of influence in the face of that of the Catholic Church: indeed it became a veritable counter-Church with its own clergy, catechism, and rites: 'The secular religion produced in France has sometimes taken the form of a Catholicism without Christianity,' writes David Martin (1979: 24). Pierre Bouretz sees in 'the copycat rivalry between the dogmatic unity advocated by the Catholic Church and the idea of the republican nation as an organic whole that borrows ideas from the Church while fighting it' one of the keys to understanding post-revolutionary French history (Bouretz 2000: 60–61).

Hence, there are certain peculiarities that characterise France in the area of the relations between the State, religions and society. 1) Church-state relations have been more confrontational in France than elsewhere: since the French Revolution and throughout the 19th and 20th centuries, the question of the place and the role of religion in our country has been a central one, generating deep and lasting divisions. 2) The question has a strongly ideological nature here with the influence, more pronounced in France than in most other European countries, of philosophical conceptions and political critiques of religions (from freethinkers, rationalists, Marxists, Freemasons and others).[1] 3) The supremacy of the State and its authority over civil life is affirmed here more strongly than elsewhere, in keeping with the tradition of a State that is on the one hand emancipating and enlightened, and on the other hand centralising and homogenising. 4) There is a strong resistance here toward public expressions of religious affiliation, and the disappearance of religious activity from public life is more accentuated in France than elsewhere in Europe. Even if one finds some of these same dimensions in other European countries – in varying combinations and with varying levels of importance – what makes France a special case in our opinion is the relevance that these dimensions have had in the social and historical configuration of our country. This is why in France, more than elsewhere, questions involving religion and its public handling are particularly sensitive ones in public opinion that can result in militant mobilisations, taking a philosophical, political and world-historical turn that often surprises foreign observers.

This was demonstrated by the debates on private schools in the 1950s and 60s with a resurgence of mass demonstrations in 1984 in favour of private schools and in 1994 in favour of the public school system; by the debates and fears stirred up

---

1   The relatively important role that the Communist Party has played in our country is yet another peculiarity in comparison with most of the other countries in Western Europe. In 2002, what struck outside observers was the significant impact of the far left, Trotskyist movements in particular.

by the cults; and by the reactions provoked by the wearing of headscarves in public schools by some Muslim girls. 'In France,' writes François Dubet with a great deal of insight, 'debates on *laïcité* quickly take on religious overtones; one talks much more easily of principles than of practices. Thus, ever since the society discovered or rediscovered its "cultural minorities", we are now faced with having to decide between the universal and the particular, between national unity and the right to difference, between the republic and democracy ...' (Dubet 1996: 85). In France, religion is put on the public agenda when, rightly or wrongly, it appears as a threat to individual liberties and to the Republic's *laïcité*. The history of France has fuelled this social representation of religion which has meant that, in our country, there has been a consistent tendency to want to 'rescue people from the dark realms of religion instead of simply creating separate spaces for Church and State' (Bouretz 2000: 31). Comparing the United States with France, Pierre Bouretz emphasises that America 'is apparently unaware of a philosophical and political conception of *laïcité* which in France seems to require that freedom be obtained through tearing oneself away from religious beliefs'. The contrast between the two countries, according to him, lies in the fact 'that on one side of the Atlantic it is religious freedom that comes first, so that separation follows as a necessary consequence, whereas on the other side, in an imagined struggle against obscurantism, the goal is emancipation in relation to beliefs, with a slight hint of largesse toward "even religious" opinions' (ibid.: 58).

The Tensions within French *Laïcité*

France is not alone in Europe in having to face the challenges represented by contemporary religious trends, characterised in particular by the appearance of religious movements of a sectarian nature and by the presence of a large Muslim minority. However, its model of integration and assimilation and its tradition of neutralising public religious activity accentuate its difficulty in rethinking citizenship under the new conditions of democracy, confronted by the assertion of cultural rights and the readjustment of the State's role given the contexts of Europeanisation and globalisation.

In the delicate area of the fight against 'sectarian deviations', given that this kind of manifestation of religious belief came at just the right moment in France to reawaken antireligious sentiments that had been taken aback by the modern and democratic reconsideration of religion, blunders and unfair, tendentious simplifications were inevitable. The struggle against sectarian deviations is legitimate when it comes from public authorities safeguarding the respect of laws and individual liberties.[2] But if the State has the duty to protect the freedom of people, it must protect religious freedom as well, which implies, as Danièle Hervieu-Léger has rightly pointed out, the respect of the right to religious radicalism: 'An individual must be able to choose freely to live in poverty, chastely and obediently, to give him- or herself a spiritual master or to enter into an order for the greater glory of God without running the risk of being put in the care of a guardian on the grounds of feeblemindedness and social

---

2   On this theme, a classic book has been written by Beckford (1985).

maladjustment' (Hervieu-Léger 2001: 185). What struck us is that, under the guise of the struggle against sectarian deviations, a hostile attitude has been rekindled toward what participation in religious practices could mean in terms of commitment for those who believe. Two elements – on the one hand a parliamentary report that lumped together a few problem groups with a majority of inoffensive ones, on the other the extremely partisan point of view developed by an interdepartmental team for the fight against cults (MILS)[3] – were contributing factors to an approach marked by a very restrictive and biased representation of religious beliefs. MILS, more influenced by private organisations than controlled by public authorities, was disbanded in 2002 and replaced by an interdepartmental team of vigilance in the fight against sectarian deviations (MIVILUDES).[4] Although the fight against cults does not consist merely of this kind of condemnation of nonconformist religious belief but raises, though awkwardly, the legitimate question of the respect of fundamental liberties, the fact remains that it is also an opportunity for awakening an ultra-Jacobinism through the mobilisation of the Republic against different, militant forms of religious expression that are seen from the outset as a 'danger'. The About-Picard law of 12 June 2001 'against sectarian movements infringing upon human rights', though fortunately restricted and limited in its effects by the principles of the right to certain freedoms, is nevertheless a repressive law presenting risks of arbitrary application, notes Patrice Rolland (2003: 149–66) in a detailed analysis of this law and the debates that governed its conception. Indeed, the law is one that targets 'cults' while admitting that one cannot define a cult, and which creates a crime of 'preying upon weakness' that is only slightly less fuzzy from a legal standpoint than the former crime of mental manipulation, which was finally abolished after various protests. It is a law that, significantly, wished to eliminate from its scope 'political parties, unions and professional groups' (an oral correction by its sponsor Catherine Picard) as if preying upon weakness could concern only religious groups.

This fight against sectarian deviations has effectively reactivated the tendency of public authorities to go after non-conformist movements and limit the right of individuals to choose their own lifestyles and educational priorities; that these choices are based on religious loyalties only encourages the State's zeal. This is why we think that the forms taken by the fight against cults in France can be analysed alongside those of the 'republicanist deviations' mentioned by Michel Wieviorka who notes that 'the visibility of various distinct identities in the public sphere and the affirmation of the right to difference are taken as attacks on the nation's unity and, hence, as attacks on the Republic' (Wieviorka 1999: 11). Faced with a religious pluralism that is heightened under the influence of both globalisation and individualisation, the French state has rediscovered its old reflexes of profound suspicion regarding

---

3   *Mission Interministérielle de Lutte contre les Sectes*, created in 1998, whose chairman was the former minister Alain Vivien.

4   *Mission Interministérielle de Vigilance et de Lutte contre les Dérives Sectaires.* The disappearance of the term 'cults' (*sectes*) is a welcome one. Speaking of 'sectarian deviations' is one way of signifying that such deviations can occur in any religious group and that there is not on the one hand suspicious religious groups thought of as 'cults' and, on the other hand, groups beyond reproach identified consequently with traditional religions.

religious sentiment, which is still considered as a worrisome threat to the State's prerogatives and the allegiance that the individual must demonstrate toward it before anything else. The State's acceptance of cultural pluralism has been difficult, especially when a particular custom appears to be connected with a foreign culture; its acceptance of religion has also been difficult when a particular belief is unwilling to remain limited to a private setting or a pure role as a religion. Behind the fight against cults, something else has in fact become apparent: the intolerance of public authorities and the general population toward those individuals who have chosen to live differently in the name of a religious ideal and to educate their children along those lines. In France the limited tolerance of non-conformism becomes even more limited as soon as a religious aspect manifests itself. This profound suspicion toward militant and all-encompassing forms of religious expression is, in our view, one of the repercussions of the highly confrontational nature of the relations between the State and religions in our country. Nevertheless, this trend is counterbalanced by the increasing role of the legal regulation in religious matters. In July 2007, for instance, Catherine Picard, President of an anti-sect association, was found guilty of slandering the Jehovah's Witnesses (according to *Le Monde* 24 November 2007, she had said that the Jehovah's Witnesses were structured 'like the Mafia'). Jean-Pierre Roulet, President of the MIVILUDES and Jean-Pierre Brard, a deputy involved in anti-cult actions, have also been prosecuted for slander by diverse religious groups.

The other subject that seems to reactivate tensions among some defenders of *laïcité* is Islam. These reactions are of course reinforced by the impact of September 11, the situation in Iraq, the conflict between Israel and Palestine; and the worries regarding terrorism. All of these lead public authorities to deal with Islam in a context of heightened security, slowing and complicating the smooth integration of this religion into the religious landscape in France. The fact that the Muslim population belongs to the most underprivileged and vulnerable sections of society only makes matters more difficult; the integration of this population cannot simply be reduced to a matter of religion. Let us recall that 'Muslims form the majority of the prison population; the rate often goes beyond 50 per cent, sometimes approaching 70 per cent, even 80 per cent in the prisons closest to the suburbs' (Khosrokhavar 2004a: 11). Are they the outcasts of the Republic? In any event, Muslims have the distinct sense that they are being discriminated against. The fascinating and perceptive survey carried out by Farhad Khosrokhavar among Muslim prisoners demonstrates the biases, the weaknesses and the omissions regarding the inclusion of specifically Muslim needs in the way prisoners are treated. For example, even in a prison with a majority Muslim population, special packages are allowed for Christmas but none to celebrate Eid, the end of Ramadan.[5] In their comparative study, *Muslims in Prison. Challenge and Change in Britain and in France*, Beckford, Joly and Khoroskhavar (2005) have recently shown how the treatment of Muslims in French and British prisons is dependent on more general policies and practices relating to the accommodation of religious and ethnic minorities.[6]

---

5   'the reception of a package to celebrate the end of Ramadan, Eid, is not permitted; the prison administration only accepts such packages at Christmas' (Khosrokhavar 2004a: 130).

6   On this theme, see also Beckford and Gilliat 1998.

Of the twenty-six propositions formulated by the report of the 'advisory commission on the application of the principle of *laïcité* in the Republic', only one, that relating to the wearing of religious signs in school, has been accepted as of now. It led to the law of 15 March 2004, which went into effect on 1 September 2006. 'In schools, *collèges* and public *lycées*,[7] the wearing of signs or clothes by which the students ostensibly demonstrate a religious affiliation is prohibited. School regulations state that the initiation of disciplinary procedures must be preceded by discussion with the student.' Public debate has been very lively and heated on this subject and I shall not summarise it here. I would like only to emphasise the paradox that French *laïcité* leads to. The main, central concern that lies behind this report and this law involves the Muslim population and its integration into French society. But since, as a result of the principle of *laïcité*, it is not possible to legislate in relation to a particular religion, a law was passed concerning the ostensible demonstration of religious affiliation at school that therefore included crosses, yarmulkes and other signs. Result: Sikh students, whose turbans were not a problem beforehand, now find that they are prohibited from wearing their turbans in school. This law, which therefore concerns all religions, has been and is effectively still seen as the 'law on the Muslim headscarf' in school and in public institutions. At the beginning of the school year, the number of girls who persist in wearing the headscarf and are expelled from public school is scrupulously counted. According to the authorities, this law has allowed the problem to be resolved, as a number of girls have agreed, after a period of dialogue, to stop wearing their headscarves. But some associations dispute this official position; they present the cases of girls who preferred giving up public school in order to avoid being expelled because they wore the headscarf. As a result, some Muslims, and non-Muslims as well, have got the feeling that the authorities' way of dealing with religious expression discriminates against Islam by singling out and stigmatising some of its followers. In this matter, some recall that it is not the students who are supposed to be secular, but the school and its staff as a public institution, which means that this public institution called the school should welcome all students in all their diversity. It is not surprising to note the enlargement of what I could call the headscarf prohibition zone, not only in other public institutions, but also in the school itself with the tendency to not allow Muslim mothers wearing the headscarf to accompany students with their teachers during school outings. As Khosrokhavar says, 'The combative dimension of *laïcité* is thus encouraged rather than its function as a means of integration .... From a *laïcité* of integration one moves toward a *laïcité* of exclusion' (Khosrokhavar 2004b: 48–9). Here, in the name of its ideal of integration of all people, regardless of their sex, their ethnic background, or their religion, *laïcité* runs the risk of causing the expulsion of some Muslim girls from public school. Does one expel in the name of integration? In the name of the emancipation of women, *laïcité* runs the risk of discriminating against girls, whereas young Muslim men can go to school without any trouble whether they wear a beard or not. A paradoxical consequence of the law of 15 March 2004 which wants to

---

7   The *collège* groups pupils from approximately 11–15 years of age, and goes from sixth year [*sixième*] (11–12 years) to third year [*troisième*] (14–15 years). The *lycée* goes from second year [*seconde*] (15–16 years) to [*Terminale*] (18 years of age and above). [Translator's note]

defend *laïcité* is the interest shown by some Muslim students and their family in the private school sector. At Décines, in the suburb of Lyon, a big Muslim school opened in September 2007 with 62 per cent of girls among the students and the majority of these girls are wearing headscarves (*Le Monde*, 5 September 2007).

So, there are tensions in the way in which the system of *laïcité* handles Islam, at the very moment when various quests for identity are asserting themselves, and when French society is becoming more and more diverse at the cultural and religious levels. The whole self-image of the French Republic, based upon the abstract universalism of the citizen, is thrown into question. Today, universality is no longer obtained by abandoning differences; it is founded on the very basis of those differences. This is what the French republican model, based on assimilation, has trouble admitting, especially when religious identity is involved.

French *Laïcité* and its Open-Minded *Aggiornamento*: 'a Legal Principle Applied Empirically'

Pierre Rosanvallon speaks of an 'unspoken reformism' at work in France, by which the policies and institutions of our country are modified 'without anyone openly putting these changes and their implications into words'; consequently, he adds, the gap between the facts and the way they are presented continues to widen (Rosanvallon 2004: 433). Applied to *laïcité*, this remark is profoundly valid. A rhetoric of *laïcité* that confines religious practice to the private sphere contrasts with a practical application of *laïcité* that increasingly recognises the public dimensions of religious belief. A position on national identity that holds up *laïcité* as one of the unique characteristics of the French Republic contrasts with a calm Europeanisation of *laïcité* that forces France to come to terms with the inapplicability of its version to the rest of the continent. An ideological *laïcité* whose antireligious dimensions are poorly disguised contrasts with an empirical *laïcité* that respects religious freedom and is capable of recognising the positive contributions of religions to civilisation. In its application of a *laïcité* of recognition and intelligence, France is actually more European than one would think.

If one gets beyond the rhetoric of many positions on *laïcité*, and if one pays attention to the day-to-day practice of relations between public authorities and religions as it is carried out in French cities and on the ministerial level, another face of *laïcité* in France appears. Here, instead of confining religious belief to the private and individual sphere, *laïcité* grants full recognition to its public and collective aspects. At the beginning of every year, the President of the Republic receives the representatives of different religions for a New Year's ceremony at the Elysée Palace. At the local level, let us mention an example that is far from unique. In Grasse (near Nice in the Alpes-Maritimes *département*), it is not unusual that a traditional festival organised by the city council starts with a solemn mass at the cathedral. In addition, there was a reception at the city hall after the mass for the ordination of the new archbishop. Today, many mayors of large cities take it upon themselves to organise public debates with representatives of different religions in their community in order to maintain a climate of goodwill between people of varying religious affiliations. In the name of *laïcité*, therefore, the believers of different religions are recognised by the local public authorities, which take their beliefs into account.

Emile Poulat (2001: 108) points out 'this undeniable, often neglected fact: separation is what enables cooperation and sometimes compels it'. It is precisely because Church and State are separate that they can cooperate. There was much talk about the effort put out by French public authorities to arrive at the creation of a *French Council for the Muslim Faith*,[8] a grouping whose representative nature has been debated, but which as least has the merit of existing. At the time of its creation, some people, in the name of *laïcité*, denounced what they saw as an illegitimate intervention by the State in the internal organisation of a religion. Every year in France, government figures meet representatives of the Jewish faith during the dinner organised by the *Representative Council of the Jewish Institutions of France.*[9] On 12 February 2002, Prime Minister Lionel Jospin received the president of the Conference of Bishops of France, the archbishop of Paris and the papal nuncio; the two sides agreed to establish 'a permanent structure of dialogue and cooperation', not only to examine problems of an administrative or legal nature in relations between the State and the Catholic Church, but also to discuss important issues in society like bioethics or family law.[10] This dialogue continued during the administration of Prime Minister Jean-Pierre Raffarin. The French Republic, as committed to *laïcité* as it is, is still capable of taking into account the role of churches in its international relations. The Ministry of Foreign Affairs is aware of the fact that the Catholic Church maintains diplomatic relations with 176 countries through the Holy See, and that the French Protestant churches have close ties with many churches on other continents (in particular in Africa and Polynesia). On the national level as well, the usefulness of religious representatives for dealing with delicate situations in some problem suburbs has not been ignored either. Another example of the relaxation of tensions between churches, state and society: the recognition of the contribution of religions in the area of social programmes and solidarity. In 1995, the secretary of state in charge of underprivileged neighbourhoods specifically called upon the Churches to join in with the government's efforts in this area. Even if many secular organisations take part in social programmes, religious organisations and religious figures are legitimised in their appeal to public compassion; their participation in charity programmes is important. Religions are also called upon to handle crises. The team sent to New Caledonia in 1988 to help with reconciliation was partly comprised of representatives of various religious and philosophical sensibilities (in particular, a priest, a minister, and a Freemason). Religious figures are also asked to preside over the funerals of the victims of catastrophes. Recently, representatives of the French Muslim community participated in negotiations to help obtain the liberation of French hostages in Iraq. In short, in the way relations between church and state are handled in France, religion is often far from being limited to a purely

---

8   *Le Conseil Français du Culte Musulman.*

9   *Le Conseil Représentatif des Institutions Juives de France.*

10   Xavier Ternisien, in the article in *Le Monde* discussing these facts, goes as far as to speak of an '*entente cordiale* between the Catholic Church and the State' (*Le Monde*, 27 February 2002).

private, individual choice. Since the facts will not go away, policy cannot ignore the social importance of religious practices.

Moreover, the questions raised by research in biology and genetics have been responsible for the return of ethical questions to the centre of debate in society, creating a need for ethics. 'Spiritual families' are thus included in the thinking and research carried out by public institutions like the *Consultative Committee on Ethics for the Life and Health Sciences* (created in 1983)[11] and the *National AIDS Council* (created in 1989).[12] Alongside non-religious views of humanity and the world, religions are also asked to participate in the legitimisation of human rights and the basic principles of pluralist democracies (such as they appear in the *European Convention on Human Rights*). Confronted with overt expressions of racism and anti-Semitism, we have seen an ecumenical approach to human rights at work, bringing Christians, Jews, Muslims, Freemasons and other sensibilities together in a celebration of the values of liberty, equality and fraternity.

By entrusting Régis Debray with a mission on 'the teaching of religious facts in the secular school system' on 3 December 2001, the Minister for National Education, Jack Lang, realised that if 'a school system that is authentically and dispassionately secular' must allow every student to be able 'to understand the world,' that meant that teachers needed to take into account 'religions as essential and, to a large extent, constitutive elements of human history, sometimes as factors of peace and modernity, sometimes as instigators of discord, murderous conflict and regression' (Debray 2002: 9–10). Hence the need, as Régis Debray put it so well, to move 'from a *laïcité of incompetence* (religious belief, by its nature, doesn't concern us), to a *laïcité of intelligence* (it is our duty to understand it)' (ibid.: 43). To this end, the Debray report calls for a few measures that concern both the school syllabus and the training, introductory and ongoing, of secondary school teachers, in particular the inclusion of a course on religious facts and *laïcité* at the University Institutes of Teacher Training.[13] The actions taken to train teachers in the area of the history and sociology of religions are on the increase in different schools, following the creation of the *European Institute of Religion Science*,[14] under the aegis of the Ecole Pratique des Hautes Etudes.

Therefore, the system of *laïcité* does not build a wall as impenetrable as one would think between the State and religions. Thus the secular Republic gives economic support in various ways to religious groups: not only for the maintenance of religious buildings, but also, for example, by completely exempting donations and bequests to churches from registration taxes (law of December 26 1959). The law on patronage of 27 July 1987 authorising certain tax-deductible donations to churches is another example of the generous nature of contemporary *laïcité* regarding religions; some have even seen this law as an attack on the principle of *laïcité* in the fiscal domain. For the jurist Francis Messner, the legal frameworks in which religious activities have been placed (the religious associations of 1905 and, for the Catholic Church, the diocesan associations of 1923), have become much more like 'public interest

---

11   *Le Comité consultatif d'Ethique pour les Sciences de la Vie et de la Santé.*
12   *Le Conseil National sur le Sida.*
13   Les Instituts Universitaires de Formation des Maîtres (IUFM).
14   *L'Institut Européen en Sciences des Religions.*

groups' or unions than the simple associations for 'religious practices' to which some would like to limit them (Messner 1993: 92). A 'well-tempered separation', a 'benevolent' or 'positive' neutrality, a 'new pact of *laïcité*' – these are some of the expressions that indicate an evolution toward a *laïcité* free from hostility regarding religion; on the contrary, a *laïcité* that wishes to create a place and a role in society for religious belief. Since the Catholic Church no longer threatens the foundations of the republican system, that system 'is capable of reintegrating the Church into the public sphere with the other religious groups, and even to grant it a regulatory function in civil society, abandoning the previous measures that isolated it' (Portier 2003: 16).

Even if such actions foster resistance and difficulties, France is now effectively committed to a new system of public policy where the role of the centralising State is less important. Taking his inspiration from the analyses of Jacques Commaille and Bruno Jobert on the contemporary transformation of political regulatory practices, Philippe Portier emphasises that, under this new arrangement, the central government, 'deprived of the monopoly on deciding what constitutes the general interest, is now just a collaborative force among others in lawmaking, in a process where all the institutions of civil society are associated ever more closely, through various contractual agreements' (ibid.: 22). If public authorities give financial support to social, cultural, and sporting activities that used to be sponsored by private interests, and if professional groups, unions and associations are publicly recognised and subsidised with public funds, Portier points out that it is unclear why 'religious groups, which are also components of civil society,' should remain 'isolated from this general tendency' (Portier 2003: 11). As the secular State gives up its absolute dominion over civil society, it is increasingly inclined to recognise the contribution of religious groups to public life. In so doing, it effectively becomes even more secular.

Despite the reactivation of a hard-line *laïcité* that would like to impose a somewhat negative neutrality toward religious practices, a more open-minded *laïcité* is developing in France, taking the form of a benevolent neutrality toward religious belief.

If one wants to be sure not to confuse the essential principles of *laïcité* with the word used to designate them, the fact that this term is hard to translate into most of the languages spoken in Europe does not mean that other countries are unaware of the realities that it encompasses. The essential principles of *laïcité* are respected in Europe: a two-part neutrality (independence of the State in relation to religions and the freedom of religious organisations in relation to public authority); the freedom of religion and of conscience, implying the absence of discrimination against people on the basis of their religion or their lack of religion; the practical implementation of these freedoms and guarantees within the limits of public order; and human rights as they are understood in democratic societies. Micheline Milot, studying *laïcité* in Quebec, insists quite rightly on the need to extract this concept 'from the French historical context where it emerged' in order to separate it from 'its ideological function' and to consider it in more political terms (Milot 2002: 23). For her, *laïcité* concerns 'the political adjustment, then the legal translation, of the place of religion in civil society and in public institutions' (ibid: 34). A political adjustment and a legal translation that, in Europe as on other continents, implements in various ways the principle of neutrality that political and religious institutions have regarding each other. As in other European countries, France is faced with social and religious changes that represent new challenges and call for certain readjustments.

References

Baubérot, J. (2004) *Laïcité 1905–2005, entre passion et raison*, Paris: Seuil.

Beckford, J.A. (1985) *Cult Controversies. The Social Response to New Religious Movements*, London: Tavistock.

Beckford, J.A. and Gilliat, S. (1998) *Religion in Prison. Equal Rites in a Multi-Faith Society*, Cambridge: Cambridge University Press.

Beckford, J.A., Joly, D. and Khoroskhavar, F. (2005) *Muslims in Prison. Challenge and Change in Britain and in France*, Palgrave: Macmillan.

Birnbaum, P. (1989) 'Les juifs entre l'appartenance identitaire et l'entrée dans l'espace public: la Révolution française et le choix des acteurs', *Revue Française de Sociologie* XXX–3/4: 497–510.

Bouretz, P. (2000) 'La démocratie française au risque du monde', in M. Sadoun (ed.) *La démocratie en France. 1. Idéologies*, Paris: Gallimard, pp. 27–137.

Debray, R. (2002) *L'enseignement du fait religieux à l'école*, Rapport au ministre de l'Education Nationale, Paris: Odile Jacob.

Deloye, Y. and Ihl, O. (2000) 'Deux figures singulières de l'universel: la république et le sacré', in M. Sadoun (ed.) *La démocratie en France. 1. Idéologies*, Paris: Gallimard, pp. 138–246.

Dubet, F. (1996) 'La laïcité dans les mutations de l'école', in M. Wieviorka (ed.) *Une société fragmentée? Le multiculturalisme en débat*, Paris: Editions La Découverte, pp. 85–112.

Goldstone, J. (1989) 'Révolution dans l'histoire et histoire de la Révolution', *Revue Française de Sociologie* XXX–3/4: 405–29.

Hervieu-Léger, D. (2001) *La religion en miettes ou la question des sectes*, Paris: Calmann-Lévy.

Khosrokhavar, F. (2004a) *L'islam dans les prisons*, Paris: Balland.

—— (2004b) 'La laïcité française à l'épreuve de l'islam', in J. Bauberot (ed.) *La laïcité à l'épreuve. Religions et libertés dans le monde*, Paris: Universalis, pp. 41–52.

Lang, J. (2002) Preface to R. Debray, *L'enseignement du fait religieux dans l'école laïque*, Rapport au ministre de l'Education Nationale, Paris: Odile Jacob, 2002.

Lochak, D. (1989) 'Les minorités et le droit public français: du refus des différences à la gestion des différences', in *Les minorités et leur droit depuis 1789*, Studies compiled by A. Fenet and G. Soulier, Paris: L'Harmattan, pp. 110–20.

Martin, D. (1979) *A General Theory of Secularization*, New York, Hagerstown, San Francisco, London: Harper Colophon Books.

Messner, F. (1993) 'Laïcité imaginée et laïcité juridique. Les évolutions du régime des cultes en France', *Le Débat*, 77: 88–94.

Milot, M. (2002) *Laïcité dans le nouveau monde. Le cas du Québec*, Turnhout: Brepols.

Portier, P. (2003) 'De la séparation à la reconnaissance. L'évolution du régime français de laïcité', in J.-R. Armogathe and J.-P. Willaime (eds) *Les mutations contemporaines du religieux*, Turnhout: Brepols, pp. 5–24.

Poulat, E. (2001) 'L'esprit d'une réflexion sur notre laïcité publique', in J. Baudoin and P. Portier (eds) *La laïcité. Une valeur d'aujourd'hui? Contestations et renégociations du modèle français*, Rennes: Presses Universitaires de Rennes.

Rolland, P. (2003) 'La loi du 12 juin 2001 contre les mouvements sectaires portant atteinte aux droits de l'homme. Anatomie d'un débat législatif', *Archives de Sciences Sociales des Religions*, 48th year, 121: 149–66.

Rosanvallon, P. (2004) *Le modèle politique français. La société civile contre le jacobinisme de 1789 à nos jours*, Paris: Seuil.

Stasi, B. (2004) *Laïcité et République*, Rapport au Président de la République de la Commission présidée par Bernard Stasi, Paris, La Documentation Française.

Ternisien, X. (2002) article in *Le Monde*, 27 February 2002.

de Tocqueville, A. (1988) *L'Ancien Régime et la Révolution (1856)*, Paris: GF-Flammarion.

Wieviorka, M. (1999) 'Dérives républicanistes', in *Le Monde des Débats*, section 'La République est-elle en danger?', September.

CHAPTER 4

French Cult Controversy at the Turn of the New Millennium:
Escalation, Dissensions and New Forms of Mobilisations across the Battlefield[1]

Véronique Altglas

It has frequently been noted that the French response to NRMs was distinctive among Western countries. Despite the small number of individuals involved and the absence of clear signs of serious and widespread problems occurring in French society, it has been indeed a passionate, conflictual and surprisingly enduring social issue. Waco in the United-States (1993), Aum Shinrikyo's gas attacks in Japan (1995), and above all the much closer – geographically and linguistically – tragic end in 1995 of the Order of the Solar Temple (OST) re-awoke in the mid-1990s a controversy that has proved to be long-running and acerbic. It also took an official turn with the State's strong involvement. A few days after OST's second collective suicide, this time in France,[2] the National Assembly hastily published a Report, *Cults in France*, renowned for its list of 172 dangerous groups provided by the police intelligence service, which drew on information from anti-cult organisations. The aim of this chapter is to give an account of transformations in the French cult controversy since the mid-nineties. It is obviously a way of furthering the empirical and analytical description initiated by James Beckford (1985), and an attempt to understand the ways in which social norms are challenged and negotiated through a dynamic process, involving individual trajectories and collective mobilisations.

1   This research has been possible thanks to a post-doctoral fellowship granted by the ESRC (2005–2006) and the unceasing support of my mentor, James Beckford. This chapter has also benefited from fruitful exchanges with Sabrina Pastorelli. It is based on the analysis of written sources: official reports, press articles, the websites of various NRMs, anti-cult movements and organisations defending NRMs, interviews conducted in France in May 2006 and March 2007; and observation of the case in appeal CAP v. UNADFI, Paris, 27 March 2007. I formally requested, by mail, an interview with the president of UNADFI for this research, but I received no response.

2   The main collective suicide of the OTS took place in Canada and Switzerland in 1994, but the controversy was inflamed a year later in France, when a group of 16 French and Swiss members were found dead in the Vercors.

The Mid 1990s: the Starting Point of an Escalation of the French Cult Controversy

To begin with, it would be worth discussing the aftermath of France's parliamentary Report on cults (Gest and Guyard 1996)[3] and its notorious list of 172 'dangerous' movements. Unfortunately, criticisms from academics (Introvigne and Melton 1996; Champion and Cohen 1997) regarding the mistakes and poor quality of the Guyard Report marginalised the sociology of religion rather than discrediting the Report. Furthermore, NRMs were unable to call to account the authors of the Report: not only did parliamentary immunity protect the latter, but the courts have not held the term 'cult' (*secte*) to be defamatory. But the list has had an impact of considerable magnitude: despite the fact the Report has no legal status, it became an official and prevailing reference, leading the public to think there was a legal definition of cults and well-identified groups, the harmful effects of which had been established. The media has systematically referred to the list and some still assume today that it is legally recognised. More importantly, the courts of justice have explicitly referred to it, as well as administrative and local authorities, with the consequence that it has prevented various groups from buying or renting public places, and resulted in individuals losing their employment or child custody cases. Was it because of this unwise and excessive use of this list that the Prime Minister, Jean-Pierre Raffarin (2005), decided to officially abolish its use? It is possible that he did not totally disavow the anti-cult policy; his official statement asserted that this list was less appropriate since the 'cult phenomenon' has become disseminated in smaller, looser, therefore less identifiable structures. Accordingly, rather than listing cults, the Prime Minister suggested drawing up a set of criteria to identify 'sectarian deviations' that could apply to any organisation. Nevertheless, in regard with the persistence of 'cult' as a social representation, it is doubtful that the now obsolete list of dangerous cults will be soon forgotten.

Indeed, the Guyard Report could serve as a watershed for strengthening French anti-cult campaigns and policies. In accordance with its proposals, the *Interministerial Observatory of Cults* was created in 1996. It was shortly after succeeded by a second committee of inquiry that published another Report, *Cults and Money* (1999), and by the establishment of the Inter-ministerial Mission to Combat Cults (MILS) in 1998. The replacement of an *Observatory* by a *Mission to Combat* clearly highlighted a reinforced government commitment to the question of cults, which was further underlined by the law known as the About-Picard Law, enacted in June 2001.[4] This Law, specifically targeting sectarian movements, allowed for the civil dissolution of such groups, limiting their right to advertise and giving associations that are accredited as having public utility the right to bring legal actions for offences committed by 'cults'. The Law's draft included a highly controversial *misdemeanour of mental manipulation*, which was removed and replaced by measures relating

---

3   An earlier Report had been written in 1983 by Alain Vivien (1985) at the request of the then Prime Minister.

4   A Bill to strengthen the prevention and suppression of cultic movements that infringe human rights and fundamental freedoms.

to the fraudulent *abuse of ignorance or weakness*, that is to say 'the physical or psychological state of subjection resulting from serious or constant pressures or from techniques that alter personal judgment'. Despite its title specifically referring to 'cults', the About-Picard Law simply reinforces the common law but appears problematic because of the subjectivity of notions such as 'weakness' on the one hand, and the lack of any definition of 'cult', which is the very object of the Law on the other hand (see Altglas 2001; Rolland 2003). The Council of Europe has asked France to reconsider the Law and clarify its terms, yet the About-Picard Law was used in 2004 to condemn the leader of a small esoteric and millenarian movement, Neo-Phare. Following the suicide of one of its members, the leader of Neo-Phare, Arnaud Mussy, was found guilty of abusing the weaknesses of four victims and received a three-year prison sentence (see Palmer 2006).

In 2002, the Inter-ministerial Mission of Vigilance and Combat against Sectarian Deviations (MIVILUDES) replaced MILS. This was the result not only of a change of government (the Prime Minister had sought to soften the debate and wished the state's involvement to be more balanced), but also of the fact that MILS's President, Alain Vivien, had been criticised for his strong line and divisive initiatives, even by some members of MILS itself. In contrast, MIVILUDES' first President, Jean-Louis Langlais, asserted that his purpose was not to target groups or doctrines in particular, but 'sectarian deviations' (acts) in whatever organisation they occur. Despite the widespread alarmism, he expressed reservations about the significance of sectarian activities in France and asserted that the State could not act in a militant manner (Courage and Lemonnier 2005). However, it is probably accurate to say that this soft line was short-lived. His successor, Jean-Michel Roulet, has laid stress on the continuity of the State's anti-cult policy. Criticising the moderate approach of his predecessor, he is proud to declare that the struggle against cults has been strengthened,[5] and wishes to see early condemnations of cult leaders under his presidency (Ternisien 2006a).

> When some organisations – cults – claim that we totally fantasise and that nothing actually happens, when we will have proved that they're wrong, that they lie shamelessly, that damages do exist … then we will have really done our job. And I really wish that we'll be able to do it, because victims and families expect it. The expectation is huge.[6]

---

5   In this regard, relations between MIVILUDES and sociologists are quite telling. Under Langlais' presidency, research projects and collaborations were implemented, a seminar on 'Cults and *Laïcité*' involving academics was organised, with the proceedings published by MIVILUDES (2005). Following the change of presidency, the anthropologist Nathalie Luca resigned from MIVILUDES because of its strong line, and collaboration with sociologists of religion ceased. 'MIVILUDES is not a research group', insisted J.-M. Roulet, 'there have been deviations during these past six months. Parliamentarians were complaining, organisations defending cult victims were complaining too. MIVILUDES is back at work. It will fulfil all the missions expected by the decree of its creation' (Ternisien 2005). A few months later, Sébastien Fath, a French scholar studying Evangelical Protestantism, was asked to join MIVILUDES by its president, but he refused, pointing to MIVILUDES' lack of genuine interest in sociology of religion and the risk of its misuse.

6   Interview with J.-M. Roulet, 2 May 2006, Paris.

There can be no doubt that, despite the recent emphasis on 'sectarian deviations' rather than on listing specific groups, the commitment of the State against 'cults' in France is neither weakening nor abandoning the targeting of particular NRMs. In June 2006, a third parliamentary commission was commissioned to investigate the influence of cults on children. This was one of the main concerns expressed in MIVILUDES' previous annual Report; the work of this new commission was intended to be complementary to MIVILUDES' initiatives, granting legitimacy to the anti-cult policy on account of its parliamentary nature.[7] Drawing on interviews with various professionals and ex-cult members, as well as an unexpected visit to *Tabitha's Place* (the Twelve Tribes' movement's community in the South of France) in order to assess the children's learning and health, the Commission presented its Report in December 2006. Alarmed by the thought that a minimum of 60,000 to 80,000 children might be raised in a cult in France,[8] the authors recommended fifty measures to control home schooling, assess children's health, and limit isolation within the parental environment. These propositions inspired several amendments regarding childcare that were eventually approved by the National Assembly in January 2007, including the power to punish parental refusal of vaccination and to limit home schooling.

The Extension of the Battlefield

The strengthening of the legal and official dimensions of the anti-cult conflict is probably its most obvious distinctive feature, but there are some other trends that have recently become more apparent. One of these is the extension of the battlefield beyond the scope of what sociologists call the NRMs. The finger is now also pointed at certain kinds of large-group training and the proliferation of post-psychoanalytical therapies as popular spheres of influence of sectarian organisations. 'There may be problems with a training programme by dint of the content, methods or objectives, without it being possible to actually identify or establish links with a cult movement …' (MILS 2001: 89). It is suggested not only that cults in disguise try to surreptitiously penetrate the health sector and professional training, but also that a wide range of popular methods might themselves be sectarian deviations. This allows the anti-cult approach to considerably enlarge its scope and depict a distressing situation in which the cult phenomenon mutates and spreads through small, fragmented and unidentifiable structures into the domain of new types of medicine, psychology, diets and training.[9] These additional areas have become core topics in the anti-cult campaign: MIVILUDES' 2005 Report recounts complaints and concerns about, for

---

7   National Assembly, Creation of a Parliamentary Commission relating to the influence of cults on children. Official Account, 28 June 2006, First Session.

8   These dubious figures are based on an estimation of 45,000 children whose parents are Jehovah's Witnesses, and 'there might be 30 or 40,000 children who belong to other groups' – a statement that suggests an implicit list of cults. Emmanuel Jancovici, interviewed by the Commission, 12 July 2006.

9   Both J.-M. Roulet and Catherine Picard evoked the worrying 'atomisation' and blending of the sectarian phenomenon in 'Quelle est la réalité des sectes?' Licht 2005; and

example, Energetic Therapies, Psychogenealogy, Shamanism, Reiki, macrobiotic Zen, and Kinesiology (2005: 29–30). In its 2006 Report, no less than twenty pages are devoted to the sectarian risks of Transactional Analysis; many post-psychoanalytical, holistic therapies and alternative medicines are cited as examples of dubious and potentially dangerous methods, encouraged by New Age thinking and involving one or more features of sectarian deviations. Consequently, anti-cult policies now also concern individuals involved in a wide range of professional activities in the field of training and therapy.

Strikingly, this evolution of the French cult controversy has probably been made possible by the end of 'cult' listing. This was justified not only by the dissonance between a legal definition of 'cult' and the principle of state neutrality towards religion and belief, but also by the fact that, in the opinion of anti-cult supporters, the so-called cults reject being labelled a cult, and so represent themselves as therapy or training groups[10]. As a result investigators now target *any* kind of cultic practice. This extension of the battlefield has to be understood in the light of a wider social debate concerning the regulation of the psychotherapeutic profession in France. Since 2003, draft Bills have been introduced with the aim of regulating the diverse and unregulated field of psychotherapies and personal growth trainings. Trapped between powerful lobbying forces, the new legal arrangements have undergone numerous discussions and reviews during the past four years and are not yet in force at the time of writing (Champion 2005). Incidentally, the regulation aiming at institutionalising and medicalising psychotherapy has explicitly been justified as a way to combat the cults' influence: directly referring to the MILS Reports, the initial draft Bills were explicitly motivated by the need to prevent cults from using psychotherapeutic techniques to manipulate individuals.[11] It is no surprise that MIVILUDES and UNADFI, the main anti-cult movement in France, supported the implementation of these regulations, considering the regulation to be a new weapon against the cults.

Golden Partnership between Anti-Cult Movements and State Agencies

The escalation and strength of the French cult controversy can be further explained by one of its long-standing dominant features, which is the quasi-official status of anti-cult movements (ACMs), collaborating with state agencies. Indeed, the voluntary organisations, such as UNADFI and CCMM, are involved and formally represented in the state agencies monitoring 'cults', enabling them to provide information, propose and support initiatives (they also do so directly to Ministries, local authorities and the police intelligence service). In this regard, they are a very influential lobby. The quasi-official status of these militant organisations has already been noted (Beckford

---

Les nouveaux charlatans de la santé, retrieved 14 February 2007 from UNADFI's website: http://www.unadfi.com/spip.php?article198.

10   National Assembly, Second reading and enactment of the Bill About-Picard, official account of the session of 30 May 2001.

11   B. Accoyer, draft Bill on psychotherapies, National Assembly, 26 April 2000; Bill introduced by B. Accoyer, art. 18 of the Law on Public Health, 8 October 2003.

1985: 286–71; Champion and Cohen 1997), but what is staggering is the trajectory of social players involved in both militant anti-cult organisations and state-based initiatives. Socialist Party politician, Alain Vivien was nominated President of MILS (1998–2002) while he was chairing the *Centre Roger Ikor Contre les Manipulations Mentales* (CCMM), one of the main French ACMs (whose current president is Daniel Groscolas, a former General Inspector for Education who, in the mid-1990s, was appointed by the Minister of Education to monitor the influence of cults in the field of education). Groscolas was then nominated to chair MILS and is currently a member of MIVILUDES' Council of Orientation as a representative of CCMM. Another significant example is Catherine Picard, who drafted the 2001 Law with centrist Senator Nicolas About (who has also been nominated to MIVILUDES). She now chairs the *Union Nationale des Associations de Défense de la Famille et de l'Individu* (UNADFI) and thereby participates in MIVILUDES' Council of Orientation. It might also be noted that the main parliamentarians who reported on the influence of cults on children (Jean-Pierre Brard, Martine David and Georges Fenech) are also members of MIVILUDES' Council of Orientation.

This circulation of powerful key-players ensures an efficient collusion between ACMs and parliamentary and inter-ministerial initiatives; that is to say a collusion between the militants on the one hand, and the state on the other hand. The authority of these stakeholders makes possible the political and juridical outcome of anti-cult campaigns, and gives them legitimacy, as long as the collusion remains discreet. Indeed, MIVILUDES downplays the importance of the relationship, nowadays presented as communication and exchange of information between two independent bodies. Yet *Les sectes en France* mentioned UNADFI and CCMM as 'experts' in the field (Gest and Guyard 1996: 27); according to MILS, 'carry out a real public service mission and comprise two associative pillars inextricably linked with the action of the authorities in their own field of competence' (MILS 2001: 5–6*)*. And indeed these ACMs are state-funded on the principle of public benefit; and the About-Picard Law allows them to bring legal actions for offences committed by NRMs. As we shall see further on, this golden partnership does not prevent the anti-cult front from being divided and attacked.[12] Indeed, because of their non-governmental nature, these voluntary organisations are the anti-cult front's weakest link as well as its most contentious.

---

12   Janine Tavernier, former President of UNADFI recently denounced the radicalisation and politicisation of the anti-cult milieu, now weighing doctrines. It is the result, according to her, of the involvement of Freemasons in UNADFI, originally founded by 'opened Catholics' (Ternisien 2006c). It is probably accurate to state that while the opposition to NRMs in the 1980s came predominantly from the Catholic Church, the anti-cult front of the 1990s is more secularist and draws on Enlightenment ideals. More interesting is the statement she made, soon after she resigned, about what she called a 'witch-hunt': 'some use the cult phenomenon to make denunciations and create rumours. Basically, if one has issues with his neighbour, he accuses him of being a cult member' (Veillard 2001). Her defence of an open and neutral approach as well as her current opposition to cult listing would probably surprise every sociologist who had studied UNADFI's activities during the 1990s.

The State and NRMs: the Politics of a Double-Headed Eagle

At the same time as the golden partnership between the State and militant organisations reinforces the power and influence of anti-cult campaigns, it threatens to undermine the legitimacy of such collaboration. The ACMs' militant approach indeed entails a dissonance with the principle of State neutrality in religious matters. Unsurprisingly, this dissonance is most challenged by the state agency which has the responsibility of guaranteeing public liberties and state neutrality in religious matters. This Department of Religions (*Bureau des Cultes*), founded as a result of the Law of Separation of Church and State (1905), administrates religious organisations, controlling their finances and overseeing the maintenance and the use of religious public assets. In some ways like the British Charity Commission, it registers 'religious organisations' and 'congregations', granting them benefits and legal privileges such as the right to receive donations and legacies, and tax exemption. This administrative department of the Ministry of the Interior embodies and enshrines the core principles of the 1905 Law: it stipulates that the Republic ensures freedom of religion, neither recognising nor supporting any particular religion. Accordingly, the *Bureau des Cultes*, as a principle, can define neither religion nor 'cult'.

The contrast between this department and the Inter-ministerial missions combating the cults should not be overstated as both can be normative. Indeed, the *Bureau des Cultes*' supervision of religious organisations was historically a legal arrangement to normalise and redefine the State's relations with the Catholic Church, and is, therefore, challenged by the modern diversification of religions. Furthermore, the indirect recognition of historically known forms of religious life has been depicted not only as the result of the French cultural heritage, but also as a means for the State to discriminate against 'cults', by not according them the tax and legal benefits of 'respectable religions' (Messner 1997: 337), giving way to the exercise of discretionary power. The *Bureau des Cultes*' representative himself acknowledged that it has not always been liberal: whereas the notion of '*culte*' was enlarged in order to recognise Buddhist congregations and associations, legal recognition was originally denied to the Jehovah's Witnesses on the grounds that their refusal to engage in military service and rejection of blood transfusions threaten public order (Council of State, 1985).[13]

However, despite the fact that the State has occasionally used its discretionary power over the granting of tax and legal benefits to religious organisations, it can be argued that the *Bureau des Cultes* is not inherently discriminatory and that NRMs are potentially assimilable by the French system of legal recognitions of religions. Indeed, the *Bureau* recently disavowed MIVILUDES, thereby contradicting its anti-cult policies. The cleavage became publicly apparent as a result of a controversial interview of Didier Leschi, the representative of the *Bureau des Cultes* by the Parliamentary Commission on the influence of cults on children. Leschi first stressed the *Bureau des Cultes*' role in guaranteeing the freedom of conscience and of religion – this, he insisted, entails the right of parents to raise their children according to their

---

13   Didier Leschi at the Parliamentary Commission on the influence of cults on children, Paris, 17 October 2006.

own standards. By referring to these fundamental rights guaranteed by the *Bureau des Cultes*, he explicitly criticised MIVILUDES for pronouncing judgements on doctrines and arbitrarily targeting groups such as the Jehovah's Witnesses, the Plymouth Brethren and the Lubavitch, emphasising a shift away from impartiality and towards a cleavage between recognised and stigmatised religions:

> I really fear that the stigmatisation of movements such as the Lubavitch and the Plymouth Brethren might become enacted by people who will take advantage of an anti-cult righteousness to justify malevolent or anti-Semitic actions. In this regard, we observe an increase of aggression against the Jehovah's Witnesses; in other words, I really fear that this stigmatisation, this type of denunciation constitutes at the end of the day a threat to public order or at least manifestations of intolerance towards one of the most fundamental liberties of all human beings and all citizens, the freedom of conscience.[14]

This somewhat provocative statement outraged the members of the Commission, who surprisingly reacted most strongly to Leschi's explanation of the *Bureau des Cultes'* policy concerning the Jehovah's Witnesses: in accordance with the Council of State's jurisprudence, and as long as there is no factual evidence to prove that the Jehovah's Witnesses breach public order, the local associations of this organisation will be granted the legal benefits provided by the 1905 Law. What has been erroneously interpreted as an 'official recognition of the Jehovah's Witnesses' religion'[15] generated immediate hostility, resulting in a heated exchange between Leschi and the parliamentarians. It was then followed by hostile pronouncements in the press, condemnations of the *Bureau des Cultes'* complacency and connivance with the Jehovah's Witnesses, and unsuccessful pressure on the then Minister of the Interior, MP Nicolas Sarkozy, to dismiss Leschi from MIVILUDES's Council of Orientation (Licht 2006; Ternisien 2006b). However, Leschi reiterated his stance, saying 'that the Ministry of the Interior is too liberal in regards to the freedom of conscience is a judgement that I consider to be positive'. He added:

> Since 2000, there is on this point a continuity of the administrative practice with four successive Ministries of the Interior: when there's no evidence of public order offences, there's no reason, in the legal frame of the 1905 Law, not to grant this or that religious group the benefits provided by the status of a religious association. (Anciberro 2006)

While Leschi is the first representative of the *Bureau des Cultes* to make such a public stand (he later explained to me his sensitivity to the question of persecution), the *Bureau des Cultes* had indeed been consistently responding to the radicalisation of anti-cult policies when these threatened to infringe fundamental rights. Its legal approach led it to disavow the list of cults published in the Guyard Report: massively solicited after its publication, the *Bureau des Cultes* has clearly indicated that this list has no legal standing whatsoever and all groups, whether religions or labelled as 'cults' in common parlance, are subject to common law. As far as the Bureau was

---

14   Leschi at the Parliamentary Commission, Paris, 17 October 2006.

15   G. Fenech (President of the Commission and previously the Judge of the long trial against Scientology in Lyon, in the 1990s), and A. Gest (Secretary of the Commission), Interview of Didier Leschi, Paris, 17 October 2006.

concerned, being included in the list in the Report did not constitute a public order offence. The Bureau affirmed that 'no group has ever been categorized as a "cult" by the Republic',[16] a statement that shed light on an occasional (yet significant) cleavage between it and the state agencies for combating 'cults'. The *Bureau des Cultes* had also contradicted MILS in the late 1990s: Alain Vivien had instructed local representatives to forbid organisations to call themselves 'religious associations' until a decree allowed them to benefit from the legal and tax benefit of the 1905 Law (as most of them do not, it was a means to prevent the formation of religious associations). The *Bureau des Cultes* immediately sent a counter-directive insisting on the illegality of these instructions: not only was the president of MILS not entitled to give such instructions to local authorities, but these directives contravened the right of association, a fundamental liberty guaranteed by the Ministry of the Interior.

These examples cast doubt on the alleged unanimity of the French State's response to the so-called cults. Rather the *Bureau des Cultes*' and MIVILUDES' divergent roles and approaches seem to make of the French state a double-headed eagle, undeniably bringing contradictory administrative and political responses to the issue. This institutional double-headed eagle primarily epitomizes the unresolved dissonance, firstly between the State's neutrality in religious matters (the official principle guaranteed by the *Bureau des Cultes*) and its anti-cult policies (MIVILUDES' function) and secondly between the guarantee of public liberties and the protection of citizens, described as cult victims by MIVILUDES and used as a justification for monitoring the so-called cults.[17] Ultimately, it is also the contradiction between defiance towards religion and liberal conceptions of individual conscience, both implied by *laïcité*, that are outlined by the French state's double response to 'cults'.

NRMs Strike Back, Reflecting their Nemesis

Doubts raised over the legitimacy of anti-cult campaigns have, however, been rare, and their impact in counterbalancing representations and legal arrangements regarding cults has been practically nonexistent. Hence small and powerless NRMs tend to avoid social visibility, refrain from advertising their activities and meetings, and adopt a low profile. In contrast, movements that have adequate human and financial resources such as the Church of Scientology or the Jehovah's Witnesses seem eager to battle on the legal and media fronts. The Universal Church of the Kingdom of God, Scientology and the Jehovah's Witnesses obtained the disclosure of the notes written about them by the police intelligence service and which had been transmitted to the National Assembly for the writing of the Guyard Report and that had thereby justified their presence in the list of dangerous 'cults' (because the tribunal considered the notes to be 'administrative' and not 'parliamentarians documents', it ruled that they must be disclosed to the public on demand).[18] The

---

16   J.-P. Gioux, representative of the *Bureau des Cultes*, letter, 10 March 1998.

17   *Laïcité* itself entails paradoxical relations with religion (see Baubérot 1997; Beckford 2004).

18   The administration is compelled to make available certain administrative documents. Accordingly, MIVILUDES was concerned as no less than forty requests were made in 2006

Jehovah's Witnesses have taken numerous legal actions against the administration: to benefit, for example, from the 1905 Law as a religious association; to be allowed to construct places of worship or to rent public buildings. Several trials for defamation have also been brought by diverse organisations (from the Jehovah's Witnesses to Anthroposophy) mainly against ACMs and the media. By and large, while civil rights played a minor role in the 1980s (Beckford 1985: 272), the cult controversy has significantly shifted to the legal realm.

NRMs have also elaborated new forms of mobilisation in founding 'cult-defensive groups' (see Barker 2007), resulting from the impossibility for outcast organisations to respond directly and publicly to the anti-cult discourse. The first attempt was FIREPHIM, the International Federation of Religious and Philosophical Minorities, created in 1992 by Raël, the founder of the Raelian movement, and Danièle Gounord, the French representative of Scientology. FIREPHIM was said to represent several movements (Scientology, Raelians, the Children of God, the Unification Church, Sri Chinmoy Centre, Wicca Occidental, and the Jehovah's Witnesses). At the time, it only led the public to assume the so-called cults were all involved in a conspiracy against society. FIREPHIM was then followed in 1996 by another federation of NRMs with the aim of confronting ACMs and MILS, the *Omnium of Liberties*, which sprang from the publication of the Report *Cults in France*. Other 'cult-defensive groups' were yet to come as anti-cult campaigns strengthened.

These organisations' names and goals refer to freedom of thought, equality and tolerance: the defence of fundamental liberties was the official aim of FIREPHIM,[19] while the *Omnium of Liberties* tried to launch an Investigatory Commission for the Violation of Human Rights. While by using terms such as 'inquisition' and 'witch-hunt', they obviously borrow from the vocabulary of human rights and religious persecution discourse in order to universalise and legitimate their cause, their purpose is more specifically to challenge the ACMs and state agencies monitoring cults. Yet at the same time they have adopted a mimetic strategy and reflect their nemesis. As an example, in 1996, FIREPHIM announced the creation of a National Observatory of the Study of Cults, a duplicate that scandalised anti-cult partisans for its alteration of the official Observatory of Cults. More broadly, the riposte of cult-defensive groups seems to mirror their opponents' discourse and practice. While the suffering of the victim is the pivotal justification for MIVILUDES' and the ACMs' campaigns, cult-defensive groups also identify themselves as 'victims' whose rights have been violated. They too collect and publish personal testimonies and offer their support to people subject to discrimination because they belong to a 'cult' – an association 'to help UNADFI's victims' was launched in 2005.[20] They too denounce, expose their nemesis harassingly, and challenge their opponents on legal grounds: while UNADFI has often sued its detractors, the *Omnium of Liberties* had sued Vivien

---

about the budget of MIVILUDES and the ACMs, and correspondence between MIVILUDES, ACMs and Ministers (MIVILUDES 2006: 105–106).

19 The organisation's deed was retrieved 1 March 2007 from http://www.prevensectes. com/firephim.htm#cartel.

20 Association d'Aide aux Victimes des ADFI, retrieved 1 March 2007 from http://aava. blogspirit.com.

for defamation before CAP (Coordination of Associations and People for Freedom of Conscience) brought a legal action against UNADFI. Finally, they challenge the anti-cult front by promoting and spreading an alternative source of information about the so-called cults. Hoping for a great movement of solidarity between members of different spiritual paths, CICNS (Information Centre on New Spiritualities, a former branch of CAP) focuses on providing information online and reflecting on the role of spirituality in society.[21] In this regard, these cult-defensive groups generally seek support from academics who in their view produce an impartial and legitimate discourse on NRMs. It is no surprise that ACMs recently expressed their concern about these 'new sectarian strategies'. Accusing them of being a mask behind which criminal cults are kept out of sight (especially and obsessively Scientology), ACMs and MIVILUDES recently denounced their promotion of religious freedom as a forgery and accused CAP especially of instrumentalizing justice and using lobbying strategies.[22]

Indeed, for the first time a cult defensive group successfully gained the attention of the public in France when CAP took legal action against UNADFI (2005). CAP's strategies are partly rooted in the personal background of its founder and spokesperson, Thierry Bécourt (1960–), a graduate in psychology and the science of education who works as a librarian in a state school. Since he was a teenager he has been deeply interested in Eastern philosophy; he had explored Alice Bailey's Theosophical teachings and belonged to the esoteric organisation the Lucis Trust. Trained in Sophrology and Transpersonal Psychology, Bécourt founded in 1987 a small therapy group: the Psychanimie Institute. He is also involved in different voluntary associations looking at environmental issues and humanitarian aid, as well as having been an active union and staff representative. It is possible that the fact that his spiritual interests do not exclude social activism helps to explain his key-role in the response against ACMs. Nevertheless, the impact of the anti-cult campaign on his personal life was decisive. In 1995, Bécourt's therapy group was cited in the Parliamentary Report's list. Labelled as one of the 172 dangerous cults, his position in public education was at risk, and his union was not ready to defend a 'cult case'. Bécourt asserts that he had to take legal action to keep his job, and he now does not expect to receive any promotion. He also lost contact with his children following his divorce in 1998: UNADFI provided a Report on his therapeutic activities that was responsible for denying him custody of his children and, he claims, eventually persuaded his ex-wife to refuse him visitation rights.

Fighting ACMs became Bécourt's new battle. In 1996, he became an active member of the *Omnium of Liberties*, then he created CAP in 2002. Aiming at promoting the coordination of actions and help for individuals and organisations who have been unfairly discriminated against, CAP calls upon politicians to demand the repeal of the About-Picard Law; the cessation of public funds for ACMs; the modification of MIVILUDES' policy, which according to CAP infringes state neutrality in matters of religion; and the creation of a neutral, academically oriented

---

21   CICNS, retrieved 5 March 2007 from http://www.cicns-news.net.

22   UNADFI, Derrière la CAP, *Bulles,* n°88, 2005, retrieved 1 August 2006 from http://www.unadfi.com/bulles/bulles88/bulles888.htm. MIVILUDES 2006: 116–134.

observatory of new religions. CAP has organised an annual rally for the freedom of conscience for three years, and its website publishes a newsletter on the anti-cult campaign, press articles, and investigations into its detractors. It also collects testimonies, as well as court decisions and law articles on freedom of religion and human rights, and advertises academic books and events related to religion.[23] CAP represents 250 to 300 members, mainly individuals, half of whom belong to the alternative therapies milieu. Indeed, CAP has distinctively strengthened its position in gathering individuals, rather than trying to federate NRMs. While its predecessors had difficulties in uniting movements whose aims, problems and strategies could be radically different, CAP's membership of individuals is more flexible and inclusive. Its cause draws on personal cases, as opposed to claims from pariah organisations. Finally, while this does not prevent NRMs from collaborating with, and supporting CAP, its independence protects CAP from being held accountable for malpractices committed by any so-called cult.

What makes CAP distinctive is also its legal line of attack. In September 2005, on the assumption that the ACM's malpractices infringe freedom of conscience, CAP asked the Court of Paris to order the dissolution of UNADFI. The case was based on testimonies of eleven complainants who alleged that they had been suffering from discrimination because of denunciations made by UNADFI. It was argued that precisely because of its charitable status and the significant resources granted by the state, UNADFI had a duty to verify the information it disseminates. In response, UNADFI's barrister (Michel Tubiana, a former President of the League of Human Rights) questioned CAP's motives and its hidden agenda behind bringing the case. He claimed that, as a smokescreen for the cults, CAP's motive was to prevent UNADFI from disclosing its criminal activities and thereby silence the organisation – 'you have the right to know' were his closing words.[24] Not only did the Tribunal consider that CAP's request was without grounds, it condemned the plaintiffs for abusive procedure. CAP had to pay UNADFI's legal costs and to publicise the court's decision. This condemnation was no surprise: Bécourt feared a mild judgement that would have simply acknowledged 'mistakes' by UNADFI. His ultimate aim is to bring the case to the European Court, hoping that, in the meantime, new plaintiffs and lawyers will join the battle. At the time of writing (May 2007), CAP had lost its appeal. The court of appeal considered the plaintiffs had not provided evidence of UNADFI's responsibility for any discrimination they suffered. The first judgement was confirmed. It was, however, partially invalidated by the cancellation of the fine for abusive procedure.[25] This was a victory for Bécourt in that, thanks to the case, CAP successfully captured the attention of the media, who for the first time gave neutral accounts of the testimonies and arguments (Robert-Diard 2005; Riffaud 2005).

It is hoped that this account has convincingly illustrated the importance of collecting empirical data for the understanding of cult controversies, which are dynamic processes involving the constant elaboration of new mobilisations, strategies

---

23 CAP-LC: http://www.coordiap.com
24 Appeal session, Court of Paris, 27 March 2007.
25 Judgement of Court of Appeal, Paris, 29 May 2007.

and discourses. While it has been too often assumed there was unanimous agreement within the fight against the so-called cults, this empirical work has shed light on the diversity of social players involved and the conflictual nature of the debate, concealed by the legitimacy of an as yet small number of key social players whose voices are better heard than those addressing the legitimacy of anti-cult initiatives (see Arweck 2006). The responses of the State itself are contradictory, between its administrative practice and its political initiatives. Furthermore, the conflictual nature of the French cult controversies might well be amplified, paradoxically, by the strengths of the anti-cult front; in so far as it has gained a greater legitimacy through an alliance with powerful social players, it has achieved successes in implementing legal arrangements targeting the so-called cults, and it has enlarged its scope by addressing new themes. But at the same time, its successful campaign and politicalisation has aroused criticisms and provoked dissent; it has also given rise to cult-defensive groups that are countering the anti-cult front with some of its own weapons. Finally, targeting new fields (such as alternative medicine, professional training, education) as well as older organisations (such as Anthroposophy, Rosicrucian AMORC and now the Plymouth Brethren, the Lubavitch and some evangelical churches) has unavoidably raised reactions from new and diverse segments of society (such as the higher levels of the state administration, the Federation of Protestants, therapists, and associations for home schooling), even among those who might share its views on 'cults'. At the turn of the third millennium, clearly, the French cult controversy has not lost its fierce energy.

References

Anciberro, J. (2006) 'Division face aux sectes' (interview with D. Leschi), *Témoignage Chrétien*, 1 February.

Altglas, V. (2001) *Cults and State in France, a Misdemeanour of Mental Manipulation?* Paper presented at the annual meeting of the Association for the Sociology of Religion, Anaheim, California.

Arweck, E. (2006) *Researching New Religious Movements: Responses and redefinitions*, London: Routledge.

Barker, E. (2007) 'What should we do about the cults? Policies, Information and the perspective of Inform', in P. Côté and T.J. Gunn (eds) *The new religious question: state regulation or state interference?* New York: PIE-Peter Lang, pp. 371–94.

Baubérot, J. (1997) 'Laïcité, sectes, société', in F. Champion and M. Cohen (eds) *Sectes et démocraties*, Paris: Seuil, pp. 314–30.

Beckford, J. (1985) *Cult Controversies: the social response to New Religious Movements*, London: Tavistock.

—— (2004) '"Laïcité", "Dystopia", and the reaction to new religious movements in France', in J.T. Richardson (ed.) *Regulating Religion: Case Studies from Around the Globe*, New York: Kluwer Academic, pp. 27–40.

Courage, S. Lemonnier, M. (2005) 'Les nouveaux pièges des sectes' (interview with J.-L. Langlais), *Le Nouvel Observateur*, 19 May.

Champion, F. (2005) *France's 'illegitimate' psychotherapists in search of professional recognition: a difficult process of constructing legitimacy*, Report in English, retrieved 14 February 2006 from http://www.cesames.org/spip/article.php3?id_article=102.

Champion, F. and Cohen, M. (eds) (1997) *Sectes et démocraties*, Paris: Seuil.

Gest, A. and Guyard, J. (1996) *Les sectes en France, Rapport fait au nom de la commission d'enquête sur les sectes*, no. 2468, Paris: Assemblée Nationale.

Introvigne, M. and Melton, J. G. (1996) *Pour en finir avec les sectes: le débat sur le rapport de la commission parlementaire*, Paris: Dervy.

Lasterade, J. (2006) 'Il serait dangereux de reconnaître les Témoins de Jéhovah comme un culte', (interview with George Fenech), *Libération*, 1 November.

Licht, D. (30.09.2005) 'Quelle est la réalité des sectes?' (interview with J.-M. Roulet), *Libération*, 30 September.

Messner, F. (1997) 'la législation culturelle des pays de l'Union européenne face aux groupes sectaires', in F. Champion and M. Cohen (eds) *Sectes et démocraties*, Paris: Seuil, pp. 331–58.

MILS (2001), *Report in English 2001*, (Retrieved 25 February 2007 from http://www.miviludes.gouv.fr/rubrique.php3?id_rubrique=125).

MIVILUDES (2005) *Sectes et Laïcité*. Paris: La Documentation Française.

—— (2006), *Rapport 2005*. Paris: La Documentation Française.

—— (2007), *Rapport 2006*. Paris: La Documentation Française.

Palmer, S. (2006) '*France's About-Picard Law and Neo-Phare: The First Application of 'Abus de Faiblesse'*', CESNUR International Conference, San Diego, 2006. Retrieved 25 February 2007 from http://www.cesnur.org/2006/sd_palmer.htm.

Raffarin, J.-P. (2005) *Circulaire du 27 mai 2005 relative à la lutte contre les dérives sectaires*, Journal Officiel, no. 126, 1 June.

Riffaud, G. (2005) 'La révolte des suspects', *Le Point*, 1724: 76.

Robert-Diard, P. (2005) 'Les méthodes d'une association antisecte contestées au tribunal', *Le Monde*, 23 September.

Rolland, P. (2003) 'La loi du 12 juin 2001 contre les mouvements sectaires portant atteinte aux droits de l'Homme', *Archives des Sciences Sociales des Religions*, 121: 149–65.

Ternisien, X. (2005) 'Durcissement à la mission de lutte contre les dérives sectaires', *Le Monde*, 20 December.

—— (2006a) 'Les protestants s'inquiètent du regard soupçonneux antisecte', *Le Monde*, 14 March.

—— (2006b) 'Querelles autour du statut des Témoins de Jéhovah', *Le Monde*, 20 October.

—— (2006c) 'Il faut distinguer les mouvements religieux des vraies sectes', *Le Monde*, 17 November.

Vcillard, J. (2001) 'Sectes: Une hystérie française' (interview with Janine Tavernier), *Technikart*, November, no. 57.

Vivian, A. (1985) *Les Sectes en France: Expression de la Liberté*, Paris: La Documentation Française.

CHAPTER 5

Two Different Types of Manifest Secularization:
Belgium and France Compared

Karel Dobbelaere

Up to the eighteenth century many laws were inspired largely by Christian ethics, especially in the Catholic countries of Western Europe, where the Church had acquired authority over institutions such as education, the family and medicine. In the nineteenth century, things started to change; a process of *manifest* secularization (Dobbelaere 2002: 19–21), in French called *laïcisation*, is to be found in France, Italy, Portugal, Spain and Belgium, which makes Champion (1993: 593–602) suggest that 'the logic of *laïcisation*', which implies conflict, is typical for countries with a Catholic tradition. In Protestant countries, on the contrary, changes do not develop in an atmosphere of conflict; there we find rather a process of *latent* secularization, where internally related changes in different social sub-systems and religion occur simultaneously (1993: 592). However, although in Belgium and France the term *laïcisation* is used to describe the conscious and intended process of functional differentiation between religion and the so-called secular spheres – among others, polity, education, medicine and the family – the outcome is quite different.

The *Laïcisation* of France

The concept of *laïcisation* is of French origin and is linked to the particular history of France. The principles of *laïcisation* were proclaimed at the French revolution, but the institutionalization took time. The foundation was laid in the Declaration of Human Rights (1789), the third article declaring that sovereignty comes from the nation, and that there is no longer any divine right of kings. This 'de-sacralization of authority' is the foundation of *laïcité* according to J. Baubérot (2005: 7). It was Napoleon Bonaparte who initiated the possibility of the *autonomization* of two institutions: medicine and education (2005: 16, 23). In 1803, a law created the notion of the 'illegal practice of medicine', which gave the medical profession a monopoly over illness and death, and, in so doing, this law dispossessed the Church of its medico-religious role. And by creating an autonomous educational institution at the secondary and higher levels, Napoleon emancipated an institution from the Catholic Church which the Church had itself created. In fact, the law of 1806 stipulates that 'no one may inaugurate a school or teach publicly if he is not a member of the university and a graduate of its faculties'. Furthermore, the civil code, the so-called code Napoleon, organized the State, the family, contracts, and others, as totally autonomous from the Catholic religion (Champion 1993: 594); and the establishment of a municipal registry office secularized the certificates of birth, marriage and death, which had previously been registered by the Church.

The *laïcisation* of primary schools was a gradual procedure, which was established by law only in 1882. According to Baubérot (2005: 31), Belgium was the country that pointed the way forward with its law of 1879, which laïcized primary education (see below). The 1882 French law did not result in a peaceful situation, the fight of militant Catholics against the secularized primary schools persisted for a long time (2005: 48–53). By the end of the nineteenth century, a certain degree of appeasement was reached in France after the elections had confirmed the *laicizing* measures taken in the 1880s, such as the abolition of discriminatory measures on the basis of the religion of the deceased in municipal cemeteries in 1884, and of the Catholic theological faculties organized by the State in 1885 (Baubérot 2005: 60–61).

At the turn of the century the conflict between the *deux France* was exacerbated again. In 1902, a coalition of left-wing parties won the elections, and 10,000 schools run by religious congregations were closed. Nearly 6,000 quickly reopened when lay people took over with the help of so-called 'secularised' members of congregations – that is, religious persons who had abandoned the habit and congregational life with the consent of the bishops – and *l'école libre* (the private Catholic school) was born. The secularists reacted and wanted the instauration of the monopoly of the state schools: they opted for a *laïcité intégrale* (an integral *laïcité*), but this was not achieved (2005: 69–72). By 1905, *laïcité* and 'freethinking associated with freemasonry' tended to become synonymous (2005: 77). On 21 March 1905, the Chamber of Representatives started to discuss a proposal concerning the separation of Church and State. The Rapporteur of the Parliamentarian Commission, Aristide Briand, rejected an alliance between the Republican State and freethinking. According to him, freethinking had only to rely on 'the power of its own propaganda, on the strength of its arguments'. Implicitly, suggests Baubérot (2005: 78–9), Briand pointed out that freethinking, just like the Churches, would be separated from the State. The law on the separation of Religions and the State was promulgated on 9 December 1905 and was the work of a pragmatic elite in the socialist party – Briand, Jaures and Pressensé (2005: 80–81). It stated in the first two articles that the Republic assures the freedom of conscience and guarantees the free exercise of worship; furthermore, that the State does not recognize any religion, neither subsidizing religions, nor paying wages to ministers of religion. Article 4, which was of major importance to realize the separation of Church and State, was borrowed from the legislation of Scotland and the United States of America. It stipulates that public buildings for worship are allocated to 'religious organizations', which have to 'conform themselves to the general rules of their religion'. This implied that the Catholic religious organizations had to respect the authority of their bishops, or else they would be materially and symbolically penalised by the Republic. The radical parliamentarians considered this a 'pseudo-separation' since the article implied a recognition of the 'ultramontane Church' (2005: 81–2).

It took the Catholic Church in France and the Holy See nearly twenty years before they accepted the law (Baubérot 2005: 83–6). After the Second World War, in which persons of different convictions had worked together in the resistance, the end of the frontal conflict between the *deux France* was manifested in the constitution of the Fifth Republic (1958, revised in 1962). There it is clearly stated that France is a *République laïque*. Already in 1945, the Assembly of cardinals and archbishops of France had accepted the *laïcité* as the 'sovereign autonomy of the State', rejecting an anti-religious *laïcité* as in the USSR, and condemning also clericalism as 'a tendency that a spiritual society might have to use public power to satisfy its will of domination' (2005: 103–104). Did that mean the end of all conflicts between the Church and the lay Republic? Not entirely, since in the preamble to the constitution it was also stated that 'The organization of public education, gratis and *laïque* on all levels, is an obligation of the State' (my italics).

Jean-Paul Willaime (2007) stresses that 'in the war of the *deux France*, the school has always had a central place'. Referring to the law of 1882, he underscores that this law 'replaced "moral and religious instruction" by "moral and civic instruction"' (see also Baubérot 1997). The role of the schoolmaster was very central, he was the 'priest' of the laicized Republican faith and Balandier (1997: 124–7) depicts the impact of the ecclesiastical model on the laicized school: its laicized catechesis, its Republican hymns, and its proper rituals, where the speeches replaced the sermons. Laicized values were sacralized, and laicized virtues honoured.

To establish a basis for a lay morality and to diffuse a *laïque* spirit, Durkheim was very instrumental in the early twentieth century. In his analysis of Durkheim's life and work, Steven Lukes (1977) underscores his efforts to diffuse the *esprit laïque*. Durkheim had founded at Bordeaux an association of university teachers and students called *La Jeunesse Laïque* and in 1902 he was appointed *chargé de cours* in the Science of Education at the Sorbonne. Durkheim's pedagogy lectures to future schoolteachers, his efforts to develop a national system of secular education, and his new Republican ideology constituted his contribution to national reintegration. Nizen, Duveau, and others pointed out that the sociology of Durkheim triumphed in the *écoles normales* (teacher training colleges), and his ideas were consequently systematically disseminated throughout the schools of France (Lukes 1977: 320–60). According to Lukes:

> Durkheim believed that the relation of the science of sociology to education was that of theory and practice; and, in this respect, it would become a rational substitute for traditional religion. Teachers should be imbued with the 'sociological point of view' and children should be made to think about 'the nature of society, the family, the State, the principal legal and moral obligations, the way in which these different social phenomena are formed'. (1977: 359–60)

Durkheim also developed a new Republican ideology that was both scientifically grounded and pedagogically effective. 'What he produced amounted to a distinctive form of liberal and reformist socialism framed in solidarist terms' (Lukes 1977: 356). In evaluating his success, Lukes writes:

> One key element in his success was certainly his aggressive secularism, his desire to establish and inculcate a doctrine that would replace, and not compromise with, religion. Certainly, his view of existing religious beliefs did not allow him to favour any kind of

eclectic compromise between the religious and the secular (such as that attempted by his old teacher Boutroux or his rival Bergson), or any attempt to secularize or modernize the teachings of the Church. Like his equally rationalist colleague and close friend, Octave Hamelin, he held that 'in a rational morality God could not intervene as the source of obligation'. (1977: 358)

One can easily see that the Catholic private schools, with their religious meaning system and a morality based on God, were, and still may be, a thorn in the flesh of the secularists. In the 1959 law Debré integrated the contributions of the private denominational schools in the public service of National Education by instituting permanent contracts permitting private schools to retain their proper character and be financed by the state under certain conditions: to adopt the educational program of the public schools, and to accept all pupils whatever their religion. The *Comité national d'action laïque* (CNAL) protested with a petition of more than 10,800,000 signatures, but to no avail. CNAL then put all its hopes in the socialist candidate for the presidency, Mitterrand, who had promised a 'unified public service for national education'. However, on 24 June 1984 more than one million people demonstrated in the streets of Paris against the law – as it had been amended by the National Assembly to satisfy the critiques of the *laïques*. The President announced the withdrawal of the law (Baubérot 2005: 108–11). In 1994, ten years later, there was a new impressive demonstration in Paris, this time in favour of the state schools. The *revanche symbolique* (symbolic revenge) was a protest against an attempt by the government to allow local collectivities to finance expenses for investments in private educational establishments with more than the 10 per cent that the law had previously permitted. The Constitutional Council nullified the contested law (2005: 112). The two manifestations suggest to Willaime (2007) that the recurrent conflicts of the past, which were virtually defused, could still emerge on certain occasions. Referring to these events, Champion (2006: 160) underscores that *la querelle scolaire* (the school dispute) is more and more focused on the question of the financing of the private schools and still structures the political identities of the left and right.

The dispute re-emerged in connection with the *foulard musulman* in 1989 (Champion 2006: 161–7). In 2004 a law was approved that prohibited ostentatious signs or dress expressing any religious affiliation in the state schools. It seems to me that this is not only inspired by the so-called neutrality of the public schools, but is also partly due to a typical French reaction against communitarianism. There is a strong tendency in France to stress a Republican equality. Sintomer (2001: 287) cites Robert Badinter, a former Minister of Justice, who provided a vivid expression of this position: 'All are citizens, nothing more than citizens. That is the foundation of the Republic. She has never been a mosaic of communities neither a juxtaposition of different components. The Republic knows only individuals, human beings and citizens without any discrimination'. Another specification of the idea of Republican equality was given by a member of Parliament who stated that 'one of the greatest conquests of the Republic since the revolution is that the subject of the law in our Republic is neither man nor woman, neither Jew, black nor white, neither young nor old, neither owner or not, neither rich nor poor: it is the human being as such' (ibid.: 287). This *anti-communautarisme* or anti-communalism is also present in the evaluation of re-Islamization, of Muslim youth on a communal basis, which does not promote integration that has to occur on an individual basis in line with the French Republican tradition, and the headscarf is seen as a *droit à la différence* and an expression of communalism.

The *Laïcisation* of Belgium

The First Wave of Manifest Secularization and Pillarization as a Reaction

After Belgium's independence in 1830, Liberals and Catholics worked together to organize the State. However, after an initial period of cooperation, called Unionism, the radical liberal wing, under the influence of anticlerical Masonic Lodges, resented the authoritarian Catholic hierarchy and the guardianship of the priests over culture, education and poor relief. For example, in the primary schools organized by public authorities, the Church had by law obtained control over the nomination of teachers and over the handbooks that were used. However, in the second part of the nineteenth century, under the impact of changing parliamentarian majorities, the radical Liberals were able to implement a secularist policy with the help of an emerging socialist party (Wils 1977). By law, Liberal governments reduced the impact of the Church in charitable work, in poor relief, and in allocating study grants. The cemeteries were laicized and the regular clergy lost their exemption from military service. Ultimately, each municipality was obliged by law (1879) minimally to establish one school where religious instruction was not part of the compulsory curriculum and, from then on, the school-teachers in these schools had to be certified by a state school, which excluded teachers who had studied in Catholic Teachers' Training Colleges. This policy was implemented through skillful nominations of the governors of the provinces, the commissioners of administrative departments, and mayors and aldermen in cities. The press also played an important role in crystallizing opinion and mobilizing the population, which often involved street disturbances. The Church for its part reacted strongly in sermons, and by making enquiries in the confessionals and refusing the sacraments. The conflict over the schools stimulated Catholic leaders to erect private Catholic schools.

Confronted with the secularization of the social system, some churches reacted with a counter-offensive. At the end of the nineteenth century, adapting to the modern world, a process of pillarization became institutionalized in certain countries of Western Europe to protect believers from the secular world. In the Netherlands, a Catholic and a Protestant pillar emerged, and Catholic pillars were gradually established in Austria, Belgium and Switzerland (Righart 1986), and also in Germany and Italy. Pillarization started in Belgium by duplicating the state school system, which had been established by the law of 1879, with a Catholic private school system, the result of 'the first school war'. And to protect Catholics from the 'world' and from a growing number of opportunities that were developing, the Church erected its own associations. At first, religious associations or associations with a charitable purpose were organized for the bourgeoisie, the middle classes and the farmers. But from 1883 on, some bishops stimulated the creation of associations with the purpose of promoting the interests of the working classes: saving clubs, organized medical insurance and trades unions. Associations were also created to promote separate social contacts for men, women and youngsters with the purpose of keeping them out of public houses where an informal social life had been developing. In fact, bit by bit the Catholic world became integrated in a pillar that comprised schools (from kindergarten to university), youth and adult organizations for the different social classes, cultural organizations, a Catholic press, hospitals, trade unions, sick funds, banks, cooperatives, and so on. When in 1921 a Catholic political party was formed, the organizations of the corporate channel were interlocked with a political party which was able to protect, even to promote, the development of the pillar and its constituent organizations.

The Catholic party has formed part of Belgian governments for 70 years, from 1884 until 1954 – apart from a short period of twenty months. In 1954 a socialist-liberal coalition government relegated the Catholic party to the opposition, and promulgated a new law on education in 1955. The law affirmed the right of the State to erect schools at all levels of the educational system, and it reduced the subsidies for Catholic schools that the preceding Catholic government had introduced to help the schools which had found themselves in financial difficulties as a result of the increased numbers of students following the democratization of education since the late 1940s. The law also instituted a tighter control over the Catholic school system, and introduced a restriction on the number of teachers certified by a Catholic Teachers' Training College who could teach in state schools. This law started the second 'school war'. Only the Belgian bishops tried to define this school war as a religious war. The Catholic party argued for equal rights for the two networks on the basis of the principles of 'freedom, equality and democracy', and did not use religious arguments in its public statements. More specifically, the party argued for 'equal opportunities and freedom of choice', the latter meaning freedom of choice for the parents on the basis of their ideological convictions, be they religious or based on freethinking convictions. Jaak Billiet (1976: 248) is correct when he points out the secularizing undertone of the arguments when these are compared with those used before 1945, at which time reference was made to the 'right of the Church' in matters of education.

In 1958 the liberal-socialist coalition lost the election and the Catholic government prepared with the opposition parties a 'school pact'. The two networks, the State and the Catholic, were recognized by law and paid by the state, and a law in 1959 introduced the requirement for a class of either 'non-denominational ethics' or religion at the primary and secondary levels in state schools. The 'school pact' recognized in principle and *de facto* pluralism *qua* meaning systems in Belgium and gave them both equal rights before the law. The notion of 'free choice' legitimized the pacification policy of a pragmatic elite (Billiet 1976: 249).

The internal secularizing tendency in the so-called Catholic pillar became still more evident in the 1960s. The State, paying for Catholic schools, by law imposed minimum qualifications for teachers. Priests and religious personnel were no longer sufficiently qualified, on the basis of their studies in theology and philosophy, to teach certain fields in secondary schools, which resulted in the recruitment of university trained lay teachers whose reference was no longer the Church but their profession. The same was true in Catholic hospitals where lay nurses replaced religious personnel, who as a result lost control over the medical practices. In Catholic hospitals, specific church ethics concerning abortion, sterilization, artificial insemination and birth control were increasingly being called into question under the pressure of medical rationality. Medical doctors pointed to the complexity of these problems and the specificity of their field; they sought to solve them by using a broader ethical framework and their specialized knowledge. In other words, the democratisation of education and the professionalization of the teaching, and medical professions, latently promoted the secularization of Catholic institutions. Other factors also played a role (Dobbelaere 1988: 83–90), but the point here is that democratization and professionalization were important factors in *latently* secularizing Catholic institutions (Dobbelaere 1979).

To survive as a complex organization, the Catholic pillar generalized its collective consciousness. Research had demonstrated that the core philosophy of the pillar no longer consisted of the strict religious rules of the Catholic Church, but referred rather to the so-called typical values of the gospel such as social justice, a humane approach toward clients and patients, well-being, solidarity between social classes with special attention to marginal people, and *Gemeinschaftlichkeit*. These are values that have a universal appeal, and which are not specifically Christian. However, by backing them up with a religious source, the gospels, and occasionally solemnising them with religious ritual, they acquired a sacred aura. This new collective consciousness is still symbolised by a capital 'C', referring to Christian, that is evangelical, rather than to Catholic, the latter being considered to have a more restricted appeal and to be more confining. This 'Socio-cultural Christianity' functions now as the sacred canopy for the segmented Catholic world of olden days (Billiet and Dobbelaere 1976: 59–78; Dobbelaere and Voyé 1990: 6–8; and Laermans 1992: 204–14).

Growing Pluralism and the Second Wave of Manifest Secularization

On the societal and organizational level, even in the so-called Christian pillar, religion became socially less and less relevant. Furthermore, an increasing number of women and men became a- and anti-religious. Studies on institutionalized religion have pointed this out. The regular Sunday mass attendance dropped drastically, for example in Belgium from 43 per cent in 1967 to 11 per cent thirty years later, and this erosion was documented throughout Western Europe (Norris and Inglehart 2004: 87). In Belgium, this resulted in a significant difference between the youngest and the pre-war generation in 1999 (Voyé and Dobbelaere 2001: 162). In the youngest generation, born after 1970, only 6 per cent are core members of the Catholic Church and 55 per cent have declared themselves as being unchurched. This percentage of the unchurched is more than twice as large as it was in the pre-war generation.

Personal beliefs also eroded; for example, belief in God dropped significantly from 77 per cent in 1981 to 65 per cent in 1999, and a *bricolage* of beliefs developed; for example, in 1999 only 42 per cent of those believing in God conceived Him as a person, conforming to the Christian tradition, with others seeing Him rather as a spirit or life force (Voyé and Dobbelaere 2001: 155). People construct their religious worldview, if they still do, by mixing religious beliefs and practices. In a study of Belgian Christians *am Rande* (marginal Belgian Christians), Voyé (1995: 199–204, esp. 201) suggested that individual religiosity is characterised by a 'mixing of codes'. This is reflected in a threefold manner: references and practices blending the institutional and the popular; occasional borrowings from scientific discourses as well as from religious sources; and inspiration sought from diverse, notably oriental, religions.

Finally, ethical attitudes have changed, especially those concerning life and death (suicide, abortion, homosexuality, euthanasia and divorce), the so-called bodily self-determination. In Belgium, the non-religious are most liberal in such matters and regularly practising believers most restrictive; the less or not practising believers are in between. However, over the years (measuring points from the European Values Study being 1981, 1990 and 1999), the three categories of believers we distinguished have all become more liberal (Elchardus *et al.* 2000: 156–61).

The decline in church involvement, the related increase of religious pluralism, and the growing bodily self-determination were favourable factors for a new wave of *laïcisation* which started with the law on the partial liberalization of abortion in Belgium in 1990. The Socialist parties, which were coalition partners of the Christian parties, joined the opposition to lead with the Liberal parties an alternative majority to approve the draft law in the Chamber and the Senate. A number of the leading members of the Socialist and Liberal parties are members of Masonic Lodges which are atheistic. The Christian parties voted against the law. After the adoption by parliament of this law, the Belgian bishops (1990: 8) issued a public statement. In an appeal to the population at large, they expounded their doctrinal and pastoral position and warned Catholics that persons who co-operate 'effectively and directly' in abortions 'exclude themselves from the ecclesiastical community'.

In a letter of 30 March 1990, King Baudouin notified the Prime Minister that his conscience prevented him from signing the law, which was incumbent upon him for it to have the force of law. This nearly led to a constitutional crisis. Referring to Article 79 of the Constitution, the King was declared temporarily unable to reign. The Council of Ministers, exercising the constitutional prerogatives of the King in conformity with Article 82 of the Constitution, sanctioned the law and thereby ratified it. As a result, the Ministers of the Christian parties were forced by the King to sign a law for which their parties had not voted. The opposition between a Christian view on abortion (the Bishops, the King and the vote of the members of the Christian parties) and the view of freethinkers, leading the Liberal and the Socialist parties, came clearly to the fore. Senator Eric Gryp (2001) expressed the humanist view by stating that 'In a pluralistic society, only the respect for the philosophy of life of dissidents can be the basis of a humane solution for ethical problems.'

In 1999, and again in 2003, the Christian parties lost the elections and thus have not been part of the federal government for the past eight years. During this period, more measures of *laïcisation* were adopted. In 2002, two laws were passed on the liberalization of the use of drugs and on euthanasia, and, in 2003, a law on the marriage of homosexual couples. Belgium was one of the first countries to change its legislation on euthanasia and to legalize homosexual marriages, two matters that are very sensitive issues for the Catholic Church. Indeed, in 1994 the bishops had anticipated such changes in the law and had published a letter on *L'accompagnement des malades à l'approche de la mort* [The accompaniment of the sick at the approach of death], and a letter on *Choisir le marriage* [Choosing marriage] in 1998.

In the latter letter the bishops referred to some changes in Belgian society, such as the decreasing number of marriages and the prevailing attitudes towards alternative forms of partnership. Since parliamentary commissions were discussing adaptations of the law, such as had occurred in some neighbouring countries, the bishops expected that the law would be changed to accommodate the new situation, and this prospect they regarded as legitimizing their intervention. Consequently, they vigorously defended marriage and the family, and expressed their opposition to any equality of treatment for alternative forms of sexual union. In their letter on dying, the bishops justified their intervention by referring to the fact that a range of arguments existed in public opinion in favour of euthanasia 'out of compassion' – which has a strong resonance – to 'claiming the individual right to die' (1994: 6–7). Another argument was given at the press conference: the bishops felt obliged to speak out, 'since euthanasia is creeping into Belgian society quietly and without resistance'. They argued in their letter that euthanasia was consciously to kill a person, an act which they confronted with the ancient law, 'thou shall not kill'. They furthermore asserted that life was a gift and that people were here 'for one another' and, consequently, should not decide to end their own lives.

The counter argument of the legislators was that they did not force people to live in alternative forms of marriage, to take drugs or to perform euthanasia. In a pluralistic society, it is up to each individual to act according to his or her ethical principles as long as they respect the limits set by the law. The explicit legitimating argument of the advocates of these laws was a reference to ethical pluralism in society, and they did not present their legislative act as *un combat contre l'Église* [a fight against the Church] as had been done in the first wave of *laicisation* in the nineteenth century. However, in analyzing some secondary measures taken by the government and pinpointing the 'supporters' for these measures, it becomes clear that the target of the *'laïcising'* measures is still the place of the Catholic Church in Belgium. Traditionally, a *Te Deum* has been sung in the Cathedral in Brussels, inaugurating the celebration of the National Holiday (21 July) and the Feast of the King (15 November). In the past, representatives of the Constituent Bodies (such as the government, parliament and the judiciary) had been expected to take part in the ceremonies. The celebration has been continued but for some years it has been defined by the government as a 'private' celebration. Consequently, the government, is no longer constrained to attend. A public lay celebration now takes place in Parliament where the presence of the Constituent Bodies is required. There is also a public discussion about the criterion for financing the recognized religions if this is not based on their actual membership. In fact the Humanist Societies suggest that the Catholic Church receives too much money considering the drop in church attendance. Finally, a discussion is on the table concerning the protocol established by Napoleon (which is still in use), since it gives the first place of honour after the King to the Belgian Catholic Cardinal. Humanist Societies insist on a revision which would result in a demotion of the Cardinal of more than ten places. It seems that the government does not want to agree to this during the term of office of the present Cardinal.

Also the reaction in some newspapers concerning the letters of the bishops is symptomatic of Belgian's laïcising tendencies. Both Christian and non-Christian newspapers reported on the bishops' letters; however, the non-Christian newspapers were critical and published at the same time contrary arguments. For example, on 1 February 1994, *Le Soir* published an interview with a representative of the 'Association for the right to die in dignity' who called the bishops' letter on *L'accompagnement des malades à l'approche de la mort* 'A very timid move of relatively little importance' since the Church still denied the will of sick people and negated their agony. The representative argued further that the medical actions of Christian and non-Christian medical doctors are the same and that the differences are only 'in the mind?' At the press conference, the Cardinal had pointed out the precise importance of what is 'in the mind', to wit the ethical *attitude*, and he condemned *deliberate* killing. The Church's line of reasoning was based on deeds with a double consequence, while accepting the risk of an early death if this were the unintended consequence of a particular medicine administered to alleviate pain. On the same day, the newspaper *De Morgen* published the opinion of a freethinking professor of medical ethics, who made similar remarks. It is clear that there is an active group of persons in Belgium who want the laws on certain ethical questions to be liberalized and that freethinkers are very active participants. This group has also defined the Church's standpoint as resolutely contrary to the factual trends such as the increase in cohabitation, conveying that the bishops are engaged in a rearguard battle (for a more detailed analysis see Dobbelaere 2001: 27–30).

Conclusion: Similarities and Differences

Françoise Champion (2006: 80) is correct in stating that the terms *laïque* and *laïcité* make sense in France and Belgium, but only to make the point that there is an 'ideological camp, a conviction and militancy'. However, the institutionalization in the two countries is quite different. In France these terms refer to the nation-state, the *République Laïque*, and refer to a constitutional and legal principle (Voyé 2005). Conversely, in Belgium the terms refer to a particular group, which has been institutionalized as a 'recognized cult' (Javeau 2005) alongside six recognized religions (Catholic, Protestant, Jewish, Anglican, Orthodox and Islamic). These recognitions are legitimated by the social utility of the religions, that produce a series of public services for the population (education, health), the '*laïque* cult' offering moral assistance (Voyé 2005). In Belgium, much importance is given to intermediate structures, contrary to France, where, as we have seen, the Republic is constituted by individuals, not by a 'mosaic of communities'.

The institutionalization of the *culte laïque* has taken some years (Haarscher 1996: 51–2). In 1970 the State recognized 'the non-denominational philosophical communities'; since 1981 the *laïque* centres have been financed by the State; and in 1991 a corps of moral counsellors was created in the army and financed by the State. Finally, in 1993, the revised Article 181 of the Constitution concerning the remuneration of the clergy includes the provision for 'the delegates of the organisations recognized by law who offer moral assistance based on a philosophical non-denominational conception'. The *'laïque* cult' is particularly visible on Sunday morning when, together with the religions, it has its own television programme, which would be inconceivable in France; it also organises rites of passage such as burials.

In France there never was an important Catholic party and an integrated pillar like there has been in Belgium (Hellemans 1988: 274–6) where the pillar was related to a Catholic party that was for decades governing Belgium either alone or as part of a coalition. It was only when the Christian pillar started to crumble, diminishing the power of the Christian party, that the Liberal and Socialist parties were able to re-start a manifest secularization policy with reference to the growing religious pluralism of the country. Unlike the situation in France, there is not a cleavage between the political left and right since, in Belgium, the Liberal parties, defined as right, are, with the Socialists, on the side of the *laïques*.

Since the step-wise recognition of a *'laïque* cult' in Belgium, one sees a clear competition between the Catholic Church and this cult, supported by the Humanist Societies, which are integrated in a Centre for *Laïque* Action, and anti-religious Masonic lodges, as was described above. One could say that the *'laïque* cult' now tries to influence the legislation as the Catholic Church has done in the past. Both try to incorporate their vision of life, death and marriage in the Belgian legislation.

Epilogue

The European Religious and Moral Pluralism study (RAMP) in eleven Western and mid European countries studied also secularization-in-mind or compartmentalization.[1] Indeed, societal secularization may have an impact on the way individuals themselves view the relationship between religion and other spheres of life: the educational, the economical, the juridical, the familial, the medical, the political and the scientific. The question addressed was whether individuals think that the so-called profane sub-systems are autonomous and that any interference of religion in these sub-systems should be rendered void and disallowed, or do they think that institutional religion should inform these sub-systems? In the RAMP survey of 12,342 interviewees, the measurement of compartmentalization was based on their views about the relationship between church and state, law and religion, religion and education, and on their acceptance of financial support for religious schools and religious bodies (Billiet *et al.* 2003: 141–2). The major result from the multi-regression analysis was that people with a high commitment to their church think less in terms of secularization and are much less opposed to the impact of religion on the other sub-systems than persons with a low degree of commitment to a church. The non-religious had the highest degree of compartmentalization and were more prone to oppose secular institutions being affected by religious influences. Differences between members of the different traditional Churches were not found (Billiet *et al.* 2003: 152–3). According to a study by Norris and Inglehart (2004: 76–8), the religious participation trend shows a much lower religious participation in the post-war generations compared to the

---

1   For information on RAMP, see Dobbelaere and Riis 2002.

pre-war generation in post-industrial societies such as Belgium. Given the results of both studies, we may expect that leftist governments in the so-called Catholic countries will follow the same manifest secularization policy of recent Belgian governments. The voice of the population confirms that: in Italy, there is a demand for a legal statute for homosexual couples; in France, the demand for a law on the liberalization of euthanasia was increasingly voiced during the electoral campaign for the presidency; and the Portuguese parliament recently liberalized its abortion law after a positive vote in a referendum.

References

Balandier, G. (1997) *Conjugaisons*, Paris: Fayard.

Baubérot, J. (1997) *La morale laïque contre l'ordre moral*, Paris: Le Seuil.

—— (2005) *Histoire de la laïcité en France*, 3rd enlarged edition. Paris: Presses Universitaires de France, Collection Q*ue sais-je*, No.3571.

Belgian Bishops (1990) *La loi relative à l'interruption de grossesse*, Brussels: Licap.

—— (1994) *L'accompagnement des malades à l'approche de la mort*, Brussels: Licap.

—— (1998) *Choisir le marriage*, Brussels: Licap.

Billiet, J. (1976) 'Beschouwingen over het samengaan van secularisatie en verzuiling', *De nieuwe maand*, 19: 244–57.

Billiet, J. and Dobbelaere, K. (1976) *Godsdienst in Vlaanderen: van kerks katholicisme naar social-kulturele christenheid*, Leuven: Davidsfonds.

Billiet, J., Dobbelaere, K., Riis, O., Vilaça, H., Voyé, L. and Welkenhuysen-Gybels, J. (2003) 'Church Commitment and Some Consequences in Western and Eastern Europe', in R. Piedmont and D. Moberg (eds), *Research in the Social Scientific Study of Religion*, 14, Leiden/London: Brill.

Champion, F. (1993) 'Les rapports Eglise-Etat dans les pays européens de tradition protestante et de tradition catholique: essai d'analyse', *Social Compass*, 40: 589–609.

—— (2006) *Les laïcités européennes au miroir du cas britannique. XVIme – XXIme siècle.* Rennes: Presses Univesitaires de Rennes, Collection 'Sciences des Religions'.

Dobbelaere, K. (1979) 'Professionalization and Secularization in the Belgian Catholic Pillar', *Japanese Journal of Religious Studies*, 6 (1–2): 39–64.

—— (1988) 'Secularization, Pillarization, Religious Involvement, and Religious Change in the Low Countries', in T. Gannon (ed.), *World Catholicism in Transition*, New York: Macmillan Publishing Company.

—— (2001) 'The Functions and Dysfunctions of the Belgian Bishops' Public Interventions', in A. Walker and M. Percy (eds) *Restoring the Image: Essays on Religion and Society in Honour of David Martin*, Sheffield: Sheffield Academic Press.

—— (2002) *Secularization: An Analysis at Three Levels*, Bruxelles: P.I.E. Peter Lang, Series 'Gods, Humans and Religions', No.1.

Dobbelaere, K. and Voyé, L. (1990) 'From pillar to postmodernity: the changing situation of religion in Belgium', *Sociological Analysis*, 51 S: 1–13.

Dobbelaere, K. and Riis, O. (2002) 'Religious and Moral Pluralism: Theories, Research Questions and Design', in R. Piedmont and D. Moberg (eds) *Research in the Social Scientific Study of Religion*, 13, Leiden: Brill.

Elchardus, M., Chaumont, J.-M. and Lauwers, S. (2000) 'Morele onzekerheid en nieuwe degelijkheid', in K. Dobbelaere, M. Elchardus, J. Kerkhofs, L. Voyé and B. Bawin-Legros (eds) *Verloren zekerhei: De Belgen en hun waarden, overtuigingen en houdingen*, Tielt: Lannoo.

Gryp, E. (2001) *Boudewijn en de abortuswet: De koningscrisis van 1990*. http://www.crk.be/N/Boudewijn_abortuswet_N.php [accessed 27 November 2007].

Haarscher, G. (2004) *La laïcité*, 3rd enl. ed. Paris: Presses Universitaires de France, Collection Q*ue sais-je*, No. 3129.

Hellemans, S. (1988a) 'De katholieke zuilen buiten België', in J. Billiet (ed) *Tussen bescherming en verovering: Sociologzen en historici over zuilvorming*, Leuven: Universitaire Pers Leuven, Kadoc-studies 6.

Javeau, C. (2005) 'La laïcité ecclésialisée en Belgique', in J.-P. Willaime and S. Mathieu (eds), *Des maîtres et des dieux. Ecoles et religions en Europe*, Paris: Belin.

Laermans, R. (1992) *In de greep van de 'Moderne Tijd': Modernisering en verzuiling, individualisering en het naoorlogs publiek discours van de ACW-vormingsorganisaties: een proeve tot cultuursociologische duiding*, Leuven: Garant.

Lukes, S. (1977) *Emile Durkheim. His Life and Work: A Historical and Critical Study*, Middlesex: Penguin Books.

Norris, P. and R. Inglehart (2004) *Sacred and Secular: Religion and Politics Worldwide*, Cambridge: Cambridge University Press.

Righart, H. (1986) *De katholieke zuil in Europa: Een vergelijkend onderzoek naar het ontstaan van verzuiling onder katholieken in Oostenrijk, Zwitserland, België en Nederland*, Meppel: Boom.

Sintomer, Y. (2001) *Délibérer, participer, représenter. Vers une sociologie de la justification politique*, Mémoire d'habilitation à diriger les recherches en sociologie, Université de Paris V.

Voyé, L. (1995) 'From Institutional Catholicism to "Christian Inspiration": Another look at Belgium', in W.C. Roof, J.W. Caroll and D.A. Roozen (eds), *The Post-war Generation and Establishment Religion: Cross-cultural Perspectives*, Boulder Co: Westview Press, pp. 191–223.

—— (2005) *Laïcité 'à la Belge': Une histoire de compromis, un statut de 'pilier'*, Paper presented at the Colloque International: 1905–2005: Cent ans de séparation. Enjeux, actualité et perspectives. Toulouse, Université du Mirail Toulouse II and Université des Sciences Sociales Toulouse I: 8–10 December 2005.

Voyé, L. and Dobbelaere, K. (2001) 'De la religion: ambivalences et distancements', in B. Bawin-Legros, L. Voyé, K. Dobbelaere and M. Elchardus (eds), *Belges toujours. Fidélité, stabilité, tolérance: les valeurs des Belges en l'an 2000*, Bruxelles: De Boeck Université.

Willaime, J.-P. (2007) 'Religion et politique en France dans le contexte de la construction européenne', *French Politics, Culture & Society*, 25 (3): 37–61.

Wils, L. (1977) 'De politieke ontwikkeling in België 1847–1870' and 'De politieke ontwikkeling in België 1870–1894', in *Algemene Geschiedenis van de Nederlanden*, Haarlem: Fibula – Van Dishoek 1977, 12: 267–304 and 13: 164–206.

PART II
Religious Insertions in Society

CHAPTER 6

The Inner-World Mysticism and a Successful Social Integration of the *Sikh Panth*[1]

Enzo Pace

This paper aims to investigate the social success of immigrants belonging to the Sikh religion (*Sikh panth*), with the aid of the main studies carried out on the various Sikh diaspora in the West (Ballard and Ballard 1977; Ballard 1982; Helweg 1979; Larke *et al.* 1990; La Brack 1988; Cowar 2000; Kaur T.O. 2005) and, in particular, in Italy (Tarozzi and Bartolini 2002; Denti *et al.* 2005), where the Sikh presence has grown considerably since 1980, especially in the north of the country. The hypothesis we put forward is that there is an *elective affinity* between the Sikh conception of ethics and religion and the spirit of adaptation to the social and economic order *of this world*. In particular, our thesis is that social success in an 'out-of-context' situation can be linked (but not in a deterministic way) to the *inner-world mysticism* of the *Sikh panth*.

Gurnam Kaur (1990) claims there is a vital connection between the Sikh ethic and the spirit of capitalism. On the basis of the moral precept whereby *work is worship* for Sikhs, she states that this is a question of inner-world asceticism, thus casting doubts on the ideal type of the Calvinist entrepreneur which Max Weber had identified as he traced the moral genealogy of modern capitalism. In other words, according to this theory, the Sikhs have created a form of Puritan religion able to instil in its followers a moral *habitus* for the rationalization of social and economic action: the Sikhs act to obtain economic success because they feel they are individually invested with a duty to achieve union with God, in the world and through the world. Apparently, therefore, this constitutes an ascesis in the world, that is, a rational and religious discipline which pervades the whole of individual and collective life.

In point of fact, the least convincing part of the theory outlined above is the use of Weber's category of inner-world ascesis. If we take a closer look at the fundamentals of their doctrine, we see that Sikhs believe neither in predestination, nor in the idea that the only chance the individual has of salvation is to live life as a vocation (*beruf*), in a continuous challenge between God and him- or herself, that is, without any degree of certainty as to salvation, which might console human reason. The risk that dominates the theological universe and the economic efforts of

---

1 A version of this paper was presented at the Association for the Sociology of Religion's Annual Meeting in Montréal, 10–12 August 2006.

the Protestant entrepreneur is not part of the Sikh horizon of meaning. The analogy is, therefore, an extrinsic one. It is just as extrinsic as comparing the Reformed Church and the Sikh religion with respect to the central nature of the Holy Book. Although the notion that, for the believer, the Holy Scripture is the only authority *on Earth* appears similar in both cases, the relationship between the believer (both individually and collectively) and the Holy Book is completely different. For the Sikh, it is 'the living manifestation of the ten Gurus and symbolizes the unity of their spirit' (Kaur G., 1990: 172). The Book (*Adi Granth*, the First Book) is the terminal point of a line of belief handed down and deposited in a canon that constitutes the source of spirituality even today. By contrast, for the Reformed Church, the Bible is an inspired text recording the Word of God, on which every believer is called upon to meditate.

Let us now look at another apparent analogy between Protestantism and Sikhism. For Protestants and Sikhs alike, there are neither holy mediators nor institutions of salvation that stand between the believer and the Book. For Sikhs, in fact, since the death of Gobind Singh (1666–1708), the Holy Text constitutes the only true institution in existence. As the tenth and last guru, Gobind Singh decreed the end of the cycle of living masters and the drafting of the official corpus of Sikh belief, the *Adi Granth*: the institution of the Word, revealed through the gurus to humankind (Mann 2001). To use Weber's terms again, the charisma of the spiritual heads of the community was handed down from the first guru, Nanak, to the tenth, Gobind Singh. This succession was regulated by the Sikhs, who left aside solutions, such as the strictly dynastic one (according to *jus sanguins*, the principle so dear to Shiite Muslims), that of personal transmission (as in the case of Lamaistic Buddhism), as well as the transformation of personal charisma into official or functional charisma (as occurred in Catholicism and the khalifs of Sunnite Islam – *khalifa*). Instead, the Sikhs adopted the solution of objectifying the authority of the charismatic power of the entire series of ten gurus in the Book (Kaur G. 1990). The tenth guru ended the human succession and established the principle of the *lignée croyante* (Hervieu-Léger 1996), an authoritative, institutionalized religious memory worshipped by the community. The authority of the Book is legitimate *per se*: it needs no clergy or specialists of the sacred; neither does it require a body of hermeneutics or jurists to translate the religious principles contained in the text into contingent social norms, as occurs among Muslims and Jews.

If we wish to make a parallel, in my opinion, it should be made with the Sufi, at least with the confraternity or brotherhood (*turuq*) that developed a work ethic as radical as that found in the Sikh *panth* (McLeod 1967: 307). One example well known to scholars is that of the Senegalese Muridiyya (Schmidt di Friedberg 1994; Cruise O'Brien 1983). Another, less well-known example is that of the Safawiyya, the confraternity of the Safavide, founded by Sāfi al-dîn (1252–1334), which is the origin of Shiite Iran. The comparison is also legitimate in the light of the historical origins of the Sikh movement. Its founder, Guru Baba Nanak (1469–1539), is said to have received his first initiation from a preacher who belonged to a movement that combined the teachings of the tantra yoga school with those of the mystic Sufi (Piano 1996: 258; Peca 2005). The Pañjab, the geographical area where the Sikh movement started, has long been a crossroads of diverse forms of spirituality. It is clear that the Sikh way is different from the stricter religious ethics of Hindu religious discipline, and closer to forms of mystical Sufism. Unlike the former, the Sikhs have not developed an ethic of separation from the world, but are considerably closer to the spirit of the Muslim confraternity, particularly as regards the type of relationship between master and disciple, spiritual guide and believer, along the path toward mystical union with God (Pace 2001; Popovic and Veinstein 1998).

The Sikh system of belief is mystical in origin. Guru Nanak is basically a bearer of charisma (a *sant*) who discovered he was a mediator, the bearer of the extraordinary Word. According to the historical sources, he went on to found a community of 'saints' (*sangat*) called upon to lead their individual lives based on the model of a pious person entirely devoted to God *Who spoke in a sacred language*. The achievement of mystical union, however, does not come about through fleeing this world. On the contrary, the central teaching of the Sikh religious ethic is engagement in the world, wholehearted participation in the various activities which give substance to human life (in the family, economy, politics and cultural spheres). Therefore, it contrasts sharply with the *Bakhti* Hindu tradition, as Niharranjan Ray reminds us:

> Neither the leaders of the Bakhti movement nor of the Nathapantha and the Sant synthesis attempted to do what Guru Nanak did .... These leaders seem to have been individuals working out their own problems towards achieving their personal, religious and spiritual aims, and aspirations. (Ray 1970: 56)

The combination of the mystical dimension and engagement in the world, therefore, favoured the adoption of an ideal type which Max Weber called *inner-world mysticism*.

In his typology of asceticism and mysticism, after distinguishing the two, Weber (1976: 587–8) speaks of inner-world mysticism, whose specific characteristic or ideal type is the particular form of rationalization of the world it reflects. The world is not rejected; it is the sphere in which contemplative virtues are practised and the search for a mystical union with God takes place. Thus, in everyday life and practical work, the inner-world mystic lives in the world, respecting the internal autonomy of the various spheres of life, without allowing this recognition to turn itself into an internal conflict between 'faith and work'. In actual fact, for the Sikh, it is a problem solved: there is no conflict between the (mystical) path to God and keenness to carry out well your work in the world. The inner-world mystic is, from this point of view, a person who, as Weber (1976: 621) puts it: 'can die satiated with life' (not 'weary of life'), in the sense that the cycle of existence is planned along a rational path leading to the achievement of mystical union with God (even though it may take several lives to achieve this aim, following the Sikh belief in metempsychosis). And if this world is not seen as a realm of sin, and human beings are not seen as vitiated by a natural propensity to evil, then inner-world engagement becomes for the mystic *joie de vivre*. Moved by the smile of the spirit, she/he is not a heartless reveller, but is closer to the *perfect delight* proposed by the Franciscan Order (Weber 1976: 625).

The problem for sociologists of religion arises when we attempt to understand the passage from a model of spirituality of this nature to some form of socio-religious organization. Jean Séguy (1997) developed the concept of *voluntary groups of religious intensity*, which is broader and more flexible than the typologies proposed by Weber and Troeltsch. It is an abstract type characterized by a number of convergences of elements, such as the individual's decision to join a group, reference to a spiritual master who guides the disciples toward an internal discipline, ascetic and/or mystical in nature, as well as *'la finalisation de la vie quotidienne de leurs membres'* (Séguy 1997: 57). Weber had already glimpsed something of this when he investigated Hinduism and Buddhism (Weber 1976).

In his discussion of whether the term 'religion', with its Western conceptual categories, should be applied to Hinduism, Weber notes that the concept is entirely alien to the Hindu tradition. Nevertheless, a Sanskrit term exists, according to Weber, which can be compared with the concept contained in the term religion. This word is *sampradaya*, which Weber translated as a community of belonging that is not acquired through birth. In this sense it is thus an *open-door caste*. People belong to it because they share common religious purposes and common paths to salvation, not the caste rules. The learned Hindi called this community a *theo-fraternity* (Weber 1976: 652–3). Perhaps if Weber had studied the origins of the Sikhs, he would not have hesitated to apply the term to them. What is important in Weber's analysis and finds echoes in the work of Séguy as regards voluntary groups of religious intensity, is the importance given to the figure of the master. Speaking of the Hindu *theo-fraternity* and the role of their guides, Weber expressly uses the French term: *directeur d'âme* (Weber 1976: 653), corresponding to the figure of the *guru*, which is so central to the Sikh system, as we shall see.

The notion of choosing to follow a master because one believes that he can offer a way, *here and now*, to achieve union with God provides a key to our understanding. It shows us, on the one hand, how a given symbolic system of belief is constructed and, on the other, how a specific form of socio-religious organization centred on the power (never mind for the moment whether this power is visible or invisible) of the guide, the custodian of the *extraordinary wisdom of God*, because he or she has been touched by Him. Choosing to follow a master, the bearer of special charisma as the 'communicator with God', means, in many cases, that the individual is released from the social constrictions imposed on him by birth, blood or caste. The individual is received as they are, because of the choice they have made, regardless of social or religious affiliations which define his identity *by birth* and/or through primary socialization (Kaur N., 1961).

The master's claim to lead the disciple toward mystically intense contact with God gives him extraordinary power. This, on the one hand, frees the initiate of the social and religious constrictions of birth, and, on the other, creates a relationship of absolute dependence of the latter on the former. But what is more, the master also depends on the disciple's full acceptance, obedience and blind trust in the master himself.

We can now turn our attention to how the relationship of *mystical dependence* is set up. The term indicates a particular type of master-disciple relation, characterized by the meeting of a specific religious demand: the quest for the initiatory path to mystical fusion, and a specific religious offer – that is, the socially acknowledged role of the *initiator*, with his great experience of this great experience. Broadly speaking, access to the esoteric is reserved for the master. Social action is the subject of public teaching, in that it constitutes the set of ethical and social precepts that the master passes on to his disciples, in order to give both meaning to their action in the world, and rules of conduct to discipline their inner and external lives. Thus, membership of a mystical group provides a social identity, and the esoteric message is, to an extent, made clear by the disciples' actions. When this comes about, it is as if we were witnessing the social success of a mystical enterprise, as if the master were reaping the benefits of a symbolic investment through his followers' engagement in the world. The followers learn to discipline their lives by devoting themselves to the achievement of a goal that is both the practice of the virtue of obedience toward the master (the esoteric side of action), and economic and social success (the ethical and esoteric side of action). Obedience plays a central role in obtaining success in life. Everything is contained within a project of rationalizing one's actions. There is no rejection or fleeing from the world, but a search for a *test* of obedience to the precepts taught by the master.

The religious ideas developed by the nine gurus who followed Nanak had an impact on the economic ethic, which was surprising for two main reasons. First, since its very origins, the Sikh system of belief had always been a *medium* of communication with the social environment marked by great flexibility and adaptability. In other words, the founding principle runs something along these lines: always act as if change and social and economic success were a sign of divine benevolence. Do not resist change, but try to 'adjust' to the changes. You can do it, because you possess a profound symbolic resource – mystical dependence on the guru and, through him, on God – which enables you to transform what is new into 'the greater glory of God'. The contingencies of the social environment are thus reduced, because in the Sikh system of belief there is a symbolic device which translates the external complexity of the environment into inner complexity. This is the notion of *work is worship*: by giving of your best in the worldly sphere, you are elevated spiritually. There is self-realization and, at the same time, realization of the divine presence in oneself. Religion becomes a living force capable of adapting easily to changes in the social environment. The fact that, in historical terms, Nanak and the gurus that succeeded him had always preached against all forms of social discrimination (including the caste system, in theory at least), thus freeing individuals of the obligations of the *dharma* of their caste, may be interpreted as a mental precondition for the social mobility known to Sikhs in the course of time. No longer forced – at least mentally – to see themselves as an indissoluble part of a caste (although the caste system continues to function among Sikhs), the Sikhs have been able to develop an economic and social dynamism that, only in recent times, is to be found partially in the Hindu world. Furthermore, the Sikh idea of universal brotherhood fostered the introduction of *democratic* liturgical practices in the life of the religious community. There are no priests or hierarchies of the learned, separate from the faithful.

The community spirit – theo-fraternity – has thus enabled the Sikhs to build a solid transnational network in the diaspora, and maintain a degree of solidarity among immigrants which has lightened the 'burden of solitude' that sometimes typifies other immigrants.

What has to be stressed is that the changes which the Sikh *panth* has undergone in the course of time can be attributed, on the one hand, to factors outside the system of belief and, on the other, to organizational needs which arose from within, as the small voluntary groups gradually became a vast population of the faithful, spread over an increasingly wide area. For example, many of the dietary taboos linked to the symbolic distinction between the pure and the impure, typical of social relations based on castes, have fallen into disuse either by choice or tacitly, since such practices no longer seem to make sense. Therefore, in the diaspora in Europe, it is easier for the Sikhs to adopt lifestyles which approximate to those of the West, and also to open their temples to those who might be considered untouchables. Taking food in the ritual collective meal with them no longer constitutes a problem. The last frontier which seems to resist change seems to be that of endogamy, a cultural relic from the patriarchal society of past times, according to McLeod (1975: 88).

By de-sacralizing the caste system, the gurus, perhaps unwittingly, gave the Sikh system of belief a highly flexible means for interpreting social reality (the environment), capable of adapting the system's development to changes imposed by the social situation (Marenco 1974: 297).

In competition with threatening and intolerant external forces, the Sikhs have sought to define their identity by *differentiating themselves*. By so doing, they stretched the original inspiration which had guided the thoughts and actions of Guru Nanak. Tradition has it that when he received illumination, Nanak exclaimed 'there are neither Hindi, nor Muslim, only worshippers of One Single God'. The absence of dogma and of rituals strictly controlled and monopolized by a class of priests, at least until the institution of the *khalsa*, tends to support the view that the Sikh system of belief is flexible because it manages to combine the individual's choice to believe with the sense of belonging to a brotherhood of worshippers recognizing as legitimate only the Word of God, revealed through the gurus, and then set down, once and for all, in the Book (*Adi Granth*). The Sikh religion, by exalting the inner-world engagement of the believer, in search of mystical union with God, has ended up valorising the 'individual talents' that each of the faithful is called upon to mobilize for the 'greater glory of God'. Each individual seeks to encounter God 'in this world', by becoming the protagonist of their own destiny: transforming the world, if necessary, to improve life for themselves and their 'brothers' (Restelli 1990).

Conclusion

We have thus shown the nature of the inner force that lies at the heart of the Sikh system of belief. The inner-world mysticism, which characterizes the Sikh path, constitutes the fundamental principle for its functioning. It relies on two symbolic resources: a) mobilizing the individual to act in this world, and b) linking the meaning of such action to a transcendental, yet immanent, purpose (Kaur G., 1990: 193). Hence, the system of belief fosters a *rationalization of the world* that we are unlikely to come across in Hinduism or Buddhism; nor can it be found in Indian Islam, which Sikhism encountered in the sixteenth century.

This rationalization meant that Sikhism was able to emerge from a magical-sacral conception of relations between human beings and the divine. But more importantly, for Sikhs, the world has a direction, a meaning that each individual along with the community may experience within themselves and in their active lives. The worship indeed is an active contemplation of the truth, which is not abstract but is actually experienced in the search for mystical union with God, working in the world. The challenge to act concerns basically the individual and their ability to feel within themselves the Word transmitted by the Gurus and preserved in the Book. And precisely for this reason Sikh believers can uproot themselves from their original environment and put down roots elsewhere, adapting to the rules and regulations of the host society.

Inner-world mysticism may help us to understand the relative social success of the Sikhs not only in Pañjab but also in the diaspora, and to explain the recognition of their community they receive from the local population and the authorities, as has emerged from recent research carried out in Italy (Denti *et al.* 2005). Perhaps I could sum up by saying: *I loro turbanti non turbano.* Their turbans are no disturbance.

References

Ballard, R. (1982) 'South Asia Families', in R. Rapaport and M. Fogarty (eds) *Families in Britain*, London: Routledge and Kegan, pp. 179–204.

Ballard, R. and Ballard, C. (1977) 'The Sikhs: the Development of South Asia Settlements in Britain', in J. Watson (ed.) *Between two Cultures*, Oxford: Basil Blackwell, pp. 21–56.

Barrier, G. and Dusembery, V.A. (1989) *The Sikh Diaspora*, Delhi: Chanaka Publications.

Cowar, H. (ed.) (2000) *South Asian Religion in Diaspora*, Albany: Sunny Press.

Cruise O'Brien, D.B. (1983), *Sufi Politics in Senegal*, Cambridge: Cambridge University Press.

Denti, D., Ferrari, M. and Perocco, F. (2005) *I Sikh, storia e immigrazione*, Milano: Angeli.

Helweg, A.W. (1979) *Sikhs in England: the Development of a Migrant Community*, Delhi: Oxford University Press.

Grewal, J.S. (1990) *The Sikhs of the Puñjab*, Cambridge: Cambridge University Press.

Hawley, J. and Mann, G.S. (1998) *Studying the Sikhs*, Albany: State University of New York Press.

Hervieu-Léger, D. (1996) *La religion pour mémoire*, Paris: Cerf.

Kaur, G. (1990) *Reason and Revelation in Sikhism*, New Delhi: Cosmo Publications.

Kaur, N. (1961) *Blossoms in the Dust*, Chicago: Chicago University Press.

Kaur, T.O. (2005) *Sikh Identity*, Aldershot: Ashgate.

La Brack, B. (1988) *The Sikhs of Northern California*, New York: AMS Press.

Larke, C., Peach, C. and Vertovec, S. (eds) (1990) *South Asians Overseas. Migration and Ethnicity*, Cambridge: Cambridge University Press.

Mann, G.S. (2001) *The Making of Sikh Scripture*, New York: Oxford University Press.

Marenco, E.K. (1974) *The Transformation of Sikh Society*, Oregon: Hapi Press.

McLeod, W.H. (1967) 'The Influence of Islam on the Thought of Guru Nanak', in N.R. Ray (ed.) *Sikhism and Indian Society*, Simla: Indian Institute of Advanced Study.

—— (1975) *The Evolution of the Sikh Community*, Delhi: Oxford University Press.

—— (1989) *Who is a Sikh?: the Problem of Sikh Identity*, Oxford: Clarendon Press.

Oberoi, H. (1994) *The Construction of Religious Boundaries*, Chicago: Chicago University Press.

Pace, E. (2001) 'Il maestro spirituale nella tradizione musulmana', in M. Maccarinelli (ed.) *Un padre per vivere*, Padova: Il Poligrafo, pp. 173–88.

Peca, R. (2005) 'Il sikhismo. Profilo storico-dottrinale', in D. Denti, M. Ferrari and F. Perocco (eds) *I Sikh, storia e immigrazione*, Milano: Angeli, pp. 43–88.

Piano, S. (1996) 'Il sikh-panth', in G. Filoramo (ed.) *Storia delle religioni*, Roma-Bari: Laterza.

Popovic, A. and Veinstein G. (eds) (1998) *Les voies d'Allah*, Paris: Fayard.

Ray, N. (1970) *The Sikh Gurus and the Sikh Society*, Patalia: Pañjabi University.

Restelli, M. (1990) *I sikh tra storia e attualità*, Treviso: Pagus.

Schmidt di Friedberg, O. (1994) *Islam, solidarietà e lavoro*, Torino: Fondazione Agnelli.

Séguy, J. (1997) *Groupements volontaires d'intensité religieuse dans le christianisme et l'islam*, Archives de Sciences Sociales des Religions, 100: 47–60.

Singh, D. (1972) *A Comparative Study of Theology and Mysticism*, New Delhi: Sterling Publisher.

Tarozzi, A. and Bertolani, B. (2002) 'La recezione del migrante asiatico nel caso degli indiani di Reggio Emilia', in R. De Vita and F. Berti (eds) *Dialogo senza paura,* Milano: Angeli, pp. 335–66.

Trumpp, E. (1970) *The Adi Granth of the Holy Scripture of the Sikhs*, New Delhi: Munshiram Manoharlal.

Weber, M. (1976) *Sociologia delle religioni*, Torino, Utet, vol. II. (English version: *The Sociology of Religion*, Boston: Beacon Press, 1963).

CHAPTER 7

A Movement without a Crisis is a Movement with a Crisis:
A Paradox in Search of a Paradigm

J. Demerath

... social theorists who are not also specialists in the study of religion have paid little attention to religious movements .... it is mainly the decline or absence of religion that is of interest to social theory these days. (Beckford 2003: 154–5)

The study of social movements has passed through a number of transformations over the past half-century. Mid-twentieth-century sociology viewed movements as a volatile part of what was then called 'collective behaviour'. Movements were akin to unruly mobs, panics and riots – behaviourally untamed and analytically untameable. But gradually movements are being brought in from the cold and accorded positions near the organizational hearth (Davis *et al.* 2004*)*. Gradually the categories of social movements and complex organizations have begun to meld. Today it is clear that many successful movements evolve into complex organizations as they seek to 'mobilize resources' (see, for example, Zald and McCarthy 1987), 'frame' their cultural and structural power (see, for example, Snow *et al.* 1986), and respond to the identity needs of their clients (see, for example, Melucci 1989). It is no less clear that many complex organizations are best understood as congeries of movements competing for space and power within them. Just as our understanding of social movements has gained from the organizational literature, the reverse is also true (Scott 2004). It is hoped that the 'crisis theory' of movement dynamics developed here applies to other organizational forms as well.

Meanwhile, if movements generally are being welcomed into the sociological core, this is less true of religious movements, or for that matter religious organizations, or indeed religion as a whole, as Beckford indicates above. But, of course, this wasn't always true. After all, the father of organizational sociology, the otherwise childless Max Weber, saw charismatic sects, bureaucratic churches, and traditional ecclesia as kindred organizational creatures, and his students were helped to see how these different forms could develop in and out of each other (see Gerth and Mills 1958). Now we need greater realization that, just as religious sects could mellow into churches, so could fledgling political movements mature into parties, and entrepreneurial start-ups grow into corporations.

Because amongst my many sins, I am a sociologist of religion, the paper draws examples disproportionately from the world of churches, sects, and cults, though its arguments are by no means confined to them. I hold with my fellow sinner, the nevertheless esteemed James Beckford, that the gap between religious movements and social movements has narrowed, and I would extend the point to the gap between religious organizations and other organizations generally (Beckford 2001; see also Williams 2003). For the record, when I refer to 'religious movements' in what follows I shall mean a much broader category than the current euphemism for 'cults'; namely 'new religious movements' or NRMs (Barker 1989). To cite the deservedly oft-cited Beckford yet again, for me a religious movement falls within his definition of 'social movements' as

> ... collective attempts to identify, challenge and change situations that movement supporters consider unjust or unacceptable. They pursue their grievances and campaigns mainly outside (institutionalized channels). (Beckford 2001: 235)

And to give the matter a sacred, if not necessarily religious flavour, it is worth adding the secular Stanford Lyman's observation that,

> In all their various manifestations in the United States, social movements have proclaimed a salvational message; in effect, each has sought to cure the soul of either the nation, a sodality within society, or the individual (Lyman 1995: 397).

This paper's basic argument is encapsulated in its title: 'a movement without a crisis is a movement with a crisis.' Although conventional movement analysis and organizational theory see crises as dystopian threats, I emphasize how movements and organizations sometimes exploit and often depend upon crises in two ways: first, as a source of their basic missions, and second, as aids in pursuing the missions. Crises are frequently the stimuli to which both movements and organizations are responses. Externally, they present both targets of opportunity and contextual constraints in the pursuit; internally they may shape and re-shape a movement's basic vision and authority structure while assisting it to mobilize resources and stem the twin tides of inertia and complacency. In fact, virtually every institution and the movements, organizations, and professions within them are responses to one sort of crisis or another. They owe much of their success to their ability to continually remind us of the crises they are confronting and have sometimes invented. In short, movements are not only vulnerable to crises but dependent upon them. However, there are crises and there are *crises*. Not all crises are positive, and some can be simultaneously functional and dysfunctional. Crises come in different forms, and I shall offer a crisis typology as a first step in sorting them out.

Starting From Scratch

Imagine that you have had a long-time yen to be a religious leader at the head of your own religious movement. To my knowledge not a single sociologist of religion has put his or her expertise to work in this manner, with the possible exception of Rodney Stark. In any event, the Vatican would likely be beyond your grasp, as would the long-standing mainline church on your downtown street corner, the suburban franchise of a sectarian denomination or an already established cult. Instead you decide to start a truly 'new religious movement', and begin to ponder what might be necessary. Charisma shouldn't be a problem; after all, your parents always said you were unusual. But something else is required that would set you apart from other unusual leaders and other religious movements. A vision would help, but a vision of what? Something positive would seem reasonable, and there are few things more positive than correcting a negative. In short, you need to find a crisis to expose.

Since the world abounds in crises, the question is what sort of crisis will work for you? Ending war and securing peace seems too ambitious, and besides – with a few all-too conspicuous exceptions – everyone is trying to do that. No, you need something closer to home and more specific. Remember those religious groups mentioned above? Perhaps you can find something that has gone wrong or gone missing in one of them – maybe a hint of heresy or a glint of corruption. Once found, you need to join the movement and wait for a propitious moment to announce the 'crisis' and denounce the culprits. When the organization's response is inadequate, as it surely will be, you lead your flock out of the old group and into your new one as destiny awaits.

At first you and your converts bask in the flush of excitement and public attention. But soon you begin to realize that the movement's spirit may be willing but its flesh is weak. You then announce a new crisis afoot within the movement itself, and your assurance that God will provide but only for those who help themselves. You convert this crisis of resources into a test of faith and an opportunity for salvation, and you send your small band of members out into the community to proselytize. There they offer succour to strangers as an end to their crises of sinning ways and personal woes, and the membership grows. However, after a while, it begins to tail off, at which point rumours of dubious origin begin to circulate of illicit behaviour within the movement and a possible police investigation. You respond with charges of being victimized by members of the mainline church from which you separated. This new crisis allows you to fan a mood of deepening commitment and renewed effort; it reverses the decline of members and resources.

This quick scenario includes a variety of crises, each of which deserves more sober consideration of its own. But instead of taking them up randomly, a slightly more systematic procedure may help. In the table below, four basic categories are defined by two cross-cutting distinctions between internal and external and structural *versus* cultural. Each of the resulting cells includes several crises – some functional, some dysfunctional, and some both. The four cells are elaborated in the four sections that follow.

Table 7.1   Crisis Typology

	Cultural	*Structural*
External	Cultural Targets and Tactics	Resource Competition *vs.* Generosity
Internal	Sacralization *vs.* Secularization	Leadership and Member Motivation

Cultural Targets and Tactics

Name an institution of virtually any sort, and it is not hard to conjure up the possible and continuing crises to which its various organizations respond and to which they owe their very existence. Religion responds to the crisis of sin; government to the crisis of anarchy; medicine to the crisis of illness, and education to the crisis of ignorance. Although Emile Durkheim's celebrated 'functions of crime' did not include providing the basic justification for the legal profession and the justice system, it was no doubt a rushed oversight (Durkheim 1982). In any case, it is important to note how the institution itself repeatedly reminds us of the importance of the crisis it confronts and averts. In some cases, the institution may be said to have actually invented the crisis – as is almost certainly true of religion's role in developing the doctrine of original sin, not to exclude Hinduism's contribution to the caste system, and *vice versa*. It is also worth noting that, within each institutional sphere, different branches or movements focus on different sub-crises from which they derive their special missions, often in opposition to larger and more established organizations. That is surely the case in religion as churches may interpret sin in one way but their sectarian offspring may have very different perspectives. From the standpoint of social movements, a crisis often looms because of some form of alleged neglect in the culture at large or some alleged malfeasance on the part of established organizations in the field.

Meanwhile, once a movement is launched, other external cultural crises begin to develop. There are also implications of another form of external cultural crisis. By their very nature, social movements run against the grain of their cultural contexts. This is true whether the cases involve religious sects or cults, new political initiatives, economic entrepreneurial start-ups, or efforts to change the rules and procedures of larger organizations. But it makes a difference what kind of response a movement elicits. From the movement's own standpoint, conflicts, snarls and confrontations are often preferable to isolation, yawns and avoidance. Whereas the former pattern can be a functional tonic, the latter combination can be a dysfunctional death knell, and even polite tolerance can be a slow poison.

As counter-intuitive as it may seem to those reared in a culture that favours democratic pluralism, hostile combatants frequently have more success than respectful aberrants (Hammond 2000 on Mauss 1994). An active conflict gives a movement a high profile and attracts members who would otherwise be unaware or uninterested. As Rhys Williams and I noted in our account of religious movements in Springfield, MA, 'cultural power' requires headline grabbing media attention (Demerath and Williams 1992). And while it is true that such power is most effective when it outflanks the opposition in moral legitimacy, even a massive edge in legitimacy may come to naught when a movement recedes into the shadows of the public arena.

Cultural power can be an important weapon in the hands of the underdog and the outmanned. But as demonstrated by both Mahatma Gandhi's *satyagraha* in India from 1920 to 1947 and the American civil rights movement of 1957–65, non-violent appeals are most effective when they are brandished by the powerless in order to provoke illicit responses from the powerful (see Gamson 1990 and McAdam 1996). Non-violence is not necessarily non-aggressive.

In fact, movements sometimes require enemies more than friends, even when the need for enemies can cut off potential friends. The rise of the 'Black Power' movement within the civil rights struggles helped to shift those struggles into a higher gear, though it put a wedge between the more radical Southern Non-Violent Coordinating Committee and the older, more temperate and more integrated National Association for the Advancement of Colored People (Demerath *et al.* 1971). As another example, Christian Smith (1998) has pointed out that the recent surge of American evangelicalism has occurred because it is 'embattled', not in spite of it. In fact, many religions appear to cultivate paranoia in order to maintain tension with their opponents, and Rodney Stark and William Bainbridge (1985) have pointed out the greater success of 'high' *versus* 'low tension' sects.

Ordinarily, the media are helpful allies to beleaguered and beginning movements. After all, movements make more waves and hence more news when they swim against the cultural tide rather than with it. However, there are also cases when the media fail to carry a movement's cultural appeal or convey it as illegitimate. Consider the case of Al Qaeda in the West. While there is little doubt that the movement has grown in the West despite great mainstream opposition in the media and societies at large, this has been the result of contestation alone without widespread cultural legitimacy. In the Middle East, the story is quite different. Here the USA has played into Al Qaeda's hands by amping up the 'clash of civilizations' just as Bin Laden might have hoped. The conflict alone has enhanced Al Qaeda's standing and recruitment in *masjids* and *madrasas* across the Koran belt. Alas, even the tragic events of 9/11 in New York and Washington have abetted the radical Islamic cause.

Crises of Resources: Competition *versus* Generosity

In moving from the cultural to structural issues facing movements from outside, it would seem to go without saying that the more external resources mobilized the better. But not so fast. An overflowing treasury can lead to overweening complacency, and according to the laws of 'goal displacement' – whereby means to ends often become ends in their own right – a balanced budget can produce the illusion of a successful program while the original goals are neglected.

Moreover, resource mobilization is not just a matter of degree. Circumstances that condition and constrain resources can be crucial and deceptive. Resources generously provided in ample amounts often carry donor constraints or at least the implicit imprimatur of a movement's more affluent elite. Mainline religious congregations and well-established civic movements often reveal the problems that occur when wealthy endowments are accompanied by conservative influences. Sometimes leaders must take considerable risks to maintain organizational integrity and commitment. While we don't usually consider classical music as a social movement, it offers a case in point here. The Boston Symphony Orchestra (BSO) is currently facing the loss of several thousand long-time subscribers and their substantial annual donations because its conductor, James Levine, insists on playing more than token contemporary music, including as standard fare a number of challenging a-tonal works by composers such as Arnold Schoenberg and Elliot Carter.

By contrast, there is something to be said for movements with a 'lean and hungry look', forced to compete with other movements for scarce resources. This competitive isomorphism takes many forms, including the frequent cheek-by-jowl location of franchise food stores on a typical city's 'schlock strip', the jousting among Protestant congregations for their share of local adherents, and the flood of membership and fund-raising appeals among competing movements in such diverse clusters as environmental conservation, civil rights or political campaigns. As the saying goes among those who study resource mobilization among social movements, '... it's a Darwinian jungle out there' for, among the many movements born, only a few survive (Zald and McCarthy 1987).

But it is also worth remembering the Darwinian mantra regarding the 'survival of the fittest'. Movements that compete well in the struggle for resources tend to be those best adapted to the competitive fray. Movements that start poorly must change quickly to avoid going under. Looming crises require adaptations that may be wrenching in the short-run but advantageous over the longer haul. The point is illustrated by Benton Johnson's (1963) dynamic formulation of the church-sect distinction. Sectarian movements are often precarious at the outset, but over time those that survive do so by taking on churchly characteristics. This may involve a shift from lay to professional clergy, from loose to tight structure and, above all, from lower to higher status adherents with more resources to contribute. Yet it is also important to bear in mind the downside of such a dynamic and the possibility of overplaying a churchly hand. Some sects become so churchly that new sectarian movements grow within their ranks and finally break away out of protest.

The history of every major religion is dotted with examples of this sort of dynamic. And just as it is not restricted to Christianity, it is also not restricted to religion. In fact, the cycle of surviving small movements to developing into larger organizations which in turn spark new small movements can be found in virtually any institutional field involving, for example, political movements *versus* parties; economic start-ups *versus* corporations; or intellectual innovations *versus* paradigms. The latter cues a shift away to a new set of crises involving internal cultural matters.

Crises of Sacralization and Secularization

Anyone familiar with developments in the sociology of religion over the past twenty-five years knows that there has been a budding revolution in the ranks; once a placid scholarly backwater, the field has become a rushing rapid. The issue concerns secularization as a phenomenon once taken for granted but now often referred to as a 'disproven hypothesis'. This is not the place for a thorough review of the dispute (see Demerath 2007). Essentially the revolutionaries argue that prophets of secularization from the eighteenth to the late twentieth century mistakenly predicted the demise of religion, when recent evidence both in the West and around the globe suggests, if anything, resurgence. As one caught in the 'middle' of the dispute in both senses of that word, I have argued that reality scorns any all-or-nothing formulation in either direction. Secularization is alive and well, but so is its dialectical opposite: namely, 'sacralization'. In the latter, some forms of religion may take on new or renewed urgency, and other matters once neglected or treated as ordinary take on a new sacred salience. In fact, the oscillation between secularization and sacralization is redolent of the church-sect dynamic described above.

For the most part, these issues have been debated at either the *macro*-level of whole societies and 'civilizations', or the *micro*-level of individuals. But they are also pertinent at the *meso*-level of movements and organizations. In fact, each tendency represents a common crisis faced not just by religious groups but also by groups of all stripes in all fields. Movements born with a particular set of shared commitments and understandings often experience both secularizing and sacralizing tendencies. From a movement's perspective, each may be either functional or dysfunctional, depending upon the circumstances. Let's consider each in turn.

Over time any organization's sacred rituals and tenets – again, not necessarily religious – may begin to give way. If a movement's founding vision and agenda are militantly hostile to the mainstream, secularization may be a positive development that allows the group to reconsider its course and renegotiate its relationship to the opposition. As noted earlier, this is a natural tendency for sects of all sorts who face resource scarcity or depletion. Movements that mellow and moderate may have a better chance at survival. They cast a wider appeal and antagonize fewer opponents who may be in a position to reduce their opposing tactics and even provide actual aid.

At the same time, this *aggiornamento* may come at a stiff price. Secularization becomes dysfunctional when it robs the originating mission of the priority needed for effective implementation or shucks the mission off entirely. Once again goal displacement rears its ugly head. While secularization may be the easy path, it can also be destructively seductive. Movements may lose their initial energies and commitments while settling into comfortable routines. They may also lose their sharp edges and distinctive callings while submitting to isomorphic pulls toward greater conformity with other movements and organizations in their social environment.

Sacralization offers a different set of crises. Certainly it can seem dysfunctional when it characterizes splinter groups within a movement which develops competing sacred goals and tactics. But conflict can also be functional, as pointed out in Georg Simmel's classic work (see the compilation by Coser 1956). Conflict tends to flesh out differences among members that might otherwise fester until infected. It also sharpens alternatives that might otherwise be left cloudy or overlooked entirely. Sacralization is surely an important counter to secularization, and even if it poses a crisis of change, such change may be necessary if the movement or organization is to regain its dedication and adapt to new conditions.

Crises of Leadership and Member Motivation

Finally, our fourth category of crises involves a series of internal-structural issues, beginning with crises of authority well-known to students of social movements. Weber himself talked about the crisis that occurs when a founder dies and there is a transition from the original leader's personal charisma to a more stable charisma of office that adheres to every succeeding occupant of the position. This applies widely, from Popes to Presidents.

But while many movements owe their beginnings and successes to top-down leaders and moral entrepreneurs with a charismatic flair, this is not always the case. For example, unlike cults or NRMs that tend to have dominant authoritarian leaders, many religious sects are suspicious of strong power-wielders at the top, hence their common emphasis on 'the priesthood of all believers' and their rotation of lay leaders who rise from and return to the congregation. Movements vary depending on whether their tone and activities are poured over the rank-and-file by elites at the top, or percolate up from the bottom where they entered as a result of either selective or accidental member recruitment.

Crises lurk in all of the above. Top-down leadership pathologies are hardly uncommon, and some organizations lack the procedures for coping with or removing them. This is especially the case in social movements where rational-legal authority is rare. Again as noted by Simmel, persistent crises are a bane, but rapidly developing and rapidly dispatched crises can be a boon. Sometimes the crisis resolution is initiated and sustained from below. The clash between top-down and bottom-up may be explosive in the short-run but a source of needed change in the long run. Often bottom-up change is the only change available when change is required.

But recruitment is itself crisis-laden. Often it produces a tension between loyalty to the older, original members and their ideals, on the one hand, and eagerness to bring in new members with little sense of the movement's past and new perspectives of their own, on the other hand. In fact, these set up competing priorities. Some churches are more cloistered in cleaving close to their continuing traditions and members; others are more evangelical and conversionist in seeking out new members while counting on the church's ability to mould them. Both of these tendencies can become crises when they go too far or not far enough. The conflict between them is another crisis that is dysfunctional in the short-run but functional over time.

Finally, having described some of the exigencies of recruiting members and raising support from outside a movement, it is important to note how crises help to raise motivation and money inside a movement. Lawrence Iannaccone (1994) notes the advantages of 'strict churches' warding off 'free riders', and I have described how declining mainline liberal congregations may 'snatch defeat from victory' by averting crises at all costs (Demerath 1997). Without suggesting that savvy movement leaders routinely concoct rumours of outside hostility and prejudice towards their mission, I would not be astonished to hear of such cases given the tendency of many movements towards what I earlier referred to as 'cultivated paranoia'. Without suggesting that pastors suffering from the 'edifice complex' resort to arson to produce a crisis supporting the fund-raising for a new church building, I would not be shocked to discover that it has happened. Among most social movements, fund raising is constant, and this is because it is constantly problematic. One can imagine the gasp of delight followed by the sigh of disappointment when the old pastor stood up and announced: 'I am pleased to report that we have all the money we need. Now all we have to do is give it.' But the sense of a chronic crisis is not all bad.

Movements need to be continually reminded of their special challenge. Successful movements are often beleaguered movements.

Summary

This paper is a humble contribution to a perverse classical genre involving the counter-intuitive and unintended positive consequences of negative phenomena – whether crime by Emile Durkheim (1982), conflict by Georg Simmel (see Coser 1956), inequality by Kingsley Davis and Wilbert Moore (1945), poverty by Herbert Gans (1995), the inept by William J. Goode (1967), or even bureaucracy by Max Weber (see Gerth and an organizational form that has been commonly demonized by so many scholars, including Max's less well-known brother, Alfred). In pointing out the functional aspects of crises for social movements and other types of organizations, I have also tried to honour another tradition of penetrating behind the facades that often mask organizational reality. Still, I have not excluded dysfunctions and have noted that in some cases a crisis may have both functions and dysfunctions, even simultaneously.

Virtually all social movements, organizations, and professions can trace their origins and continued justification to a perceived crisis that is either already upon us or just ahead. Beyond this, many of these same organizations owe their internal dynamics to other sorts of crises that are more inherently organizational. A simple typology helped to frame four different sorts of crises pertaining to matters external and cultural (involving targets and tactics), external and structural (involving resource competition *versus* generosity), internal and cultural (involving sacralization *versus* secularization), and internal and structural (involving leadership and member motivation). It is true that movements and organizations following my lead are in for a storm-tossed voyage during what Beckford (2001) has called a 'free floating' trip for religious groups. However, as has been argued at several points, functional crises may lead to short-run difficulties but long-run advantages. Some will reach port safely.

References

Barker, E. (1989) *New Religious Movements: A Practical Introduction*, London: Her Majesty's Stationary Office.

Beckford, J.A. (2001) 'Social Movements as Free-Floating Religious Phenomena', in R.K. Fenn (ed.) *The Blackwell's Companion to the Sociology of Religion*, Oxford: Blackwell's Press.

——— (2003) *Social Theory and Religion*, Cambridge, England: Cambridge University Press.

Coser, L.A. (1956) *The Functions of Social Conflict*, New York: Free Press.

Davis, G.F., McAdam, D.E., Scott, W.R. and Zald, M.N. (eds) (2004) *Comparative Perspectives on Social Movements*, New York: Cambridge University Press.

Davis, K. and Moore, W. (1945) 'Some Principles of Stratification', *American Sociological Review*, 10, 2: 242–9.

Demerath, N.J. III. (1997) 'Snatching Defeat from the Jaws of Victory in the Decline of Liberal Protestantism', in N.J. Demerath III, P. Hall, T. Schmitt, and R.H. Williams (eds) *Sacred Companies: Organizational Aspects of Religion and Religious Aspects of Organizations*, New York: Oxford University Press.

—— (2007) 'Secularization and Sacralization Deconstructed and Reconstructed', in J.A. Beckford and N.J. Demerath III (eds) *Sage Handbook for the Sociology of Religion*, London: Sage Publications.

Demerath, N.J. III., Marwell, G. and Aiken, M.T. (1971) *Dynamics of Idealism: White Students in a Black Movement*, San Francisco: Jossey-Bass.

Demerath, N.J. III. and Williams, R.H. (1992) *A Bridging of Faiths: Religion and Politics in a New England City*, Princeton, N.J.: Princeton University Press.

Durkheim, E. (1982) *Rules of the Sociological Method*, New York: Free Press.

Gamson, W. (1990) *The Strategy of Social Protest*, 2nd Edition, Belmont, CA.: Wadsworth Press.

Gans, H.J. (1995) *The War Against the Poor*, New York: Basic Books.

Gerth, H. and Wright Mills, C. (1958) *From Max Weber*, New York: Oxford University Press.

Goode, W.J. (1967) 'The Protection of the Inept', *American Sociological Review*, 32: 5–19.

Hammond, P.E. (2000) *The Dynamics of Religious Organizations*, Oxford, Oxford University Press.

Iannaccone, L. (1994) 'Why Strict Churches Are Strong', *American Journal of Sociology*, 99, 5: 1180–1211.

Johnson, B. (1963) 'On Church and Sect', *American Sociological Review*, 28: 539–49.

Lyman, S. (ed.) (1995) *Social Movements: Critiques, Concepts, Case-Studies*, New York: NYU Press.

Mauss, A. (1994) *The Angel and the Beehive*, Urbana, IL: University of Illinois Press.

McAdam, D., McCarthy, J.D. and Zald, M.N. (eds) (1996) *Comparative Perspectives on Social Movements*, New York: Cambridge University Press.

Melucci, A. (1989) *Nomads of the Present: Social Movements and Individual Needs in Contemporary Society*, Philadelphia: Temple University Press.

Scott, W.R. (2004) 'Reflections on a Half-century of Organizational Sociology', *Annual Review of Sociology*, 30: 1–21.

Smith, C. (1998) *American Evangelicalism: Embattled but Thriving*, Chicago: University of Chicago Press.

Snow, D. *et al.* (1986) 'Frame Alignment Processes, Micromobilization, and Movement Participation', *American Sociological Review*, 51, 4: 464–81.

Stark, R. and Bainbridge, W. (1985) *The Future of Religion*, Berkeley, CA.: University of California Press.

Williams, R.H. (2003) 'Religious Social Movements in the Public Sphere', in M. Dillon (ed.) *Handbook of the Sociology of Religion*, New York: Cambridge University Press.

Zald, M.N. and McCarthy, J.D. (1987) *Social Movements in an Organizational Society*, New Brunswick, N.J.: Transaction Books.

CHAPTER 8

The European Court of Human Rights, Minority Religions, and the Social Construction of Religious Freedom[1]

James T. Richardson and Jennifer Shoemaker

Introduction

In a recent publication (Richardson 2007) the social construction of human rights was discussed, focusing particularly on the relatively new right of religious freedom. Beginning with a discussion of the social construction of international human rights, following Donnelly (1999), the article briefly examined the construction of the concept of religious freedom, pointing out that it first developed within a particular historical and geographic context in Western Europe as a means to deter bloody religious conflicts that had broken out there. The Peace of Westphalia in 1648 is the first time religious freedom was guaranteed in a formal legal document. Somewhat later the idea of religious freedom was given great impetus with the establishment of the United States, a new nation so divided religiously that its founding fathers were willing to try a 'lively experiment' by making religious freedom one of the building blocks of the new society.

This 2007 paper critiqued the somewhat negative assessment of Philip Lucas (2004) concerning the status of religious freedom in the contemporary world, and took a more optimistic view, noting that religious freedom seems to be on the upswing in many regions.[2] Cited were such developments as increasing pluralism worldwide, the global increase in judicial autonomy and the globalization of judicial systems, including the European Court of Human Rights (ECHR), and the spread of

---

1   A summary of this paper will appear in the proceedings volume of 'State-Church Relations in Europe: Contemporary Issues and Trends at the Beginning of the 21st Century' that took place in Bratislava, Slovakia, November, 2007. The research on which this paper is based was supported by a Scholarly Activities Grant from the College of Liberal Arts, University of Nevada, Reno, for which I am grateful.

2   See Robbins (2003) for another quite negative assessment of religious freedom in the contemporary world to which the critique offered of Lucas' position in my 2007 chapter also applies to a considerable extent. Robbins' major point is that religion has become much more important and therefore controversial in the modern world, a point echoed forcefully in Jim Beckford's fine *Social Theory and Religion* (2003) analysis. However, Beckford would not, I think, agree with Robbins that this controversy over religion has led directly and automatically to limitations of religious freedom.

adversarialism in judicial systems, among other things. In this treatment a number of examples were used from post-Soviet times in former communist countries. We want to return to this geographic location and to recent decisions of the ECHR to expand on this earlier argument by examining the developing pattern of specific case decisions by the ECHR that concern religious freedom.

Another article (Richardson 2006b) also examined social structural and historical factors that contribute to the development and maintenance of religious freedom, drawing on some major concepts from the sociology of religion and the sociology of law to develop theoretical assertions about sociological and historical conditions that would foster religious freedom and which might undermine such concerns. For instance, the rise of pluralism, the development of strong nation states, and the development of typical methods of regulating religion by modern governments (such as the establishment of formal hierarchies of religions) were discussed. From the sociology of law were drawn concepts such as the pervasiveness, centralization, and autonomy of legal systems. It was noted that most modern states had experienced expanding and centralizing legal systems, and that modern movements toward more autonomous judicial systems usually would, under certain conditions, play a major role in protecting religious freedom, assuming decision makers shared such values and other social conditions supported them as well.

This article, 'The Sociology of Religious Freedom' (2006b), relied in part on the theoretical work of Donald Black (1976; 1999), making particular use of his variables 'cultural intimacy' and 'status' to help explain how religious groups might fare when involved in legal and judicial systems. Those religions of high status and which share cultural intimacy with decision makers within society and the legal system would be expected usually to prevail in legal actions involving them. Black and Baumgartner's (1999) concept of 'third party partisanship' was also useful in helping understand rare times when minority religious groups lacking social status and cultural intimacy might prevail in legal actions. Attention was also paid to the considerable discretion that operates within legal systems (Richardson, 2000), and the significant impact of decisions made by key functionaries in the legal system (such as on admissibility of certain kinds of evidence) on the outcomes of legal actions involving religious groups and individuals.

Another recent publication (Richardson 2006a) focused particularly on former Soviet countries and on the role religion played in the overthrow of that officially atheistic regime. This chapter examined particularly the role of constitutional courts in a few of those nations, and how they were able in most cases to promote the ideal of religious freedom with their rulings. Particularly this has been the case in Hungary and to a lesser but still important extent in Russia. However, in Poland the Constitutional Court has been dominated more by Catholic values, thus causing some conflict with other more secular values and with some minority faiths. Nonetheless, this analysis demonstrated the important role that courts can play in protection of religious freedom under certain circumstances.

In the latter paper (2006a) and in the more recent one (2007) it was noted the important role of relatively autonomous judicial systems in promoting and maintaining religious freedom. The former focused on constitutional courts, and the later publication briefly discussed the role of the European Court of Human Rights

(ECHR). Indeed, this article even referred to the ECHR as functioning as a 'third party partisan' on behalf of minority religions with its recent (since 1993) spate of cases concerning such religions. It is this last point that we want to expand herein.

The European Court of Human Rights

Our overall theme is that the social construction of religious freedom in the modern world, including especially former Soviet countries, involves the ECHR as a major contributor. The ECHR, working in loose concert with constitutional courts in the region of Eastern and Central Europe, has shown support for religious freedom for groups and individuals in that part of the world during the post-Soviet period. Arguably the ECHR is the most important court of human rights in the world, given that it is the court of last resort for some forty-six nations and nearly one billion people, and that its decisions are considered persuasive in many other nations, as well.[3] Thus it is clear that decisions of that court can contribute much to the modern social construction of religious freedom.

This has not always been the case. As noted in numerous publications (see Richardson 1995; Evans 2001; Edge 1998; Gunn 1996, for examples), it was not until 1993 that the ECHR finally found a violation of Article 9 of the European Convention on Human Rights, which supposedly guarantees religious freedom to all those individuals in nations that are Member States of the Council of Europe (COE). Thus the Convention was in force 43 years before a violation was found of Article 9.[4] The Court regularly deferred to decisions of Member States on matters of religion, granting them a considerable 'margin of appreciation' that meant in practice that the Member States could do what they pleased as they regulated religion. However, that posture changed with the *Kokkinakis* case in 1993, when the Court found (on a split six to three vote; see Richardson 1995 and Evans 2001 for discussion of this watershed case) that a Greek statute criminalizing proselytizing was violative of Article 9 of the European Convention on Human Rights. Since that time there have been a number of decisions affirming in various ways the right of religious freedom, although the pattern of decisions is not consistent and has been criticized (Evans 2001; Gunn 1996; Richardson and Garay 2004), at least Article 9 cases are receiving

---

3   Note that a recent U.S. Supreme Court decision allowing sexual activity between same sex consenting adults, *Lawrence v. Texas*, cited as a major justification for its decision ECHR case law.

4   Article 9 of the European Convention on Human Rights states:

1) Everyone has the right to freedom of thought, conscience, and religion; this right includes freedom to change his religion and belief, and freedom, either alone or in community with others and in public and private, to manifest his religion or belief, teaching, practice, and observance.

2) Freedom to manifest one's religion or belief shall be subject only to such limitations as are prescribed by law and are necessary in a democratic society in the interests of public safety, for protection of the public order, health or morals, or for the protection of the rights and freedoms of others.

attention now, instead of being almost automatically dismissed, as they were for decades.[5]

One criticism germane to this discussion is that offered by Richardson and Garay (2004: 233). In the conclusion section of that paper we made the following statement:

> ... there is something odd about these more recent (post-*Kokkinakis*) cases, namely that most of them involve Jehovah's Witnesses and most cases come from Greece (including some non-Witness cases) and former Soviet Union countries ....
>
> It does seem that the 'margin of appreciation' generally afforded Member States by the ECHR is weakening, but in an interesting way. There still seems to be considerable deference shown to dominant and original members of the Council of Europe, but Greece seems to be being used as an example for other newer states, particularly those from the former Soviet Union.

Another possible interpretation is offered in this 2004 chapter: that Greece and former Soviet nations have much more punitive approaches to minority religions than do original Member States, and that this posture requires intervention by the ECHR, thus leading to what on the surface looks like possible discrimination against those nations. But, as noted above, it could also be the case that Greece, with its criminalization of proselytization, is being used as an example of what these newer COE Member States should not be doing. Therefore, a possible 'double standard' might be posited concerning recent ECHR cases which treat cases from some nations differently than similar cases from other more established COE countries. This paper will examine more recent cases than were included in the earlier publication, in a tentative attempt to ascertain if this possible pattern still exists, and if the 'double standard' interpretation seems justified.

New ECHR Cases

In Richardson and Garay (2004), ECHR cases with final rulings or settlements that occurred between the 1993 *Kokkinakis* case and late 2001 were discussed, which led to the tentative conclusion that a double standard might be in operation, and that Greece, with its numerous cases involving the Jehovah's Witnesses (JWs), was being used as the exemplar and precedent for cases from those former Soviet nations. Nine of the dozen post-*Kokkinakis* cases where religious freedom was supported were from Greece, with seven of them involving JWs. The other cases with final decisions for plaintiffs were from Spain, Bulgaria, and San Marino.[6] Also, during this time period four cases, all involving JWs, were settled favourably for the plaintiffs after

---

5   The timing of the *Kokkinakis* case, coming shortly after the demise of the Soviet Union, raises an interesting question of whether the ECHR was perhaps preparing for the anticipated move of former Soviet nations into the Council of Europe by establishing a precedent, and in effect announcing that the 'margin of appreciation' doctrine that had prevailed for years was no longer the norm.

6   The case from Spain is particularly interesting for students of new religions because it involved a deprogramming case, with attendant claims of 'brainwashing', where the Court

being granted admission by the Court. Two were from Greece, and two were from Bulgaria (Richardson and Garay 2004: 229–30).

In sharp contrast to this pattern of favourable decisions for plaintiffs from minority faiths, we noted that two cases involving the JWs in France had been dismissed (not granted admissibility), and also that in a major 1996 case, *Wingrove v. United Kingdom*, the ECHR ruled in favour of U.K. authorities who had banned an allegedly blasphemous film, using as a basis a justification not appearing in the European Convention – 'the right of citizens not to be insulted in their religious feelings.' (Evans 2001: 71). A similar result occurred in another case involving an original member of the COE, Austria. In *Otto-Preminger v. Austria* (1994) the ECHR ruled in favour of a ban on a film that mocked religious figures citing '"respect for the religious feelings of believers as guaranteed in Article 9" despite the fact that nowhere in Article 9 is such respect explicitly guaranteed.' (Evans 2001: 70).

At the time the research was completed for the 2004 Richardson and Garay paper a number of other Article 9 cases were before the ECHR, including at least 14 JW cases from Bulgaria, Austria, Romania, France, Georgia, and Russia. Also, one case involving Scientology and one involving the Unification Church against Russia were before the Court. We noted that what happened to these and other cases would indicate whether a 'double-standard' pattern was in fact real. A fuller study of all ECHR cases implicating religion will not be possible herein given space limitations. However, a report of case dispositions obtained from the ECHR Library shows that between 1999 and 2006 a total of 13 cases have resulted in decisions finding a violation of Article 9. It is noteworthy that this includes four from Greece, two each from Bulgaria and Ukraine, one each from Latvia, Moldova, Russia, Turkey, and San Marino. Also, a report from *Human Rights Without Frontiers* shows several other judgments rendered already in 2007, with three against Russia, and one each against Moldova, France and Georgia.

These data continue to raise the question of whether a double standard might exist since so many of the rulings are against former Soviet dominated countries, but only much closer comparison of cases from these nations with comparable ones (in terms of facts) from older Member States of the Council of Europe would reveal definitive proof on this important question. Herein we will examine the disposition of selected cases since this last report, focusing particularly on Russia and France, to note any apparent differences in how cases have been handled from those two nations. Russia was selected because it is the dominant nation of the former Soviet Union, making any cases involving that nation a test of the political will of the ECHR to exert authority over former Soviet nations. France was selected because it was a founding member of the Council of Europe, and also it has been severely criticized in recent years because of its treatment of minority religions (Beckford 2004; Duvert 2004, Richardson and Introvigne 2004; Introvigne 2004; Davie 2003).

---

found a violation of Article 5–1 against false imprisonment. See Richardson (1996) for a fuller discussion of this fascinating case.

Russian ECHR Cases

A number of legal cases involving religion have developed in Russia during the turbulent times since the fall of the Soviet Union, leading to a conclusion that the situation for minority religions has been decidedly mixed in that country during the decade following the fall of the Soviet Union (see Richardson *et al.* 2004 for one summary of major cases).[7] This mixed (but mostly negative) message has led to several key cases being filed with the ECHR from Russia in recent years. This was possible because Russia had joined the Council of Europe, along with a number of other former communist countries, thereby agreeing to subject itself to the jurisdiction of the ECHR. The case filings concerning Russia with the ECHR since it joined the COE have led to some remarkable decisions rendered against Russia within the last two years.

Moscow Branch of the Salvation Army v. Russia (2006)

This case (Application # 72881/01) derived from application of a key provision of the new 1997 law governing religion that replaced the much more liberal law passed in 1990 that had allowed a number of foreign religious groups to register with the Russian government and its political subdivisions. That provision required all already approved religious organizations to reregister following new provisions. Initially granted official status in 1992, the Moscow Branch of the Salvation Army (SA) had reapplied under provisions of the 1997 law, but was rejected. This decision led to efforts by authorities in Moscow to dissolve the SA, which then fought battles with the bureaucracy and in the courts for years, winning some of them but not achieving success with registration. In spite of a major victory for the SA in the Russian Constitutional Court that effectively voided the key provision of the new law (February 2002), the SA was still refused re-registration. Eventually the SA filed a claim with the ECHR asserting violations of Articles 9, 11, and 14.

On 5 October 2007 the Court issued a unanimous ruling in the case, making this the first such judgment against Russia in the ECHR since it became a member of the Council of Europe in February 1996. The Court found a violation of Article 11 (freedom of association) in conjunction with Article 9 (freedom of religion), and awarded costs to the Salvation Army as well. The ruling was quite critical of the arguments raised by Russia in its defence and of the failure to make clear what process was to be followed for re-registration. The ruling also criticized other aspects of the 1997 law, including the provision that prohibits foreign nationals from being founders of Russian religious organizations.

---

7   The lack of autonomy of the legal system and growing nationalism in Russia have contributed to a severe problem for minority religions attempting to exercise what seemed to be fairly liberal laws at the outset of the decade of the 1990s (see Shterin and Richardson 1998; 2000). The change of laws dealing with religion in 1997 resulted in even more difficulties for minority faiths (Shterin and Richardson 2002).

Kuznetsov and Others v. Russia (2007)

This complicated case (Application # 184/02) involved efforts to break up a meeting of over 100 deaf Jehovah's Witnesses by police and government authorities in Chelyabinsk. The background of the case involves lengthy efforts of the JW congregation to register during which 12 different applications were submitted between 1997 and 2001, with all being refused. Only after the JW group took their case to court did they achieve registration by order of the Chelyabinsk Regional Court, which upheld an earlier decision by a District Court. As this battle was taking place, the JWs were also under criminal investigation by the Chair of the regional Human Rights Commission who claimed that the group had '... "lured" young children into their "sect"' (Paragraph 10 of ECHR ruling). The investigation by the local prosecutor was quashed once but reopened at the behest of the Commissioner, but then quashed again '... on the ground that no evidence pointing towards a criminal offence could be found.' (Par. 13)

The JWs had negotiated a lease in February 1999 for the use of a vocational training school to use school facilities for meetings of the group, and had been using the facilities for over one year when the event in question took place. On 31 March 2000 an order had been issued to all educational establishments that no school property could be used for religious purposes. Shortly thereafter the Commission and a police officer visited the technical school and attempted to persuade the principal to cancel the lease immediately. The request was refused, however. On Sunday 16 April 2000 the Commissioner returned with several others, including two police officers, and after some discussion and harassment of a group leader, Mr. Kuznetsov, forced the meeting to disband before its appointed time of adjournment. The next day the JW group was informed that the lease had been cancelled and that they could no longer use the school facilities.

Mr. Kuznetsov and others filed complaints with the local prosecutor against the Commissioner and police officers for their actions, but these complaints were dismissed. An action was then filed in the District Court of Chelyabinsk complaining that the actions violated the group's right of religious freedom guaranteed under the Russian Constitution and the European Convention. The District Court ruled against the plaintiffs and this ruling was upheld on appeal in the Chelyabinsk Regional Court. The JW group then appealed to the Ombudsman of the Russian Federation for relief, who sent a strongly worded letter to the Prosecutor General of the Russian Federation, condemning the actions taken by the local prosecutor and other authorities in the matter. The Ombudsman complained that the Prosecutor's Office had itself been implicated in the case by virtue of use of a letter from a deputy prosecutor recommending some very biased materials as authoritative to the Commissioner whose actions led to the confrontation when the service was disrupted. Mr Kuznetsov and others involved then filed a claim with the ECHR, claiming violations of Articles 6, 8, 9, 10, and 11.

The ECHR unanimously found in favour of Mr. Kuznetsov and others (ruling of 11 January 2007), finding violations of Articles 6 (fair hearing) and 9 (freedom of religion), and awarding damages to the plaintiffs. In its decision the Court cited two precedents from the Supreme Court of the Russian Federation in which that

Court had over-ruled decisions disallowing other JW meetings. The ECHR ruling also included criticisms of the Russian local and regional courts that handled the case, stating that they had not allowed a fair hearing of the case.

Church of Scientology Moscow v. Russia (2007)

This rather remarkable case (Application # 18147/02) also involved a re-registration effort brought on by the passage of the 1997 law in Russia which was implicated in the Salvation Army case described above. Scientology had registered as a religion under the law approved in 1990 in Russia, achieving registration in January of 1994. The new law forced Scientology and many other groups to reregister, and Scientology officials in Moscow attempted to do so a total of ten times after the new law came into effect. However, the organization was unsuccessful in these efforts, and the convoluted trail of applications, court cases, and appeals followed by Scientology resulted in its being thwarted at every turn for reasons that were disingenuous and involved obvious subterfuge. The tortured history of these efforts by Scientology even involved some lower court rulings in their favour, but subsequent decisions clearly demonstrated the lack of autonomy and authority of the judicial system in Russia; any favourable initial rulings were ignored by the Moscow Justice Department, or overturned on review by higher judicial authorities.

Another regional Scientology branch filed a case with the Russia Constitutional Court, claiming that the 1997 law was unconstitutional in that it violated provisions of the Russian Constitution that guaranteed religious freedom and the ability of religious groups to function. Although similar suits were won before the Constitutional Court by the Salvation Army, Jehovah's Witnesses, a Protestant group, and the Society of Jesus, Scientology's suit was dismissed on a technical ground that also seemed somewhat disingenuous (Richardson *et al.* 2004).

Having failed to achieve re-registration through use of the legal system of Russia after years of trying, Scientology carried its case to the ECHR. The Scientology case was admitted by the Court, and in April of 2007, the ECHR ruled in favour of Scientology, finding a violation of Article 11 (freedom of association) in light of Article 9 (freedom of religion), and ordered the Russian government to register the organization. Modest money damages were awarded as well. The opinion recounts the convoluted history of the ten attempts to reregister, the many court cases and other machinations engaged in by the government entities involved, and in very strong language castigates the Russian government for its refusal to intervene and effect a re-registration. The opinion also makes it clear that the series of events involved with this effort were violative of the international agreements to which Russia was a signatory, including especially the European Convention on Human Rights, the governing document for the ECHR.

Barankevich v. Russia (2007)

This case (Application # 10519/03) involved a pastor of an evangelical Christian church ('Christ's Grace') in Chekhov in the Moscow region who was refused permission to hold an outdoor service in a park. The refusal was based mainly on the fact that the majority of citizens in Chekhov were not of the faith of Pastor Barankevich's church, and allowing his group to use the public park might cause 'discontent' among other citizens and 'public disorder'. The pastor challenged the decision of the Chekhov Town Council on the grounds that this violated his rights of religious freedom and of assembly. However, his case was dismissed by the Chekhov Town Court and by the Moscow Regional Court. The law at the time allowed the Town Council to make such arbitrary decisions, but was changed in 2004 to require only notification, not authorization, for such events.

Pastor Barankevich appealed in 2003 to the ECHR, claiming violations of Articles 9 and 11 (freedom of religion and freedom of assembly). The ECHR ruled unanimously on 26 July 2007 in favour of Pastor Barankevich, finding 'that there had been a violation of Article 11 of the Convention interpreted in light of Article 9', and also awarded monetary damages. The Court made strong statements concerning the importance of freedom of assembly to a democratic society, stating that there was no evidence offered that would support a claim that the meeting requested would cause public disorder. The Court also stated that it was the responsibility of the authorities to make sure that peaceful assemblies such as that proposed by the plaintiff would be protected and not subject to attack from those opposing the group's beliefs and values. A quote from the decision reveals the sentiment of the Court (Par. 31):

> It would be incompatible with the underlying values of the Convention if the exercise of Convention rights by a minority group were made conditional on its being accepted by the majority. Were it so a minority group's rights to freedom of religion, expression, and assembly would become merely theoretical rather than practical and effective as required by the Convention ....[8]

Thus the Court concluded (Par. 35) that '… the ban on the religious assembly planned by the applicant "was not necessary in a democratic society"'.

These four decisions, all coming within two years, have sent a strong message to Russia and other former Soviet bloc nations concerning the importance of respecting the provisions of the European Convention concerning religious freedom and associated rights such as freedom of assembly. These decisions, coupled with others against former Soviet dominated countries, are making it clear that these rights are to be respected.[9] A question remains, however, as to whether these decisions represent unequal treatment of these new members of the Council of Europe, and it is to this question that we now turn, using France as a preliminary test of whether original members of the COE have been dealt with similarly in recent years by the ECHR.

---

8   Note how sharply this language contrasts with that of the *Wingrove* and *Otto-Preminger* cases from the U.K. and Austria mentioned above.

9   It remains to be seen if Russia will in fact implement the decisions as ordered by the Court, and what will happen if it does not. Recall that the Russian Constitutional Court had in fact ordered that the Salvation Army be re-registered, but officials refused to carry out that order, leading to the case being taken to the ECHR.

ECHR Cases from France

As noted in the 2004 Richardson and Garay paper, cases involving France were likely not to garner admissibility before the ECHR. However, France has had two decisions against it in the years since we collected data for the earlier report. This is not surprising given the strongly negative posture adopted by the French government against minority faith, a situation that has been much discussed in the scholarly literature (see Davie 2003; Beckford 2004; Duvert 2004; Luca 2004; Richardson and Introvigne 2004, for examples). Also, there is another major case from France awaiting an admissibility decision, the decision of which will impact our research question directly.

Palau-Martinez v. France (2005)

This case (Application # 64927/01) involved a custody dispute brought on by a husband moving out of a home to live with his mistress. The couple was affiliated with the Jehovah's Witnesses originally, and the mother remained a member. A divorce was granted in 1996, with fault attributed to the husband alone. Custody of the children was awarded to the mother, who desired to live with them in Spain, while the father in France would be afforded some access. In summer of 1997 the children went to visit the father in France who was due to return them after the summer to the mother in Spain. He refused to return the children and instead enrolled them in school in France.

The mother had filed a legal action in 1996 seeking more contact with the children during times they were visiting the father, and later amended her pleading to seek return of the children after the father refused to return them to her. In January 1998 the Nimes Court of Appeal confirmed the divorce and awarded an allowance of 1500 FRF to the mother per month for three years, but allowed the children to remain with the father in France. The ruling by the court contained discussion of the religious affiliation of the mother and clearly took that into account in its ruling. The mother appealed this decision to the Court of Cessation, which ruled on 13 July 2000, confirming the earlier judgment to award custody to the father. The mother then filed with the ECHR, alleging violations of Articles 6 (fair hearing), 8 (respect for private and family life), 9 (freedom of religion), and 14 (prohibition of discrimination) in her complaint.

The ECHR ruled (16 December 2003) that there had been a violation of Article 8, taken together with Article 14, and also awarded damages to the plaintiff. The Court did not rule on the Article 6 or 9 claims, deeming it unnecessary to do so given the finding under Article 8. The Court was very critical of the French court's apparent heavy reliance on the fact that the mother was a member of the JWs. The Court was also critical of the rather cursory analysis carried out by the French courts of the situation in that no formal 'social inquiry report' was conducted, even though this is common practice in custody cases.

Affaire Paturel v. France (2005)

This case (Application # 54968/00) is unusual in that it was brought by a private individual (Paturel) and not by the national JW organization in France. A JW member who was also a lawyer self-published a book recounting his difficulties in having a career as a lawyer while a JW. After publishing the book he was disbarred by the local bar association and he and his family experienced severe financial difficulties, including a tax audit by the government tax authorities. He was also sued for slander by a major French anti-cult organization which Paturel had discussed in his book. Paturel was found liable in the suit and ordered to pay damages. He appealed the decision but was not successful in French courts.

Paturel then filed a claim with the ECHR claiming violation of Article 10 (freedom of expression) and Article 9 (freedom of religion). The case was granted admissibility, and on 22 December 2005 the Court found unanimously in Paturel's favour on the Article 10 claim, but did not deem it necessary to handle the Article 9 claim. Damages were also awarded to the plaintiff.

Jehovah's Witnesses v. France (pending)

As part of the official anti-sect campaign in which the French government has been engaged for years, the tax authorities have taken action against two religious groups, the JWs and Mandarom,[10] both of which appeared in a parliamentary established list of 'cults and sects' that are supposedly not true religions (Richardson and Introvigne 2004). In what the tax authorities assert was a simple tax audit, the JWs were sent a notice that they owed over $50 million dollars in past due taxes since they were not an official religion. The issue was fought in the French court system, but to no avail. Eventually a claim was filed on 25 February 2005 with the ECHR (Application # 8916/05) with claims that Articles 6 (fair trial), 9 (freedom of religion), 14 (prohibition of discrimination), 18 (limitation of rights), as well as some items of the Protocols had been violated.[11] The case awaits an admissibility decision, which is expected in spring, 2008.

It is worth noting that the French government refuses to acknowledge that this case involves any issues of human rights, including religious freedom. However, it is also the case that the law applied to the JWs (and to Mandarom) has since been changed making it clear that organizations legally defined as charities cannot be charged such taxes. Neither effort to collect past due taxes was negated by this change of statute, and efforts continue to seriously impair if not destroy both the JW organization and Mandarom in France. This is the case even though the JWs have been operating in France for over a hundred years, and are the third largest Protestant denomination in France.

---

10   See Introvigne (2004) for a discussion of the overall campaign against this small religious group in the South of France.

11   The Protocols are official documents that expand upon and interpret the provisions of the European Convention on Human Rights.

The JW organization is seeking to have France admit that the government has been discriminating against the JWs, that the national JW organization and its subsidiaries can continue to function as an officially approved religion, and, of course, they want the tax bill cancelled. France refuses to agree to any of the terms asked for by the JWs, however, and both parties are awaiting the admissibility decision. In the interim some discussions are taking place with ECHR officials attempting to serve as mediators in the dispute.

It should be noted that a very similar JW case was filed earlier with the ECHR (Application # 53430/99) but was found inadmissible in a rather convoluted opinion rendered in November, 2001. The decision stated that the JW organization could not be considered a victim under the provisions of the convention. Richardson and Garay (2004: 232) state of this earlier decision: 'This application was replete with many instances of harm that individual Witnesses and Witness organizations had encountered because of official governmental reports and actions in France.'[12] Thus, a decision to admit the newer claim, and to act upon it in a manner favourable to the JWs would potentially represent a shift in the posture of the ECHR toward France, one of the founding members of the Council of Europe.

Conclusions

This review of ECHR cases from two key nations – one an original member of the Council of Europe and one new but quite important one – seems to suggest that the hypothesis offered in 2004 by Richardson and Garay about a possible double standard operating with ECHR decisions in the area of religion remains viable. Russia, the leading nation of the former Soviet Union, has been dealt with in almost a perfunctory manner by the court, with a recent series of unanimous and strongly worded decisions against Russia in the area of religious freedom. France too has suffered two losses in the Court in the past few years. The custody dispute decision was perhaps predictable, given earlier precedents of the Court (i.e. *Hoffman v. Austria*, 1993 case[13]) and the other case involved more of a focus on freedom of expression. However, unlike the conclusion in the earlier study (Richardson and Garay 2004), at least this more recent examination has found some decisions against an original member of the COE. Whether they are of the same 'weight' as those against Russia is debatable, however.

Other caveats are in order, as well, before drawing any conclusion about the existence of a double standard with recent ECHR decisions. First, the outcome of the pending major tax case from France may reveal that the double standard does not exist, or that there has been a major shift in recent years. The 'major shift' hypothesis may be defensible, given the continued punitiveness of France toward minority faiths. Perhaps the ECHR is in the process of deciding to send a message to France about what is and is not acceptable behaviour among original Council of

---

12   Alain Garay was one of the attorneys for the JWs in this earlier case.

13   It is perhaps worth noting that this case brought by a JW mother against one of the original members of the Council of Europe, decided the same year as *Kokiknakis*, was on a split vote of five to four (see Evans 2001).

Europe member nations. Second, perhaps no double standard ever existed, and the pattern of case decisions discussed in 2004 and herein simply represents different structural and historical conditions, as discussed in the introduction (see Richardson 2006a; 2006b and 2007), in the former Soviet dominated nations (and Greece). This possibility is perhaps the most important caveat, raising an issue that can only be resolved with careful comparison of the entire range of religion cases handled by the ECHR since the demise of the Soviet Union and the affiliation of those nations with the Council of Europe. We are undertaking this large task, but the results are not yet available.

References

Beckford, J. A. (2003) *Religion and Social Theory*, New York: Cambridge University Press.
—— (2004) '"Laicite", "dystopia", and the reaction to new religions in France,' in J.T. Richardson (ed.) *Regulating Religion: Case Studies from Around the Globe*, New York: Kluwer, pp. 27–40.
Black, D. (1976) *The Behavior of Law*, New York: Academic Press.
—— (1999) *The Social Structure of Right and Wrong*, New York: Academic Press.
Black, D. and Baumgartner, M.P. (1999). Toward a theory of the third party. In D. Black, *The Social Structure of Right and Wrong* (New York: Academic Press, pp. 95–124.
Davie, G. (2003) 'Religious minorities in France: A Protestant perspective,' in J.A. Beckford and J.T. Richardson (eds) *Challenging Religion: Essays in Honour of Eileen Barker*, London: Routledge, pp. 159–69.
Donnelly, J. (1999) 'The social construction of international human rights,' in T. Dunne and N. Wheeler (eds) *Human Rights in Global Politics*, Cambridge: University of Cambridge Press, pp. 71–102.
Duvert, C. (2004) 'Anti-cultism in the French Parliament: Desperate last stand or an opportune leap forward? A critical analysis of the 12 June 2001 Act,' in J.T. Richardson (ed.) *Regulating Religion*, New York: Kluwer, pp. 41–52.
Edge P. (1998) 'The European Court of Human Rights and religious rights,' *International and Comparative Law Quarterly*, 47: 680–87.
Evans, C. (2001) *Freedom of Religion Under the European Convention on Human Rights*, Oxford: Oxford University Press.
Gunn, J. (1996) 'Adjudicating rights of conscience under the European Convention on Human Rights,' in J. van der Vyver and J. Witte (eds) *Religious Human Rights in Global Perspective*, The Hague: Matinus Nuhoff, pp. 305–30.
Human Rights Without Frontiers. Available at www.hrwf.net.
Introvigne, M. (2004) 'Holy mountains and anti-cult ecology: The campaign against Aumist religion in France,' in J.T. Richardson (ed.) *Regulating Religion*, New York: Kluwer, pp. 73–84.
Luca, N. (2004) 'Is there a unique French policy of cults? A European perspective,' in J.T. Richardson (ed.) *Regulating Religion*, New York: Kluwer, pp. 53–72.

Lucas, P. (2004). 'The future of new and minority religions in the twenty-first century: Religious freedom under global siege', In Tom Robbins and Phillip Lucas (eds), *New Religious Movements in the 21ˢᵗ Century*, New York: Routledge, pp. 341–58.

Richardson, J.T. (1995) 'Minority religions and religious freedom, and the new pan-European parliamentary and judicial institutions', *Journal of Church and State*, 37: 39–59.

—— (1996) '"Brainwashing" claims and minority religions outside the United States: Cultural diffusion of a questionable concept in the legal arena', *Brigham Young University Law Review*, 1996: 873–904.

—— (2000) 'Discretion and discrimination in cases involving minority religions and claims of ritual abuse', in R. Ahdar (ed.) *Law and Religion*, Aldershot, U.K.: Ashgate, pp. 111–32.

—— (2006a) 'Religion, constitutional courts, and democracy in former communist countries', *The Annals of the American Academy of Political and Social Science*, 603: 129–39.

—— (2006b) 'The sociology of religious freedom: A structural and socio-legal analysis', *Sociology of Religion*, 67: 271–94.

—— (2007) 'Religion, law, and human rights', in P. Beyer and L. Beaman (eds) *Globalization, Religion, and Culture*, Boston: Brill Academic Publishers, pp. 409–30.

Richardson, J.T. and Garay, A. (2004) 'The European Court of Human Rights and former communists states', in D. Jerolimov, S. Zrinscak, and I. Borowik (eds) *Religion and Patterns of Social Transformation*, Zagreb: Institute for Social Research, pp. 223–34.

Richardson, J.T. and Introvigne, M. (2001) '"Brainwashing" theories in European parliamentary and administrative reports', *Journal for the Scientific Study of Religion*, 40: 143–68.

Richardson, J.T., Krylova, G., and Shterin, M. (2004) 'Legal regulation of religion in Russia: New developments', in J.T. Richardson (ed.) *Regulating Religion*, New York: Kluwer, pp. 247–58.

Robbins, T. (2003) 'Notes on the contemporary peril to religious freedom', in J.A. Beckford and J.T. Richardson (eds) *Challenging Religion: Essays in Honour of Eileen Barker*, London: Routledge, pp. 71–81.

Shterin, M. and Richardson, J.T. (1998) 'Local laws restricting religion in Russia: Precursors of Russia's new national law', *Journal of Church and State*, 40: 319–41.

—— (2000) 'The effects of Western anti-cult sentiment on the development of laws concerning religion in post-communist Russia', *Journal of Church and State*, 42: 247–71.

—— (2002) 'The *Yakunin v. Dworkin* trial and the emerging religious pluralism in Russia', *Religion in Eastern Europe*, 22: 1–38.

CHAPTER 9

The Trumpet Sounds Retreat:
Learning from the Jehovah's Witnesses[1]

David Voas

Introduction

The Jehovah's Witnesses (JWs) mobilize nearly seven million people around the world (including a million Americans and the same number of Western Europeans) to engage in hours of direct marketing every month. Despite the movement's size, growth and global reach, scholarly interest in the group has largely focused on the legal questions raised by its distinctive doctrines on blood transfusion, military service and door-to-door proselytizing. Jim Beckford's book *The Trumpet of Prophecy: A Sociological Study of Jehovah's Witnesses* (1975) remains the key source. Indeed, this study is so authoritative that, apart from a very few papers (such as Singelenberg 1989; Wilson and Dobbelaere 1990), no one has ventured back onto the same territory until recently (Holden 2002; Barbey 2003; Dobronravoff 2007).

The group was founded by Charles Taze Russell in the 1880s, and since 1896 has been called the Watch Tower Bible and Tract Society. The more familiar name of 'Jehovah's Witnesses' was adopted by the second president, Joseph Franklin Rutherford, in 1931. JWs believe that the world has entered the end times and the destruction of governments and false religion is imminent. Teaching is based on a close, literal reading of the Bible. Members are expected to attend regular meetings during the week, to engage in Bible study, and to evangelize actively among friends, neighbours and strangers. The group is now represented in most countries in the world; only about 15 per cent of active JWs are American.

The leading proponents of the 'market model' of religion argue that the Witnesses demonstrate what a religious group can achieve if it simply adopts the right strategy (Stark and Iannaccone 1997). They depict the group as the perfect sect, one that combines all the attributes necessary for success. This view has been picked up elsewhere, for example in a recent text that devotes part of a chapter called 'Secularization in Retreat' to the JWs (Aldridge 2000: 116 ff). Likewise Stark and Finke (2002: 52) have repeated the claim that it is one of 'the world's fastest-

---

1   I am grateful to Eileen Barker, Jim Beckford and Richard Singelenberg for their help and advice in studying the Jehovah's Witnesses. As usual I have rewarded Larry Iannaccone's friendship with criticism, and I thank him for his forbearance. I also appreciate the assistance and goodwill of Witnesses in Britain and the USA, including Paul S. Gillies from the Office of Public Information for Jehovah's Witnesses.

growing religious movements'. The JWs are therefore of far more than incidental interest to sociologists of religion; they have been held up as representative of an ideal type and in consequence serve as an especially useful case study.

In their enthusiasm for demonstrating the importance of the JWs, Stark and Iannaccone were led to make bold but possibly ill-considered conjectures about the prospects for the group. They suggested that a growth rate of 4 per cent per annum over the next century was a conservative forecast. Compound growth would thus take the total number of active Witnesses from about 4 million in 1990 to 194 million worldwide in 2090. They wrote that:

> while we cannot be sure at what rate the Witnesses will grow during the next century, in our judgment the least plausible assumption is that they will quit growing or begin to decline in the near future. Continued growth is the most plausible assumption and we favour the 4 per cent projection. (Stark and Iannaccone 1997: 154)

It seems inconceivable that this global figure could apply in any developed country; the growth rates characteristic of a group in the early stages of its development cannot be maintained indefinitely. If one applies the rate of 4 per cent per annum to the current number of self-described Jehovah's Witnesses in the United States, for example, it would imply that by the end of the century most people in the country would be adherents. Not only is such an outcome implausible in itself, it is inconsistent with similar extrapolations of the current growth rates of quite different groups, from Mormons to Muslims to non-believers. In any event, the analysis had no sooner been published than it was criticised for being at odds with recent trends (Singelenberg 1997).

Stark and Iannaccone's projections were global, not national. Their theoretical argument, however, is applicable to any society, and hence it is fair to infer at a minimum that the JWs should continue to grow everywhere the sect maintains the characteristics they describe. If the group fails to grow, then there may be a better underlying model of how religious movements grow and decline. In the past decade, growth in the West has in fact levelled off. Three rival explanations could be offered: the product or the sales force is no longer as good as it used to be, the market niche is now saturated, or people are simply losing their taste for this kind of religion. Finding the right story will help us to understand the nature of social and religious change.

Recent Trends in Activity

The JWs have produced statistical summaries of their activities, country by country, for several decades. The level of detail is extraordinary; every national organisation produces a monthly 'service report' giving the number of members engaged in active evangelism, the total number of hours spent in the field, the number of Bible studies conducted, and so on. Whereas most religious organisations count many people who have ceased to be active as members, the Witnesses' statistics include only those who engage in proselytizing, known as 'publishers'. The average publisher spends eight to ten hours per month in this work; so-called pioneers contribute much more. 'Regular' pioneers are publishers in good standing who promise to spend some 70 hours or more per month in the field over the course of a year. 'Auxiliary' pioneers commit themselves for shorter periods or fewer hours, while 'special' pioneers work full time for the organization.

Growth in the immediate post-war period was exceptionally rapid. By the early 1960s the expansion had slowed, but calculations that led many to believe that 1975 could bring Armageddon helped to inspire a surge of activity. Although the subsequent disappointment was reflected in a dip in active membership, the group

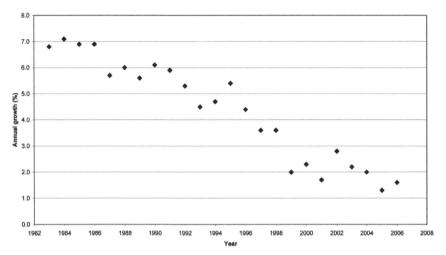

Figure 9.1   Worldwide growth rate of Jehovah's Witnesses, 1983–2006

recovered very quickly, and numbers again shot up during the 1980s. The rate of growth has steadily declined over the past 25 years, however (Figure 9.1).

Global growth in the number of publishers fell from 7 per cent per annum in the early 1980s to a low of 1.3 per cent in 2005; in consequence, growth is now only just keeping pace with that of the total world population. The major developed countries of North America, Western Europe, Australia and the Far East show remarkably similar trends, with the timing of growth and stagnation being approximately the same everywhere. The absolute numbers of active Witnesses have recently declined not only across Western Europe, but also in Canada, Australia and Japan. In the United States numbers have changed little since 1998; the events of 11 September 2001 produced a renewal of energy as the apocalypse again appeared to draw near, but the effect seems to have been short-lived. Growth in the United States jumped from zero to 2.9 per cent in the year September 2001 to August 2002, but fell back to half that in the following 12 months; a similar pattern is found in other countries.

Even more surprisingly, the countries in Latin America that have contributed so much to the global growth of the movement in recent decades show clear signs of following the same S-shaped trajectory, with growth now levelling off. Similarly very high growth in post-communist Eastern Europe appears to be coming to an end. The proportion of Witnesses in the population is declining in such countries as Argentina, Cuba and Poland. Only African countries still show strong and steady growth, though even here not without exception: the most developed of them (South Africa) now shows no growth in numbers of JWs relative to the population.

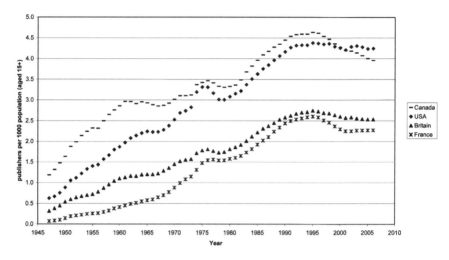

Figure 9.2   Trends in four countries since 1947

The fact that the time series are so close in cross-national comparison (Figure 9.2) is startling: possibly evidence of globalization, or a demonstration of the effects of centralised management and target-setting, or of sects having a quasi-biological life cycle.

Changes in Effectiveness and Commitment

The falling growth is not a result of individual Witnesses being less active; over the past half century the average number of hours spent in the field by each publisher has fluctuated within a moderate range. The striking change has been the declining productivity of recruitment work. Productivity can be measured by the number of hours needed to produce a Bible study (the first step towards conversion) or a baptism (performed only for adults who have committed themselves to active membership).

Looking just at the period that followed the post-1975 disappointment and subsequent recovery, one finds that the number of baptisms per 10,000 hours spent in the field has dropped in the US from 3.6 in 1982 to 1.5. In Britain the story is almost identical, with a fall from 3.5 baptisms per 10,000 hours in 1983 to 1.4 (Figure 9.3). The position is comparable almost everywhere in the world except sub-Saharan Africa. In Mexico, for example, second only to the US in its population of JWs, the number of baptisms per 10,000 hours has fluctuated around a declining trend; the rate has fallen from about 5 to less than 2 over the past 20 years.

While baptisms per 10,000 hours of field service is a good global measure of productivity, it does not provide a means of distinguishing between the two main sources of new members: publishers' children and converts. Ideally we would have evidence to help us decide whether the current stagnation is attributable to diminishing success in one or both. Even if retention of children has declined dramatically, however, that factor alone could not account for the substantial reduction in the rate of baptism; the productivity of field service must have decreased.

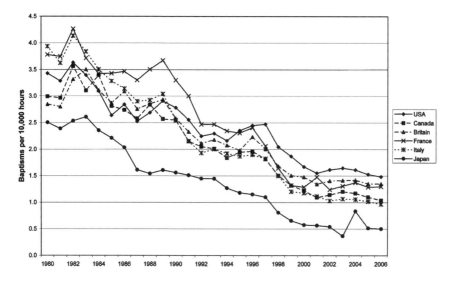

Figure 9.3   JWs' baptisms per 10,000 hours field service, 1980–2006

Beckford found that somewhat more than half of the children of JWs were retained by the sect in Britain in the mid-1970s (Beckford 1975: 194). A survey of nine Belgian congregations in the late 1980s produced similar findings (Wilson and Dobbelaere 1990: Table 7). A Witness couple with an average of 2.4 children would thus be followed in the faith by about 1.2 offspring, or 0.6 for each spouse. If retention has been at that level, we can estimate the magnitude of recruitment.

Consider someone who became an active member at the beginning of 1974 and left field service 30 years later, at the end of 2003. Statistics from the US show that the average publisher would have spent 3,352 hours proselytizing during that period. With a rate of 8.2 baptisms per 10,000 hours, this investment would have produced a return of 2.7 baptisms, from which we subtract approximately 0.6 representing the member's own progeny. Thus the average American publisher might in 1974 have expected to make at least two converts during a lifetime of field service. Even at the much lower productivity of 3.6 baptisms per 10,000 hours for 1982, an American publisher would still have had a better than even chance of making a convert at some point during a 30-year career. The current level of baptisms is such that an ordinary Witness is unlikely to make any conversions in a lifetime of knocking on doors. At current rates the 3,352 hours constitute only half what is needed to produce a single baptism, and even that addition probably results from procreation rather than conversion.

Another factor that affects growth is the level of attrition. Every year the ranks of publishers are increased by the newly baptized and those coming back from a period of inactivity, and decreased by the numbers who die, become infirm, drop out or are excluded ('disfellowshipped') because of unacceptable behaviour. By taking the ratio of one year's stock (the average number of publishers) to the prior year's stock augmented by the flow (baptisms), it is possible to estimate loss from all causes. Unfortunately it is not easy to separate losses from natural causes from deliberate inactivity. If mortality has been roughly constant over the period since 1980, any trend in attrition will reflect changes in the net drop-out rate. Conceivably the average age of publishers has increased, however, which would tend to raise the level of natural attrition.

In the USA, Canada, Britain and France attrition rose steadily from 1983 to 1997, though it has since fallen. In many countries outside Europe and North America there has been a swing from negative attrition in the early 1980s (perhaps as those disappointed in 1975 returned to the fold?) to positive attrition today.

A benefit of analyzing baptisms and attrition separately is that we can identify the sources of upswings and downturns in numbers. For example, it seems that the impact of the events of 11 September 2001 on the JWs was felt not in recruitment – the level of baptisms did not recover significantly – but in stemming (albeit temporarily) the defection of existing members, or perhaps in encouraging the return of former publishers to active service.

Although attrition is appreciable, it is nevertheless no higher than could be explained by mortality or infirmity. If (for the sake of argument) publishers were evenly distributed across 50 years of age, then 2 per cent would drop out every year, and attrition was lower than that figure in the US, Canada, France and Britain in 2006. The JWs are like all the mainstream denominations in Europe: they are stagnating or declining not because people are leaving the churches, but because too few children are following in the parental footsteps and there is little compensating recruitment of adults.

Carrying Capacity of the Population

Not only are these findings interesting in themselves, they might be claimed as evidence for some bold conjectures. Note from Figure 9.2 that although the growth rates are very close, year by year, in all developed countries, the number of JWs as a proportion of the population is variable. It seems possible that each society has a certain 'carrying capacity' for JWs. As a function of the religious environment, in other words, the sect is able to expand up to a certain level; the upper limit will vary from one country to another. Its growth to that point will follow the sort of logistic curve familiar from many applications in population biology. The carrying capacity depends on the number of potential converts, which in turn depends on the general level of religiosity. Some countries (for example, Mexico, Italy and the USA) have strong religious cultures and are conducive to high prevalence of JWs, independently of whether the competition comes from one traditional church or many alternative suppliers. Other countries are less religious (for example, Britain and the Netherlands) and so the maximum penetration achieved by JWs is much lower in relative terms. The success of the sect, then, is a function of the environment's religious resources, not the structural features of the religious market.

There is an alternative speculation about the possible trajectory of the JWs (and similar groups) that could be worth consideration. I outline the conjecture below, followed by criticisms made by Jim Beckford when I proposed the idea in 2002. I am inclined to agree with his reservations, but the issue seems worth discussing.

Equilibrium or Collapse?

With numbers of JWs in developed countries stagnating or declining after a long period of growth, one may be reminded of over-fishing in the North Atlantic, where the size of the fleet rapidly increases and then collapses. If there is a mechanism connecting poor recruitment to attrition – and the obvious suggestion is that lack of organizational success leads people to give up – then something similar could happen.

In more technical terms, perhaps the appropriate population pattern is not the simple logistic (S-shaped) curve, but an 'overshoot-and-collapse' model, which in more specific contexts may be described as a potential outcome of a 'predator-prey' system. Without wishing to be pejorative, we may think of the evangelists as the predators, and the potential converts as the prey. With plenty of fish in the sea, no problem exists: success is merely a matter of the fisherman's skill and effort and the fish's interest in what is being dangled before it. If too many people are attracted to become fishermen, however, the result is over-fishing: stocks decline, productivity drops, the return on investment falls, and eventually some people leave the business. There may still be too many people chasing too few fish, though, particularly since stocks have been reduced, and over-fishing continues even as the number of fishermen declines. The time may come when there is insufficient incentive for anyone to continue fishing, even though there are still fish in the sea. In nature the predator-prey relationship would normally be cyclical, but extinction is possible if one group or the other falls below a sustainable level.

If publishers are discouraged by failure to recruit and are more tempted to become inactive, if they do not see their own efforts and those of their fellow publishers rewarded, then the mechanism exists to produce an overshoot and collapse in total numbers. A point may be reached where diminishing returns from field service become obvious and painful (with, for example, a lifetime of effort producing no conversions). People start to drift away from active participation. The intensity of evangelism is still such, however, that occasional converts are brought in; investment remains high. Attrition continues at a high level; recruitment is no longer high enough to compensate. Numbers will continue to fall.

The proselytizing orientation of the JWs makes them vulnerable to decline when conditions become unfavourable. The rewards of membership are found in possessing and proclaiming the truth, rather than in access to rituals, emotionally uplifting worship, or a range of social opportunities. Meetings resemble training seminars more than conventional religious services. The difficulty is that if recruitment appears to be the *raison d'être* of activity, and then for extended periods not merely the individual publisher but the entire congregation experience no success, the consequential loss of morale could be substantial. If members stay firm in their faith and enjoy the solidarity that comes from mutual striving (however fruitless), the position is sustainable. If they are more like members of a pyramid scheme that must continue to grow in order to survive, however, the prospects may be bleak.

What happens after the onset of decline – whether there is a complete collapse or instead a cyclical variation around an equilibrium point – depends on the characteristics of those who become disaffected. If their time as active Witnesses has inoculated them against further spells in the organization – if, in other words, they do not return to the pool of potential recruits once they become inactive – then a major fall in numbers may result. If they simply return to occupy the same niche as before, however, and can be brought back into active service, then the prospects for the JWs are better; numbers will oscillate around the sustainable maximum.

Beckford's Response

When I first advanced this argument in 2002, Jim Beckford offered an appropriately critical response:

> 1) I question your assumption that Publishers are discouraged by 'failure to recruit'. I have always argued that the main purpose of the service work is not recruitment but confirmation of identity and commitment to the WTBTS [Watch Tower Bible and Tract Society, the JWs' corporate entity]. In fact, I would go further and claim that the poor response that JWs receive on the doorstep confirms their view that the world is corrupt and heading for disaster. This means that the phrase 'diminishing returns from field service' can't be easily reconciled with the JWs' worldview as prophetic, heroic and sacrificial. So, I question your claim that proselytization makes JWs vulnerable to decline in hard times.
>
> 2) A closely related point is your claim that 'recruitment appears to be the raison d'être of activity'. Again, I question whether this is true. The main activity is publishing the good news. I see recruitment as a useful bonus. An allied point is that the JWs are quite selective in their efforts. They have their own prejudices and stereotypes in mind. Again, this places limits on recruitment. See Munters (1971).
>
> 3) I don't have good quantitative evidence to support my belief, but it certainly used to be the case that 'cold calling' produced poor results that were compensated for to some extent by recruitment through networks of relatives and work friends, neighbours, etc. What I would dearly like to discover is the proportion of Bible studies that are conducted with people already personally known to the JWs.
>
> 4) If the JWs become demoralised, it's not because of poor responses on the doorstep. It's more likely to be because of internal scandals, official obstructions in, for example, France, and the energetic efforts of apostate groups. (Personal communication, 2 December 2002)

In a subsequent message Beckford commented further:

> You argue that the 'willingness to sacrifice may fade' if it becomes clear that the organisation is losing ground. But the JWs will certainly use such evidence to show that the 'endtime' is near and that Satan will manifest himself through attacks on Jehovah's organisation. So, the effect on morale may be surprising. (12 December 2002)

Beckford is right to argue that JWs may not be discouraged by falling recruitment, and hence that the connection with rising attrition is far from evident. At an individual level the pay-off from field service is not measured in baptisms. Even at the best of times the return on investment was so small that no one could expect to make a convert from months or even years of effort. To that extent it would make little difference to a single publisher directly if the odds of winning the doorstep lottery went from (say) 10,000 to 1 to 50,000 to 1: they were never going to win anyway.

One might still wonder, though, whether there could be an indirect effect. If recruitment declines to the point where the individual congregation and the entire circuit or district begins to shrink rather than grow, there could a psychological impact on those participating. After all, the Watch Tower publications (particularly those mainly for internal consumption, like the yearbooks or *Our Kingdom Ministry*) make great play of the onwards march from one numerical peak to the next. News of missed targets and poor results are used to exhort publishers to yet greater efforts. The value system communicated and thereby created seems to be one in which growth, at least at the organisational level, is a sign of Jehovah's power and approval.

A steady flow of converts may also help to explain the resilience of the Witnesses as the promised end time fails to arrive. 'If a movement recruits rapidly, the sense of disappointment may itself be somewhat allayed since newer members have not waited so long ... Each recruit, too, provides a new focus of interest, restoring buoyancy and zest to older members ... [who] need such re-invigoration if commitment is to be sustained' (Wilson and Dobbelaere 1990: 174–5).

Beckford is certainly right to point out that failure in the field can be given a positive spin: it shows that this old world is indeed ready for the end. The truly committed will be faithful to the last. For at least a certain proportion of the membership, though, there must be a desire to accept the teaching at face value: field service has a purpose that is real, not merely symbolic; it can bring people to the truth, and more and more are being baptised; we are beleaguered but will prevail. If it becomes clear that the organisation is losing ground, the willingness to sacrifice may also fade. The effect on morale may be similar to that of a half-empty church (Gill 2003).

As Beckford observes, publishers may achieve most by using networks of relatives, colleagues, neighbours, and so on. The statistics show a decline in the number of Bible studies relative to the hours of field service, which suggests that it may be harder to get existing friends to agree to study (a necessary step *en route* to membership). The distance between the JWs and the wider society has presumably increased: unlike other organisations (even conservative churches) the JWs remain quite rigorous in their demands and restrictions, and the gap that has to be crossed by potential converts is perhaps even larger than before.

The incidence and potency of official obstructions is unclear. On the one hand, there is perhaps less hostility to the JWs in countries like the United States and Britain than at any time in the last century; ordinary people may see them as a nuisance, but tolerance of unusual beliefs has arguably never been higher. On the other hand, Beckford points out that:

> they appear on the list of 172 'dangerous cults' in France, where the taxation authorities have imposed swingeing penalties on them. The Belgian and Spanish authorities also treat them as a major threat to social order. And, of course, in Eastern Europe they are persecuted in many countries. (Personal communication, 5 December 2002)

How far these restrictions limit growth can be debated; the JWs seemed to hold up well under pressure in the past, and a modest dose of martyrdom might help to build solidarity. The JWs appear to be highly successful in Zambia, for example, despite the severity of anti-Witness regulations there.

What remains intriguing is how similar trends have been across the developed world. The US seems to follow the same pattern as Europe and with practically the same timing. Perhaps the explanation is to be found on the supply side, and the declining success in generating baptisms reflects poor leadership or errors in strategy that have affected the global organisation. If growth has stopped because of dwindling demand, though, the phenomenon seems harder to explain.

Religious Economies or Religious Environments?

It is far from easy to account for the international variation in prevalence of JWs in terms of the theory of religious economies. The proportion of JWs in the population is relatively high in quite different kinds of religious markets: on the one hand the United States (seen as the quintessential free market for religion) and on the other the Catholic strongholds of southern Europe such as Portugal and Italy (in which the JWs faced legal barriers to operation). Stark and Iannaccone could claim to explain both, arguing that although there is strong competition in the former the market has thereby been invigorated, whereas in the latter the monopolist has deadened the market but can be outmanoeuvred by an efficient sect. Having it both ways makes it all the more difficult, however, to explain the less impressive statistics in countries like Britain and the Netherlands. These places would seem to offer the best of both worlds: a relatively free but apparently underdeveloped market.

Germany presents one of the most awkward challenges to the religious economies theory. The JWs have a long history in the country, and before the war were very strong in the East, where they had their German headquarters. Activity was suppressed during the communist period, but with the fall of the old regime the organisation returned in force. Nevertheless Eastern Germany still has a far smaller proportion of JWs in the population than the West, a situation that shows no signs of changing. In 1990, the year of reunification, not only was the ex-communist state far behind the Federal Republic in the prevalence of JWs, its number of Witnesses was growing at only 1 per cent per annum, as compared to 3 per cent in the former West Germany. The combined total has since stagnated, and the past few years have seen a decline.

To most observers, the varying degrees of Witness penetration will seem to reflect not the market structure but the contemporary culture of the countries concerned. Even Stark's first proposition is that 'New religious movements are likely to succeed to the extent that they retain cultural continuity with the conventional faith(s) of the societies in which they seek converts' (Stark 1996: 136). The religious ambience in the United States, Italy and Portugal is very different from that in Britain and the Netherlands, where much of the population now has had no religious upbringing and may be regarded as secular. Similarly the former East Germany remains the least religious part of Europe; far from being impatient for religious conquest, it has remained indifferent to the best of religious marketing.

The growth and stagnation of the JWs is better explained by the existence of a bounded niche for the type of religion that they offer. Because that niche cannot expand indefinitely (every country has a certain 'carrying capacity' for JWs, as suggested above), numbers will reach a plateau from which further increase is unlikely, unless the environment itself changes. The proportion of the population belonging to the group seems to be associated with overall religiosity, so that it is higher or lower depending on whether the country itself is more or less religious in general.

This ecological approach might provide a solution to the puzzle of simultaneous stagnation that improves not only on economic supply-side theories but also on demand-related explanations derived from a conventional view of secularization. The post-war religious decline in Europe may indeed be the result of a changing demand for religion, but the levelling out in the 1990s of the JWs seems to be happening simultaneously in countries that came early or late (or perhaps not at all) to secularization. Niche size may depend on the environment, but the pattern of niche filling appears to be independent of it. The centrally-coordinated dispersion of JWs has ensured that they reached saturation point everywhere in the developed world at essentially the same time. One might, though, have expected the onset of diminishing returns in a population to depend on the period of exposure to JWs, which varies considerably between countries.

Conditions for Growth

There are two ways of explaining the success or failure of a religious movement. One is by reference to its environment, highlighting conditions suggested by theory (of the secularization or rational choice varieties, for example). Another focuses on the characteristics of the group itself, looking for features that encourage or inhibit growth. The ten conditions held to be necessary and possibly sufficient for organisational success that were set out by Stark (1996) and then applied to the Jehovah's Witnesses by Stark and Iannaccone (1997) combine these two elements.

The propositions dealing with group characteristics are for the most part unobjectionable. They include, for example, the statements that religious movements must have legitimate leaders with adequate authority (prop. 4), that growth requires a highly motivated labour force (prop. 5), that fertility (prop. 6) and socialisation (prop. 10) must be adequate, and that members must be highly bonded while retaining bridges to potential members outside the group (prop. 8).

Proposition 2 is the familiar claim that religion is superior to magic: 'New religious movements are likely to succeed to the extent that their doctrines are non-empirical'. It would be more accurate to say that organisations should promise outcomes that are empirically verifiable in principle but are protected against falsification. Many mainstream Christian churches, for example, preach the power of prayer, with the protective proviso that God's will is unknowable. Alternative medicine, a contemporary variety of magic, does better than many religions because success counts for more than failure. For Adventist groups like the Jehovah's Witnesses, the challenge has been to create an expectation that the end is nigh without being too specific: to make empirical claims that are not exposed to empirical test. The history of the JWs shows that it is difficult to benefit from millennial excitement without suffering damage when hopes are disappointed.

Two overlapping propositions (3 and 9) assert that religious movements must maintain a medium level of tension with their environment by being strict, but not too strict. Without further specification of what level of tension/strictness is just right, this type of test lends itself to being wise after the fact. In the case of the Jehovah's Witnesses, it is not evident that strictness has changed. Tension may have increased in some places and decreased in others, but this factor is of little obvious help in explaining the cessation of growth.

The importance of the environment is most pronounced in proposition 1: 'New religious movements are likely to succeed to the extent that they retain cultural continuity with the conventional faith(s) of the societies in which they seek converts'. It is clearly true that Christian sects, for example, will do better in Christian countries than elsewhere. It is less clear why the JWs should be better represented in Catholic countries like Italy and Portugal, where the religious culture is wholly at odds with this non-Trinitarian, non-ritualistic, highly scriptural faith, than in European Protestant societies. Perhaps the conventional level of religiosity is as important as the religious heritage, but then the explanation would focus on demand rather than supply.

Finally, then, we are left with the key point of contention. Proposition 7 expresses the basic thesis of the supply-side approach: 'Other things being equal, new and unconventional religious organisations will prosper to the extent that they compete against weak, local conventional religious organisations within a relatively unregulated religious economy' (Stark and Iannaccone 1997: 150). Thus a group will do well if it operates in a free market against vulnerable competitors.

The problem is that religious markets in much of the world are more open than ever, while conventional churches are becoming weaker. Rather than benefiting from these developments, the Witnesses have seen their growth come to a halt in many countries. The theory of religious economies is successful neither in explaining cross-national differences in the stock of JWs nor in accounting for changes in the group's fortunes over time.

Stark and Iannaccone might simply say that their evaluation of the JWs on the ten criteria failed to identify some crucial weakness. Another reaction would be to concede that the conditions advanced in the theory are not in fact sufficient, and that one or more requirements (not satisfied by the JWs) need to be added. There is nothing illegitimate about either manoeuvre, though of course if too many ad hoc changes were needed one might want to go back to the drawing board.

There are other options, however. If it turns out that the JWs are running out of steam despite meeting Stark's various conditions, at least two demand-related explanations are available. One might argue that this particular niche has reached saturation point, with no more customers to whom this distinctive product appeals. While compatible with an economic perspective, this view does have an interesting implication if generalised: religion might occupy a niche in an ideological ecosystem, and this niche can be larger or smaller depending on the time and place.

The related explanation is that growth is a function of demand, not only for the specific brand but for the product/service in general. If no one is wearing top hats, the prospects for even the best and most vigorously marketed hats are not good.

The final paragraph of a recent exposition of the religious economies view reads as follows:

> Underlying the entire model are two very simple assumptions. First, effort is productive. Other things being equal, the harder a religious group works to achieve success, the more successful it will be. Second, people will only work as hard as they must to achieve their goals. ... These points seem so self-evident that only trained social scientists could doubt them. (Stark and Finke 2002: 54)

The Jehovah's Witnesses, one of the favourite examples of these scholars, now appear to be a counterexample to their theories. Surely no group works harder to achieve success. If all things are no longer equal, we have not been told how to recognize the fact. Clearly there are times when hard work is not enough (one of the sadder lessons of life); specifying those conditions may lead us to a more sociological explanation. Beyond that, the Witnesses remind us that what is labour to one may be devotion to another. If the sect survives it will not be because field service is efficient, but because it expresses and reinforces commitment. It does so partly by creating a bond between publishers. It remains to be seen whether the community that results – one based on self-denial, obedience and solidarity – can keep the modern sirens of self-fulfilment, choice and autonomy at a distance.

References

Aldridge, A. (2000) *Religion in the Contemporary World*, Cambridge: Polity.

Barbey, P. (2003) *Les Témoins de Jéhovah: Pour un christianisme original*, Paris: Harmattan.

Beckford, J. (1975) *The Trumpet of Prophecy: A Sociological Study of Jehovah's Witnesses*, Oxford: Blackwell.

Dobronravoff, P.L. (2007) *Att bli, att vara och att ha varit: om ingångar i och utgångar ur Jehovas vittnen i Sverige [To become, to be and to have been: Entering and exiting the Jehovah's Witnesses in Sweden]*, Lund University: Lund Dissertations in Social Work 28.

Gill, R. (2003) *The 'Empty' Church Revisited*, Aldershot: Ashgate.

Holden, A. (2002) *Jehovah's Witnesses: Portrait of a Contemporary Religious Movement*, London: Routledge.

Munters, Q.J. (1971) 'Recruitment as a vocation', *Sociologica Neerlandica*, 7, 2: 88–100.

Singelenberg, R. (1989) '"It separated the wheat from the chaff": The "1975" prophecy and its impact among Dutch Jehovah's Witnesses', *Sociological Analysis*, 50, 1: 23–40.

—— (1997) 'The Changing Face of Jehovah's Witnesses', Paper presented at the 11th International Congress of CESNUR, Amsterdam, Free University, 7–9 August, 1997.

Stark, R. (1996) 'Why religious movements succeed or fail: A revised general model', *Journal of Contemporary Religion*, 11, 2: 133–46.

Stark, R. and Iannaccone, L.R. (1997) 'Why the Jehovah's Witnesses grow so rapidly: A theoretical application', *Journal of Contemporary Religion*, 12, 2: 133–57.

Stark, R. and Finke, R. (2002) 'Beyond church and sect: Dynamics and stability in religious economies' in T.G. Jelen (ed.) *Sacred Markets, Sacred Canopies: Essays on religious markets and religious pluralism*, Lanham, MD: Rowman & Littlefield.

Wilson, B. and Dobbelaere, K. (1990) 'Jehovah's Witnesses in a Catholic Country: A survey of nine Belgian congregations', in B. Wilson *The Social Dimensions of Sectarianism*, Oxford: Oxford University Press, pp. 149–75.

CHAPTER 10

Theorising Conversion:
Can we use Conversion Accounts as Sources to Actual Past Processes?

Margit Warburg

The study of conversion has been a major theme in the sociology of religion since the early 1970s. Initially, this research to a large extent was motivated by public concern over the phenomenon that a minute fraction of the sons and daughters of the well-educated middle class turned away from their parental heritage and became zealous members of religious groups with colourful clothes, communal living and conspicuous new ways of proselytising. In the following two decades different theories of conversion were promulgated, debated and criticised while no single theory emerged as dominating. It is, rather, inspiration from several theories that has given a more consistent and balanced understanding of conversion to new religions in modern Western society (Dawson 1998: 72–101).

Theories of conversion cannot gain substance without data obtained by analysing actual processes of conversion. Such data are usually acquired retrospectively, because a person's conversion to another religion is rarely recorded by external observers or otherwise documented in contemporary sources. In most cases the main source of the conversion process is the convert's own, later account of the process, and sociologists have, of course, discussed the quality of the data, which can be extracted from these later accounts.

In this article I shall begin by briefly outlining some of the common elements of conversion theories. This outline leads to the main part of the article, where I discuss the reliability of conversion accounts as sources of data which can substantiate or perhaps falsify conversion theories. This discussion is not new in the sociology of religion; however, it has not been touched for several years, and it is my suggestion that it is worth reviving it to get a fresh comprehension of the theoretical positions of the past. Finally, I shall end by proposing that when formulating sociological theories on the basis of conversion accounts, it may be productive to draw parallels with sociological studies of other important re-orientations in personal life.

Processes, Probabilities and Priorities

It is a prevailing view among sociologists of religion that conversion is a *process*, and in this regard the influential model proposed in 1965 by John Lofland and Rodney Stark still holds. The Lofland-Stark process model was based on the authors' study of a small millenarian group, coded D.P. (Divine Precepts), and it proposed seven sequential, necessary and sufficient stages of the conversion process to a sectarian group (Lofland and Stark 1965). The model soon became widely applied to empirical material from diverse religious groups, and modifications were suggested to broaden its applicability (Robbins 1988: 80). For example, in the process model proposed by Lewis R. Rambo, there is no requirement for a specific sequence of events in the conversion process (Rambo 1993: 16–19). Some of the assumptions behind the Lofland-Stark process model were questioned as more empirical studies were compared and evaluated against the model (Richardson and Stewart 1978; Greil and Rudy 1984). Also Lofland himself warned against the uncritical use of a model that was based on 'rather pallid data' (Lofland 1978).

The original vocabulary of the Lofland-Stark process model tended to present converts as passive actors who were subjected to circumstantial, external forces, and this later led Lofland to call for the opposite view that studies of conversion should 'scrutinize how people go about converting themselves' (Lofland 1978: 22). It became the prevalent view that religious conversion is a normal and sensible change in a person's life resulting from his or her reflections over religious issues (Balch and Taylor 1978; Richardson 1985; Dawson 1990). This brought the sociologists' view of conversion in Western society in line with the 'intellectualistic' theory of conversion suggested by Robin Horton and J.D.Y. Peel for conversion to Christianity and Islam in non-Western societies, in this case West Africa (Horton and Peel 1976).

Although there is little evidence for regarding converts as involuntary victims of coercion, it is also true that potential converts are often subjected to social pressure from the group. This is part of the mission strategy; some groups like the Unification Church used to expose the converts to intense, all-day experiences in retreats and camps, while other groups, like the Baha'is, concentrate on continuously inviting people to various events (Barker 1984: 106–20; Warburg 2006: 319–21, 406–408). This period of familiarisation with the new creed and the socialisation into the group are general elements in a conversion process.

The later discussion and criticism of the Lofland-Stark process model has not challenged its basic and obvious assumption that there are some predisposing or background factors that may encourage or discourage conversion to a particular group, but not determine it (Lofland and Stark 1965). The fallacy is to assign these factors too much weight; for example in the well-known study of recruitment to Nichiren Shoshu and ISKCON by David A. Snow and co-workers, the authors concluded that the probability of being recruited was largely a function of circumstantial factors, such as pre-existing personal contacts through networks and what they called structural availability (Snow *et al.* 1980). Their proposition of the significance of pre-existing contacts through personal networks was valuable and evident, but the study was rightly criticised by Roy Wallis and Steve Bruce for the apparent neglect of the cognitive aspects of conversion (Wallis and Bruce 1982).

The potential convert must somehow know the group in question before the actual conversion. This typically takes place as a physical encounter with the group, but it is also reported that conversion may result by, for example, reading a book. Meeting the new religion appears as the middle of the seven key steps in the Lofland-Stark conversion process model: 'an encounter with the religious movement at a crucial turning point in life'. The encounter is an essential element in understanding the conversion process, and few convert to another religion in splendid isolation all way through the process. However, there is no reason to complicate matters by introducing the diffuse requirement of a 'crucial turning point in life' (Lofland and Stark 1965). Lofland himself has also later found this turning point troublesome (Lofland 1978).

Thus, a balanced view on conversion implies that converts should be considered social actors whose choices are influenced by the social environment of the conversion process, as well as by individual factors (Barker 1993). This means that sociological theories of conversion must consider at least:

a) Individual background variables (sex, age, education, environment of upbringing, amongst others).
b) The social environment in the period before the encounter with the group.
c) The circumstances of the encounter with the group, its social environment, and the immediate, subsequent socialisation into the group.
d) The person's own reflections and choices during the entire process.

Of course, the latter weighs heavily; otherwise the individual conversion career would resemble a deterministic or a probabilistic social process with the convert drifting passively with the stream. Converts reflect (often a lot) over the beliefs and practices of the group they may join eventually. However, when considering many conversion careers together in a quantitative study, it makes sociological sense to analyse conversion as a probabilistic social process, which is influenced – but not determined – by well-chosen social variables.

The individual background variables (item a) can generally be described and assessed in objective terms. The data which are relevant for analysing the conversion process itself (items b, c, and d), may sometimes be acquired through participant observation and interviews with neophytes. In most cases, however, the data are provided by the informant in interviews, where he or she renders a personal account of a conversion process which took place in the past.

The Reliability of Conversion Accounts as Sources – An Aborted Discussion

Evidently, conversion accounts, like other memories, suffer from problems of reliability as sources of past events and experiences which are claimed by the narrator to be crucial for his or her life later on. Among sociologists of religion, this discussion of reliability accelerated in 1978 after the publication of James A. Beckford's challenging article, 'Accounting for Conversion' (Beckford 1978). In this article Beckford noted that many of the conversion accounts rendered in interviews with members of Jehovah's Witnesses were strikingly similar and consonant with Witnesses' ideals of the conversion process. His conclusion was that the converts had gradually adapted to these ideals and therefore constructed their conversion testimony in the light of the present, rather than the past:

> Accounts of conversion are constructions (or reconstructions) of experiences which draw upon resources available *at the time of construction* to lend them sense. They are not fixed, once-and-for-all descriptions of phenomena as they occurred in the past. (Beckford 1978: 260):

Beckford's conclusion was a much needed warning against an uncritical trust in using converts' own accounts as sources for the analysis of conversion. Students of conversion generally agree that conversion accounts are by their nature backward-looking, self-reflexive, personal constructions, which are also coloured by the circumstances of the retelling (Beckford 1983). As sources for an objective historical past, conversion accounts are therefore surrounded by the same methodological problems as are other oral or written personal accounts of past events. The discussion among sociologists of religion regarding the reliability of conversion accounts as sources is also paralleled by, for example, the debate among historians concerning the use of oral sources (see Murphy 2007 on this debate).

Beckford's interpretation of the observed conformity of the Jehovah's Witnesses' accounts certainly indicates a retrospective construction of the conversion history, but it does not leave out the possibility of an alternative, plausible interpretation. It is known that the process of affiliation to Jehovah's Witnesses is carefully controlled by the group (Beckford 1975: 186–9). This could have the hypothetical effect that only those who conform to the conventions of the Watch Tower movement eventually convert, which means that the conversions may, in fact, have taken place in the way they are later recounted. This does not, of course, explain away the problem of the reliability of the sources raised by Beckford; it is just to remind us not to throw away the baby with the bath water.

Among students of conversion there has been a tendency to see conversion accounts as mere narratives, which cannot yield any objective information about the conversion process in the past, or if they can, then this information is not central to the study. A typical example is the approach taken by the anthropologist Peter G. Stromberg who studied conversion to American Evangelical Christianity. After providing an excerpt of an exemplary conversion account by an informant called Jim, Stromberg concluded:

> In this context the important point is that Jim's conversion narrative is not only or even primarily an account of events from the past, it is a creation of a particular situation in the moment of its telling. The way to look at Jim's conversion, I have come to see, is not as something that occurred in the past and is now 'told about' in the conversion narrative. Rather, the conversion narrative itself is a central element of the conversion. The way around the evidential problem I mentioned above is to abandon the search for the reality beyond the convert's speech and to look instead at the speech itself .... (Stromberg 1993: 3)

My quotation is not meant to be a critique of Stromberg's position as a basis for his own study; among Baha'is and many other groups conversion accounts and other accounts of personal religious experiences are also told to co-believers as narratives with plots that confirm a group's identity as Baha'is, sometimes by showing divine intervention in the life of the narrator (Wyman 1985: 157–68; Piff 2000: 80–84). However, I am criticising Stromberg's implicit, general endorsement of giving up the search for an historical reality beneath the conversion accounts. Just as with autobiographies, conversion accounts often provide personal observations of concrete situations, and, as with any other historical source, the reliability depends on what is being asked from the conversion account.

It is worth pursuing this problem of the reliability of the conversion accounts as sources of events and experiences of the past. These accounts may often be the only available sources to the conversion, and they are also often the most detailed. Should we really restrict our research by accepting that all reported events and experiences are to be regarded as nothing but later constructions? At the International Society for the Sociology of Religion Conference in 1991, Lorne Dawson emphasised the dilemma connected with the use of the conversion accounts as sources:

> But whatever approach is taken, the question of getting behind the institutionalized accounting frameworks, the professed reasons for conversion, to the supposed real reasons and actual past processes remains fundamental. Can we do it, should we even try? (Dawson 1991: 22).

Dawson claimed that the character of self-reflection of most conversion accounts supports his and others' position that religious conversion is an active process controlled by the person converting (Dawson 1990). I quite agree with him on this; however, it does not answer the question whether accounts of conversion are sufficiently reliable sources of 'the supposed real reasons and actual past processes', which eventually lead to conversion. If we cannot make any use of the accounts of conversion as historical sources for understanding the conversion, but only as constructions of the present, then we will be severely limited in developing theories of conversion.

Few researchers are probably ready to accept such a radical constraint on the use of conversion accounts. Also Beckford maintains that it should be possible to use the accounts as sources of more than the informants' own reflections at the time of the interview (Beckford 1983). In the following I shall explore this possibility, expanding the theoretical discussion in my own study of conversion among the Baha'is of Denmark (Warburg 2006: 298–9).

Two types of Causality in a Conversion Account

The sociologist George W. Brown and co-workers have for many years studied psychiatric disorders from a sociological perspective and interviewed patients suffering from depressions about their life stories before the onset of the disorder (Brown 2002). Quite early, Brown raised the general issue of what use sociologists can make of interviewees' accounts of past events in their lives (Brown 1983). Like Beckford, he noted the possibility of bias stemming from respondents who in their talk may create 'quite misleading patterns concerning the link between the meaning of things in their lives and what has happened to them' (Brown 1983: 35).

Brown addressed this methodological problem of possible bias by arguing that personal accounts can generally be taken as trustworthy with regard to what he called *situational* causality. He here referred to the informant's statements about where they were at a given time, whom they met, and what they said or did at that occasion. The issue of the fragility of human memory remains, of course, but there is no immediate reason to believe that such circumstances are deliberately invented. This is not the same as accepting such data at face value, of course. However, the pertinent problem arises with what Brown called *distal* causality, which occurs when there is a considerable distance in time between a set of circumstances which the informant links to his or her later reaction and the occurrence of the reaction itself.

It should be emphasised that Brown did not use the term causality to signify a tight one-to-one correspondence between given circumstances and the respondent's later behaviour. Situational causality refers to some circumstantial conditions which we also, from an external perspective, may assume to have influenced the subsequent conversion. For example, a 34-year old, male Baha'i informant told me:

> When I was a student in the late 60s, I saw an ad in the newspaper: The Baha'i library is open every Tuesday. ... I had no idea what it was and went there.

It is obvious that the advertisement was an important external factor influencing the conversion. The opposite conclusion, that the advertisement had no effect and that the young man would have converted to Baha'i anyway, would be unfounded. However, it is true that in principle we cannot be *sure* that the informant really saw this advertisement, and that it read that the library was open on Tuesdays. We are faced with the same problem as the historian who sometimes has only one source for a particular past event, and here the statement about the Baha'i advertisement stands out as a potential historical fact challenging the researcher. A consistent choice has to be made in the pursuit of historical data: either this and other statements in the interview about the past are regarded as later constructions or they are approached as something that probably did happen and which can be subjected to historical criticism; it cannot be both ways at once (Mansell 2007).

With regard to distal causality, it may sometimes not qualify as a cause at all when seen from an outsider's viewpoint, since distal causality is based on the informant's personal linking of different events over time in order to make them meaningful in the context of re-telling the conversion process. Beckford describes the convert's creation of distal causality (without using the term) with a succinct expression: 'In particular, special significance is attached to the meaning of certain events and experiences in the pre-conversion life, and the conversion account gathers them together in an *encapsulated review*' (Beckford 1983: 87, my emphasis). Here, the parallel to the autobiography as a literary genre is evident: although autobiographies may provide accounts of historical facts, they are written primarily with a focus on personal experiences and events which give meaning to the autobiographer 'when viewed in the perspective of a whole life' (Pascal 1985: 17).

Causality Analysis of a Baha'i Conversion Account

The differences between distal causality and situational causality can be illustrated by an analysis of the following, quite typical, conversion account of a 29-year-old Danish Baha'i woman, to whom I asked the question 'How did you become a Baha'i?'

> I first heard about Baha'i when I was a young assistant nurse, for a short period, at Skodsborg Sanatorium [a sanatorium north of Copenhagen]. I met a Norwegian girl there who told me about the book by Esslemont, *Baha'u'llah and the New Era*. I went to the library to look for it, but could not get hold of it. Later, in 1974-75 [the informant was born in 1952, so she was around 23 years old at that time], I was having my trainee service as part of my education as a librarian, in Sønderborg [in southern Jutland], and I found the book there. However, I did not know that there were any Baha'is in Denmark, so I left it at that. The next time I saw anything related to Baha'i was [in 1979] when I arrived by air in Søndre Strømfjord in Greenland, because at the airport the local Baha'is had put up a notice [about Baha'i]. I was working at the library in Søndre Strømfjord and courses in Greenlandic were arranged there. I enrolled in such a course, and so did two Danish Baha'is. Through these two I became a Baha'i. (The example is taken from Warburg 2006: 300–302, where the discussion is elaborated at certain points)

Applying the methods of historical critical analysis on this conversion account we can begin by stating that it is a first-hand account of four events separated in time and space. These are:

1) The meeting with the Norwegian girl at the sanatorium in Skodsborg.
2) Finding Esslemont's book *Baha'u'llah and the New Era* in the library in Sønderborg somewhat later.
3) Seeing the notice at the airport in Greenland about five years later.
4) Attending the course in Greenland where she met the two Baha'is.

The informant was personally involved in these events, and we should therefore ask whether or not she can be considered a trustworthy witness (Erslev 1972: 47–8). In all probability she can be trusted as unbiased with regard to some of the information, such as that she heard about Esslemont's book from a colleague at the sanatorium in Skodsborg, and that she found the book at the library in Sønderborg. She voluntarily gave this information, which expresses situational causalities. The informant had no motive for lying or distorting the account with regard to these times and places; for example she was not accused of anything which might encourage her to tell a lie saying that she was a librarian trainee in another town than Sønderborg! In principle, this information could be verified, because the researcher might contact the library in Sønderborg to find out if she really was employed there at the indicated time. Of course, this is not customary in the sociology of religion, and it would be quite resource demanding; but the mere fact that the information is testable influences both parties in the interview.

There are therefore good reasons to accept the Baha'i informant's trustworthiness with respect to the four situational causalities. She may not remember correctly, but she can be assumed not to be systematically distorting facts.

There is an implicated distal causality in the above account, namely that the first two events were important for the actual conversion in Greenland. The methodological problem created by using this information in a sociological study of conversion is illustrated by the following hypothetical situation: had the informant been asked to identify which of the four events was the most crucial, she might have mentioned the meeting with the Norwegian girl. The interviewer cannot assess this statement, but must note that the informant had met Baha'i through a colleague, in other words, through her personal network. However, against this interpretation stands the fact that for several years after the meeting she did *not* join the Baha'is, or even contact them. When exercising historical criticism this speaks against accepting the suggested distal causality.

This methodologically unsatisfactory situation of arbitrariness in dealing with the different possible causalities rendered in the conversion account can be avoided if we concentrate on the situational causalities. The final process towards conversion began when the informant met the two Baha'is at the language course in Greenland several years after the meeting with the Norwegian girl. Meeting the two Baha'is at the language course was what I will call the informant's *decisive encounter* with Baha'i. From that meeting onwards she was in regular contact with the Baha'is of the town in Greenland, and this contact eventually led to her becoming a member of the Baha'i community. If the decisive encounter is taken as the basis for the onset of the conversion process, the informant was recruited to Baha'i by a chance meeting with Baha'is outside her personal network.

One way or another, in a systematic study, either the informant's own judgment or the decisive encounter must be chosen as defining the onset of conversion in cases when the two do not coincide. The first (the informant's judgement) risks an analysis on the basis of a distal causality which is impossible to evaluate critically; the other (the researcher's decision of what is the decisive encounter) risks the weakness of attributing significance to circumstances that the informant might regard as insignificant. However, in a choice between the two, the circumstances surrounding the decisive encounter are at least those that both the informant and the interviewer would agree initiated an uninterrupted, *final phase* of the conversion process. I shall here repeat that the term 'decisive' is the interviewer's term; it is based on an external evaluation of the conversion process.

In quantitative studies of conversion, the significance of having a pre-defined, measurable criterion for the onset of the conversion is obvious. I can illustrate this briefly by a study of the concept of seekership among the Baha'is (Warburg 2001). I first defined a set of pre-conversion variables of attitude and behaviour for seekers and non-seekers, respectively. Thereby, it was possible to divide 88 first-generation Danish Baha'i converts into 39 seekers and 49 non-seekers. Next, I correlated seekership with different routes of conversion: inside the personal network or outside the personal network. The routes were defined from the situational causality of the decisive encounter, and these definitions were independent of the definitions of seekership. I found that among those recruited outside the personal network, both seekers and non-seekers were recruited by chance meetings, just as in the case of the informant above. However, only seekers responded to advertisements and public announcements of Baha'i events and attended them on their own initiative – thus they complied with what would be an expected behaviour of a seeker.

The study of conversion routes would have risked being significantly biased if I had not been able to define the variables 'seekership' and 'route to recruitment' by objective criteria common to all conversion accounts. It is not an extraordinary example; many other quantitative studies like the above depend on the reliability of conversion accounts and other interview material as sources for 'actual past processes', cf. Dawson above. This reliability can be established by, for example, distinguishing between situational and distal causalities and using conventional historical criticism.

Trust in Informants' Self-Reflections?

In Lorne Dawson's above mentioned discussion of the use of conversion accounts as sources, he used the words 'the supposed real reasons' (Dawson 1991: 22). Here, he claimed that conversion accounts usually provide informants' subjective reflections about motives and feelings during the period of conversion. Subjective reflections are also a core theme in autobiographies, and if evaluated critically, knowing the conditions of their genre, autobiographies may reveal important insights to the thoughts of the historical agent (Wallach 2006). Subjective reflections may also yield valuable material to the sociologist of religion who is theorising about conversion. However, there are good reasons to be on guard here: many converts are motivated both to see and to report themselves as having undergone a profound personal change in the course of the conversion process. Among some sociologists of religion this risk of bias has deemed the conversion account to be an 'unreliable source of information about any real personal effects of the conversion process' (Machalek and Snow 1993: 66).

Being on guard should, of course, not lead to an *a priori* rejection, and a separate critical assessment must be made for each case. For example, a Danish Baha'i woman described her feelings about disengaging herself from the Evangelical-Lutheran Church of Denmark after her conversion:

> It was very difficult to withdraw from the National Church. Even if I was not brought up very religiously, I felt as if I broke with my parents. Furthermore, the minister who had just buried my father was the same person I would have to meet in order to resign from the National Church. (Warburg 2006: 312–13)

There is no doubt that at the time of the interview the informant thought back on this disengagement as a hard dilemma to solve. But was it that difficult at the time when she resigned? In this particular case I consider it likely that the woman did feel it was difficult to withdraw from the church at the time when she resigned. Her reference to the minister adds credibility to her story, for example. Furthermore, there is no current discourse among Danish Baha'is suggesting that it should be difficult to withdraw from a church which most converts belonged to before joining Baha'i. Nor is there any idealisation of particular conversion patterns among Baha'is in general; for example, a compilation of 37 different conversion accounts written by North American Baha'is claims on the back cover that the 'very diversity [of the accounts] demonstrates the universal appeal of the Bahá'í teachings' (Gottlieb and Gottlieb 1985). Thus, there is no particular reason to suspect that the Baha'i informant's account about the resignation from the Evangelical-Lutheran Church reflects a later socialisation and not how the informant felt at the time.

These considerations suggest how the discussion could be approached concerning the reliability of a particular conversion account as an historical source: its validity must be critically assessed with regard to what is asked from it as source. If there remains a substantial basis for suspecting bias, such as a striking similarity between the accounts of different converts, then there is reason to reconsider the use of the account. But to take critical precautions when dealing with accounts recorded much later than when the actual events took place does not in itself justify an extrapolation of these precautions into a general rejection of the reliability of conversion accounts as sources.

From Sources to Theories

In cases where data from conversion accounts can stand up to historical criticism, they may become the basis for formulating and testing hypotheses about conversion. The data can help us to understand individual motives and individual circumstances, which can substantiate qualitative hypotheses. When looking at many accounts together, these individual circumstances may suggest some general circumstances that may raise or lower the probability of conversion. For example, it is more probable that a person converts when being a student who has just moved to a university city than it is probable that a tenured university professor with a husband, garden, teenage children and a pile of professional and social obligations will suddenly convert! The window of opportunity is almost shut in the latter case.

I will conclude by proposing a sociological comparison between conversion and love and courtship. Both processes usually involve a significant reorientation of one's life, and like the choice of a religion, the choice of a mate is correlated with sociological/demographic variables, such as class, ethnic background, and age (Davis-Brown *et al.* 1987; Lewis *et al.* 1997). Another parallel is that both courtship stories and conversion stories may be retold to give meaning to an important transformation of one's life – thus, researchers of family life claim that spouses often construct their courtship stories and narrate them to their families in order to emphasise the unique quality of their relationship and/or to capture the moment of beginning as a family (Ponzetti 2005).

In the early research on conversion to new religious movements there was tendency to seek to establish a general theory or model of conversion (Robbins 1988: 65–6). The current assumption at that time was that 'spiritual apotheosis is an unnatural and problematic phenomenon which entails esoteric processes', as Thomas Robbins sarcastically put it (Robbins 1988: 63). Thus, conversion to new religious movements seemed to call for an 'explanation' – a view building on Freud's view of religion as 'psychopathology' and Marx's view of it as 'false consciousness' (Bromley and Hadden 1993). Such approaches do not prevail anymore in the sociology of religion, and the current view is that it is futile to establish a single causal model or theory of conversion.

Sociologists have established a sociology of love, courtship and marriage patterns without disturbing themselves with a need to explain individual cases of love and marriage. It is not considered possible to establish a convincing theory which *explains* why X fell in love with Y, but it is possible on objective criteria to assign a reasonably high probability that X and Y, if they meet, may marry eventually. Conversely, it is possible to argue for a low probability that Z and V, were they to meet, would become a couple. Such arguments have for some time constituted a rationale for computerised match-making (Sindberg *et al.* 1972). Nevertheless, young people who might seem to fit nicely together, in particular in the eyes of their respective parents, surprisingly enough do not always fall in love. And it is also possible to find examples of the most 'impossible', but happy marriages. Like in the sociology of conversion also in the sociology of love and courtship it seems questionable to generally assume a rational choice in behaviour (Owen 2007).

This is a final good reason why I like the parallel between conversion and courtship.

References

Balch, R.W. and Taylor, D. (1978) 'Seekers and Saucers. The Role of the Cultic Milieu in Joining a UFO Cult', in J.T. Richardson (ed.) *Conversion Careers. In and Out of the New Religions*, Beverly Hills: Sage, pp. 43–64.

Barker, E. (1984) *The Making of a Moonie. Choice or Brainwashing?* Oxford: Basil Blackwell. (Now available from Aldershot: Ashgate.)

—— (1993) 'Will the Real Cult Please Stand Up? A Comparative Analysis of Social Constructions of New Religious Movements', in D.G. Bromley and J.K. Hadden (eds) *Religion and the Social Order. The Handbook on Cults and Sects in America*, vol. 3B, Greenwich: Jai Press, pp. 193–211.

Beckford, J.A. (1975) *The Trumpet of Prophecy. A Sociological Study of Jehovah's Witnesses*, Oxford: Blackwell.

—— (1978) 'Accounting for conversion', *British Journal of Sociology*, 29: 249–62.

—— (1983) 'Talking of apostasy, or telling tales and "telling" tales', in G.N. Gilbert and P. Abell (eds), *Accounts and Action. Surrey Conferences on Sociological Theory and Method*, Aldershot: Gower, pp. 77–97.

—— (1985) *Cult Controversies. The societal response to new religious movements*, London: Tavistock.

Bromley, D.G. and J.K. Hadden (1993) 'Exploring the Significance of Cults and Sects in America: Perspectives, Issues, and Agendas', in D.G. Bromley and J.K. Hadden (eds) *Religion and the Social Order. The Handbook on Cults and Sects in America*, vol. 3B, Greenwich: Jai Press, pp. 1–48.

Brown, G.W. (1983) 'Accounts, meaning and causality', in G.N. Gilbert and P. Abell (eds) *Accounts and Action. Surrey Conferences on Sociological Theory and Method*, Aldershot: Gower, pp. 35–68.

—— (2002) 'Social Roles, Context and Evolution in the Origins of Depression', *Journal of Health and Social Behaviour*, 43: 255–76.

Davis-Brown, K., Salamon, S. and Surra, C.A. (1987) 'Economic and Social Factors in Mate Selection: An Ethnographic Analysis of an Agricultural Community', *Journal of Marriage and the Family*, 49: 41–55.

Dawson, L.L. (1990) 'Self-Affirmation, Freedom, and Rationality: Theoretically Elaborating "Active" Conversions', *Journal for the Scientific Study of Religion*, 29, 2: 141–63.

—— (1991) 'Coping with Accounts: Towards a Hermeneutic for the Study of Conversion', presented at *International Society for Sociology of Religion Conference*, 21 August 1991, Maynooth, Eire (unpublished manuscript).

—— (1998) *Comprehending Cults. The Sociology of New Religious Movements*, Toronto: Oxford University Press.

Erslev, Kr. (1972) *Historisk Teknik* [Historical Methodology], Copenhagen: Gyldendal.

Gottlieb, R. and Gottlieb, S. (eds) (1985) *Once to Every Man and Nation. Stories about becoming a Bahá'i*, Oxford: George Ronald.

Greil, A.L. and D.R. Rudy (1984) 'What have we Learned from Process Models of Conversion? An Examination of Ten Case Studies', *Sociological Focus*, 17: 305–23.

Horton, R. and Peel, J.D.Y. (1976) 'Conversion and Confusion: A Rejoinder on Christianity in Eastern Nigeria', *Canadian Journal of African Studies*, 10: 481–98.

Lewis, R. Jr., Yancey, G. and Bletzer, S.S. (1997) 'Racial and nonracial factors that influence spouse choice in black/white marriages', *Journal of Black Studies*, 28: 60–78.

Lofland, J. (1978) '"Becoming a World-Saver" Revisited', in J.T. Richardson (ed.) *Conversion Careers. In and Out of the New Religions*, Beverly Hills: Sage, pp. 10–23.

Lofland, J. and Skonovd, N. (1983) 'Patterns of Conversion', in E. Barker (ed.) *Of Gods and Men. New Religious Movements in the West, Proceedings of the 1981 Annual Conference of the British Sociological Association Sociology of Religion Study Group*, Macon: Mercer University Press, pp. 1–24.

Lofland, J. and Stark, R. (1965) 'Becoming a world-saver: a theory of conversion to a deviant perspective', *American Sociological Review*, 30: 862–74.

Machalek, R. and Snow, D.A. (1993) 'Conversion to New Religious Movements', in D.G. Bromley and J.K. Hadden (eds) *Religion and the Social Order. The Handbook on Cults and Sects in America*, vol. 3B, Greenwich: Jai Press, pp. 53–74.

Mansell, D. (2007) 'Unsettling the Colonel's Hash: "Fact" in Autobiography', in T.L. Broughton (ed.) *Autobiography. Critical Concepts in Literary and Cultural Studies*, Volume I, London: Routledge, pp. 168–83.

Murphy, J. (2007) 'The Voice of Memory. History, autobiography and oral memory', in T.L. Broughton (ed.) *Autobiography. Critical Concepts in Literary and Cultural Studies*, Volume III, London: Routledge, pp. 116–36.

Owen, E. (2007) 'The Sociology of Love, Courtship, and Dating', in C.D. Bryant and D.L. Peck (eds) *21ˢᵗ Century Sociology. A Reference Handbook*, Volume 1, Thousand Oaks: Sage, pp. 266–71.

Pascal, R. (1985) *Design and Truth in Autobiography*, New York: Garland Publishing.

Piff, D.M. (2000) *Bahá'í Lore*, Oxford, George Ronald.

Ponzetti Jr., J.J. (2005) 'Family Beginnings: A Comparison of Spouses' Recollections of Courtship', *The Family Journal*, 13: 132–8.

Rambo, L.R. (1993) *Understanding Religious Conversion*, New Haven: Yale University Press.

Richardson, J.T. (1985) 'The Active vs. Passive Convert: Paradigm Conflict in Conversion/Recruitment Research', *Journal for the Scientific Study of Religion*, 24: 163–79.

Richardson, J.T. and Stewart, M. (1978) 'Conversion Process Models and the Jesus Movement', in J.T. Richardson (ed.) *Conversion Careers. In and Out of the New Religions*, Beverly Hills: Sage, pp. 24–42.

Robbins, T. (1988) *Cults, Converts and Charisma: The Sociology of New Religious Movements*, London: Sage.

Sindberg, R.M., Roberts, A.F. and McClain, D. (1972) 'Mate Selection Factors in Computer Matched Marriages', *Journal of Marriage and the Family*, 34: 611–14.

Snow, D.A., L.A. Zurcher, and S. Ekland-Olson (1980) 'Social Networks and Social Movements: A Microstructural Approach to Differential Recruitment', *American Sociological Review*, 45: 787–801.

Stromberg, P.G. (1993) *Language and self-transformation. A Study of the Christian conversion narrative*, Cambridge: Cambridge University Press.

Wallach, J.J. (2006) 'Building a bridge of words: the literary autobiography as historical source material', *Biography*, 29: 446–61.

Wallis, R. and Bruce, S. (1982) 'Network and clockwork', *Sociology*, 16: 102–107.

Warburg, M. (2001) 'Seeking the Seekers in the Sociology of Religion', *Social Compass*, 48: 91–101.

—— (2006) *Citizens of the World. A History and Sociology of the Baha'is from a Globalisation Perspective*, E.J. Brill: Leiden.

Wyman, J.R. (1985) *Becoming a Baha'i: Discourse and Social Networks in an American Religious Movement* (Ph.D. dissertation), Washington D.C.: Department of Anthropology, The Catholic University of America.

CHAPTER 11

From 'Visiting Minister' to 'Muslim Chaplain': The Growth of Muslim Chaplaincy in Britain, 1970–2007

Sophie Gilliat-Ray

Introduction

The development of Muslim chaplaincy needs to be understood more generally against the backdrop of the sociology (and theology) of 'religious professionalism' in Islam. It is often said that there is no clergy in Islam, (Chittick and Murata 2000; Gilliat-Ray 2000; Haneef 1979; Ruthven 1997) and up to a point this is true, mainly because Islam's religious specialists exercise no sacramental or priestly functions (Tayob 1999). There is certainly no such thing as 'chaplaincy'. Within Sunni Islam, there is no formal, structured hierarchy of religious professionals, such as may be found in the Christian churches, or in some Buddhist monastic orders, for example. In the belief that there should be no form of human intercession between God and humanity, Islam encourages all believers to know and understand their faith and to exercise their own interpretive judgement. However, Muslims are exhorted to learn from scholars with specialist knowledge of the Qur'an and Hadiths, and to emulate individuals of piety. Thus the most respected religious professionals in Islam are predominantly recognised for their *scholarship* and *moral conduct*.

However, during the course of Islamic history, individuals of scholarship and piety have also been engaged in the delivery of what we might call 'pastoral care', beginning with the Prophet Muhammad himself. So whilst it is the case that Muslims have not developed anything that formally equates to 'chaplaincy', it would be mistaken to assume that pastoral care does not exist. Quite simply it is not institutionalised, because it has rested solely on interpersonal relations between a religious scholar and his or her followers, or between family members. These individuals have no doubt been inspired by the numerous Qur'anic verses and sayings of the Prophet which exhort believers to visit the sick, to comfort the needy, to be compassionate, and so on.

> As regards the rewards for visiting the sick the Prophet (peace and blessings be upon him) informed us: 'As a Muslim calls on a sick Muslim brother, he gathers the fruits of Paradise during the entire course of his visit' (Ahmad and Tirmidhi). 'When a Muslim visits an ailing Muslim seventy thousand angels pray for him until the evening. If the visit takes place during the evening, the same number of angels pray for him until morning.

For such a Muslim there are the fruits of Paradise.' (Tirmidhi and Abu Dawud). (Siddiqui 2005: 38)

The Prophet (peace be upon him) said: 'Help your brother whether he is oppressed, or an oppressor', upon which one of the companions asked, 'We understand how to help the oppressed, but how can we help the oppressor?' The Prophet replied, 'Help him by refraining him from oppression'. (Bukhari and Muslim), (Bokhari and Gent 2005)[1]

In the light of these words, the development of Muslim involvement in chaplaincy can be seen as building upon a very well-established but less formally defined and less institutionalised understanding of pastoral care in Islam.

Having made this point by way of background, we can now move on to consider some of the key stages in the development of Muslim chaplaincy in Britain, particularly in relation to prison and healthcare chaplaincy. By singling out these two sectors, we can identify some key milestones in terms of progress and development over the last 20 years. Muslim involvement in other chaplaincy sectors, such as higher education, or the military, has a much shorter history. These are becoming no less significant, but it is hard to trace key developments over time, hence my focus upon prisons and hospitals in the discussion that follows.

Development of Muslim Chaplaincy in Britain: from 'Visiting Ministers' to 'Muslim Chaplains'

It is difficult to place an exact time-line against the development of Muslim chaplaincy in Britain because of the extent of regional and institutional variation. The evolution of Muslim chaplaincy has taken place to a greater or lesser extent in different parts of the country, and according to the politics of different local institutions (Beckford and Gilliat 1998). Despite this caveat, in general it would be fair to say that early Muslim involvement in prison or hospital chaplaincy in Britain, especially from about the 1970s up to and including the 1990s, tended to be haphazard, locally organised, and largely focussed upon meeting the basic religious needs of patients or inmates, such as ensuring the provision of halal food, making suitable arrangements for prayer facilities, and facilitating the celebration of Eid festivals (Beckford and Gilliat 1998).

Those Muslims involved in prison or hospital visiting were often termed 'visiting ministers'. Their work was often voluntary, and usually confined to several hours per week, if that. Sometimes visiting ministers were mosque-based Imams, but because many Imams working in Britain in the 1970s or 1980s could not speak adequate English, it was not unusual for visiting ministers to be so-called 'community leaders', this term often applying to Muslim (usually male) professionals with good standing in the locality, or within a particular mosque community (Burlet and Reid 1998). It was also common for the term 'visiting minister' to be applied to existing institutional staff members, such as Muslim doctors, or simply well-meaning

---

1   Ahmad and Tirmidhi, Tirmidhi and Abu Dawud, Bukhari and Muslim are Hadith texts.

members of a Muslim congregation who had time to spare and a reasonable fluency in English. The term 'visiting minister' therefore applied to individuals with a wide range of backgrounds, and their designation as 'visiting ministers' fully conveyed the fact that generally speaking they had only a marginal involvement in the life of the chaplaincy. They were simply passing through the institution on a temporary basis. They were 'on call' when necessary, but were rarely able to make strategic decisions, or to shape the context in which they were working (Spalek and Wilson 2001).

When Jim Beckford and I first began to do research on publicly funded chaplaincy in the mid 1990s, things were at an interesting point of change and development. There were still many Muslim 'visiting ministers' going into prisons and hospitals, but some institutions were starting to advertise full or part-time posts for 'Muslim Chaplains' (especially in the healthcare setting), and a new Muslim professional religious role was coming into being. The change indicated in the transition from 'visiting minister' to 'Muslim chaplain' was brought about for several reasons. A range of contextual factors all came together, which made the emergence of 'Muslim chaplaincy' possible. The driving forces for change came from a number of different sources both within and outside the Muslim community, and the 1990s was a critical decade for the beginnings of this change.

Firstly, within public institutions in the UK, there was a growing expectation of better service quality and standards for the general public in their engagement with government departments. In the healthcare context, the Patient's Charter in 1991 prioritised the religious and spiritual needs of all patients, regardless of their faith tradition. The Charter laid down patients' rights to care, standards and targets for healthcare providers to achieve, and ways of assessing the performance of the National Health Service (NHS). The first of the nine National Charter Standards stated in the Patient's Charter specifies 'Respect for privacy, dignity and religious and cultural beliefs'. As a consequence of the Charter, religion was no longer confined to what chaplains provided, and it became incumbent on every NHS employee to show respect for patients' religious beliefs. Crucially, no distinction was made between the standards of respect demanded for Christian and non-Christian beliefs (Beckford and Gilliat 1996). This Charter directive required hospitals and other healthcare settings to facilitate the provision of adequate facilities and personnel, and it was clear that meeting the requirements of the Charter demanded a new multi-faith approach. In those parts of the country with large local Muslim communities, fulfilling the requirements of the Charter began to mean the full-time, part-time, or sessional employment of a Muslim chaplain.

In our book *Religion in Prison: Equal Rites in a Multi-Faith Society* (Beckford and Gilliat 1998) Jim Beckford and I outlined in detail the history and development of prison service chaplaincy, especially in terms of the increasing and often contentious provision of facilities and personnel for members of other faiths. Just as in the healthcare setting, during the 1990s the Prison Service was under similar political, social, and legal pressures to adopt a more multi-faith approach to its chaplaincy provision. The rapidly increasing and growing over-representation of Muslim prisoners was also a catalyst for progress. It became increasingly obvious that new resources would have to be devoted to the employment of Muslim religious professionals if one of the few rights of prisoners – to practice their religion and to receive appropriate pastoral care – was to be met. Muslims currently constitute approximately 11 per cent of the prison population in the UK, but only 3 per cent of the general population (Bajwa 2007), whilst in some establishments the number of Muslim inmates rises to as much as 28 per cent.[2] There are a number of ways to account for this unusually high rate of imprisonment. For example, there has been an increase in the incarceration of foreign national prisoners, and as they make up just over a third of the Muslim prison population, an increase in their numbers is likely to impact on the overall number of Muslims (Solomon 2005). Solomon also alludes to the possibility that, given

> Muslim prisoners represent a diverse range of non-white ethnic groups, it is most likely that the 'multiplier effect' of institutional racism in operational policing, through the process of caution, prosecution, remand and bail decisions to sentencing, which has been documented in academic studies, has also been a contributory factor. (Solomon 2005)

A third consideration is that Muslims come from communities that experience high levels of social deprivation (Phillips 2006), and this is known to increase the risk of offending and, therefore, imprisonment.

In both hospital and prison settings then, the combined growth in the Muslim patient and prison population, and the increasing complexity of the issues associated with this growth, meant that personnel were increasingly needed on a full-time or part-time basis, particularly in some parts of the country. The issues were beginning to extend beyond simply advising on basic religious needs. Muslim visiting ministers, or chaplains, potentially had an important role to play, for example when family relationships had broken down between a prison inmate and his family,[3] or when the extended family support network was at breaking point in the face of terminal illness or death. It was becoming clear that a more active and informed Muslim professional input was required, to advise on a whole range of issues. And so, from the top down, and both locally and nationally, new posts were created which facilitated the development of Muslim chaplaincy.

This progress was stimulated in the prison context by the employment of a new 'Muslim Advisor' at the Prison Service Chaplaincy Headquarters in 1999. This role meant that the often serious lack of provision for Muslim inmates in terms of access to religious support, halal meals, and Friday prayers could be pro-actively addressed at a national level. The first incumbent of this post, Maqsood Ahmed, also instituted a centralised vetting system for potential Muslim chaplains, thus ensuring that new chaplaincy posts were only offered to those with appropriate credentials, and counter-terrorism clearance (Birt 2006: 699). In 2007, there were 34 full-time and 15 part-time Muslim chaplains, supporting the welfare of 8,789 Muslim inmates (Bajwa 2007) in 138 establishments in England and Wales. Additionally, nearly all prisons have access to hourly paid/sessional Muslim chaplains. In 2003, the Prison

---

2   IQRA Trust Newsletter, Issue 1, http://www.iqraprisonerswelfare.org/ [accessed 19 November 2007]

3   Interview conducted by Angelo Pittaluga with Abdelati Fergani, Muslim Chaplain at HMP Cardiff, March 2007.

Service re-named its Muslim 'visiting ministers' and conferred upon them the title 'Muslim Chaplain' (Beckford *et al.* 2005), a designation which helpfully enables female Muslim chaplains to gain professional recognition alongside their male counterparts.

The NHS has made slower progress with the appointment of Muslim chaplains, but the decision by the Department of Health to set aside funding to support the new employment and training of chaplains from minority faith groups helped to secure new posts in mid 2000. This has recently been supported by the organisation of a 'Muslim Healthcare Chaplaincy Training Course', jointly organised by the Muslim Council of Britain and the Department of Health, and delivered to 25 Muslim hospital chaplains in May 2007. Currently, there are four full-time Muslim chaplains in the NHS (1 of whom is female). Additionally, there are 39 part-timers (of whom seven are female),[4] and 23 volunteers (of whom six are female).

A second important driving force for the emergence of Muslim chaplaincy was the growing maturation and confidence of the Muslim community in Britain. During the 1990s there was a growing awareness and recognition of social needs and problems within the Muslim community. Whereas difficulties and sensitive issues had often been 'swept under the carpet' by Muslim communities, by the 1990s the British Muslim press, such as *The Muslim News* and *Q News* were starting to report problems of marital breakdown and domestic violence, substance abuse, the need for a stronger 'home grown' religious leadership, and so on. Perhaps as a response to this more open community debate, a range of British Muslim organisations were formed to directly tackle some of the social problems within the community, and especially to support the needs of young people. Against this background, the work of Muslim chaplains, especially in the reform and rehabilitation of Muslim offenders, had greater legitimacy and support because they were tackling questions and challenges that were now being openly debated within the Muslim community more widely. And so, in June 1991, *The Muslim News* devoted an entire page to the rising Muslim prison population, the opening of the first mosque in a British prison (HMP Wandsworth), and the work of one of the first Muslim imams/chaplains in Britain, Dr Ijaz Mian, who was at the time visiting Muslim inmates in a number of prisons on a full-time basis (Dhalla 1991).

Another important contextual factor that made the development of Muslim chaplaincy possible, and which reflected the developmental progress of the Muslim community in Britain, was the growing availability of suitable personnel to take up new chaplaincy posts. A new generation of British born, English speaking students were starting to graduate from their lengthy period of training in British Islamic seminaries or *dar ul-uloom*, particularly those established by the Deobandi school of thought in the 1970s and 1980s (Birt 2006; Gilliat-Ray 2006). Although they had received no formal training in the techniques of 'pastoral care' and counselling, they were knowledgeable in their faith, they could speak English and often a range of other community languages, and they had some awareness of the protocols and procedural

---

4   Part-time means offering at least five sessions per week, each session being 3.5 hours (or half a day). I am grateful to Chowdhury Mueen-Uddin, Director of Muslim Spiritual Care in the NHS at the Muslim Council of Britain for these figures.

rules governing work in public institutions, for example, confidentiality, health and safety, security, and so on. Thus some of the first key appointments of Muslim chaplains in both the prison, health (and more recently, military) contexts were from the Deobandi school of thought, and graduates of British Islamic seminaries.

The development of the 'Certificate in Muslim Chaplaincy' provided by Markfield Institute of Higher Education (MIHE) in Leicester, first offered in 2003, reflects another important social and educational landmark for the Muslim community in Britain in its engagement in chaplaincy. The course provides students with a basic grounding in chaplaincy skills and knowledge, and the opportunity to do a supervised placement under the direction of an experienced chaplain. The emergence of this course has been another important impetus for progress by giving current and prospective chaplains the opportunity for appropriate and specifically Islamic in-service training on a par with their counterparts from other faith traditions that builds upon the rather more generic training some of them receive as Prison Service or NHS employees. There are some important parallels between the MIHE course and the Islamic Chaplaincy Program at Hartford Seminary in Connecticut, in the USA.[5]

It is clear that there is also now a sufficient critical mass of part-time and full-time Muslim chaplains in Britain for a distinctive professional identity to be emerging, and this has found expression in the foundation of the 'Association of Muslim Chaplains' in 2004 (established to support graduates of the MIHE course) and the 'Muslim Chaplains Association' – established in May 2007 to represent the interests and professional development of Muslim prison chaplains. This recent development was predicted by Jim Beckford and his team in their study of Muslims in British and French prisons back in 2005 (Beckford *et al.* 2005: 241). Chaplaincy is now starting to become a career option for those Muslims in Britain who aspire to serve their community within the context of a public institution,[6] and there is a sense of greater Muslim 'ownership' of chaplaincy than was previously conceivable among part-time visiting ministers back in the 1990s (Beckford and Gilliat 1998; Beckford *et al.* 2005: 239).

A third driver for the development of Muslim chaplaincy has been the emergence of new or more inclusive national chaplaincy structures and committees that give Muslims, and members of other faiths, a voice for articulating their ideas and their concerns, and for engaging in long-term planning. The 'Islam Resource Group' within the College of Health Care Chaplains, or the Multi Faith Group for Health Care Chaplaincy are good examples. So whereas Jim Beckford and I found in the 1990s that Muslims were often marginal in national debates about chaplaincy, from about the year 2000 onwards, new or more inclusive structures made it possible for the contribution and perspectives of Muslims to be given greater recognition.

---

5   http://macdonald.hartsem.edu/chaplaincy/program.html

6   Whilst recently teaching a session for the 'Certificate in Muslim Chaplaincy' at MIHE, the author asked the assembled students (numbering 33) how many were actually working in a chaplaincy role. Only around seven were actually in a chaplaincy post, but the question and answer session that followed was indicative of their aspirations and ambitions to work as full-time chaplains as soon as an opportunity arose.

Muslim chaplains and Muslim organisations have started to become partners in national discussion, giving them a legitimate voice and a sense of real long-term inclusion.[7] Muslims have also been appointed to a number of strategically important positions. For example, in 2003, Yunus Dudhwala was appointed as a 'Faith Manager' at Newham Healthcare NHS Trust, a position carrying the potential for positive change and progress. It is probably only a matter of time before a Muslim Chaplain working in a prison is appointed as an area co-ordinating chaplain, a role that again signifies greater opportunity to shape debate and policy, and to establish the long-term inclusion of Muslims in publicly funded chaplaincy.

A fourth driver of change was a growing awareness among Muslims in Britain of their rights as British citizens, particularly during the 1990s. Against the background of the Rushdie Affair, Muslims were becoming more conscious of their rights as British citizens in a multicultural society, and were thus making increasing claims upon the state for recognition in law, education, public life, and in civil society. The growth of Muslim involvement in chaplaincy reflects a community that was becoming increasingly confident of its long-term commitment to, and aspirations for, inclusion in British society. Pressing for new Muslim chaplaincy posts was part of a wider process of capacity building, and the creation of opportunities for greater prosperity, equality, and inclusion.[8]

These important contextual factors – within public institutions, within the Muslim community, and within national chaplaincy structures – all against the background of a society increasingly aware of the need to accommodate to some extent the rights of minorities – have made the emergence of Muslim chaplaincy possible. But this development arguably has a significance that extends beyond particular public institutions. Muslim involvement in institutional chaplaincy provides a framework and an opportunity for the growing inclusion of Muslims in the public life of our society. I believe that institutional chaplaincy is potentially creating a very significant social and theological opportunity for Muslims in Britain.

The Theological Significance of Muslim Chaplaincy for the Development of a 'European Islam'

In his recent review of Jytte Klausen's book *The Islamic Challenge: politics and religion in Western Europe*, Humayun Ansari writes: 'a European Islam, theologically innovating and contextually and sociologically adapting, is emerging through a process of negotiation' (Ansari 2007: 145). I would argue that the development of Muslim chaplaincy provides very good evidence for this point, and is itself part of the process of crafting and shaping a way of being Muslim in Britain that is

---

7   In January 2007, St Michael's College Cardiff, in association with Cardiff University, hosted a national consultation on chaplaincy as a prelude to the launch in 2008 of its new 'Centre for Chaplaincy Studies'. Muslim participants – especially serving Muslim chaplains – were invited and made full contributions to the debate.

8   Other capacity building initiatives have included the Learning and Skills Council pilot scheme in 2004, which sought to train Muslim leaders in management skills, and Muslim Council of Britain training programmes (such as how to work with the media).

faithful Islamically, but is also contextually relevant. From the days of the marginal Muslim 'visiting ministers' to the recognised inclusion of Muslim chaplains in national conferences and committees, things have moved a very long way. Muslims are taking up the opportunities for engagement in British public institutions, and they are negotiating their place in the structures that govern chaplaincy. They are developing their own professional identity, career structures and educational opportunities to support their work. I am sure that over the next 20 years, a more developed 'theology' to accompany these changes will begin to emerge, and this theology is likely to be drawn not from Christian models, but from Qur'anic sources and from the traditions of Islam. There is a readily available body of Islamic literature which could be brought together, and from which a theology of pastoral care in Islam could be developed. There are already some signs that this is starting to occur, and Muslim chaplains are themselves conscious of the need to preserve the distinctively Islamic nature of their working (Beckford *et al.* 2005: 243). This provides evidence for the potentially wider development of a 'European Islam' that is both authentic and faithful to Islamic traditions and teachings, but which is also made relevant to the context in which Muslims now find themselves in the diaspora. A good example is a paper by Yunus Dudhwala to whom I have already referred, entitled *Building Bridges Between Theology and Pastoral Care* (Dudhwala 2006). His paper draws the links between the Prophetic example of visiting the sick, the theology of sickness in Islam, and the duty that all Muslims have towards those who are suffering. However, he acknowledges that, while this might have been possible in the past,

> in an ever changing world where individual priorities have taken over collective responsibilities, a new tradition of Muslim chaplaincy is evolving, a person from the faith, one who is well versed within Islam and who carries with them a spiritual presence, specifically being employed to look after the pastoral, spiritual, and religious needs of the sick. With the increase of materialism which in turn has decreased time people can give to others, this new tradition of Muslim Chaplaincy will only increase. (Dudhwala 2006)

The personal and religious qualities of those Muslims now offering themselves as chaplains makes the prospects for a theologically innovating and sociologically adapting Islam very promising. Far from inciting radicalism as some have supposed, those pioneering Muslims most deeply involved in chaplaincy tend to have the essential combination of religious knowledge, faithfulness, resourcefulness, and pragmatism, and their work has been shown to be valuable in combating extremism (Marranci 2007). Furthermore, Muslims who are working at the interface of their own faith communities, and in the multi-faith public institutions of our society, are perhaps the most important theologians at the disposal of the Muslim community. Let me cite some examples to illustrate this point.

Whilst doing some background reading for this chapter, I came across a short personal reflection written by Maulana Sikander Pathan, an experienced Imam working in the prison service. Reflecting on his journey into chaplaincy he reported an incident that occurred in his early days in chaplaincy. Just as he was about to perform one of his obligatory prayers, his senior Christian colleague asked whether he would mind him reading his Bible in the same room. To which he replied: 'Tony, I would find it offensive if you do not sit beside me on my prayer mat whilst I perform my prayers' (Pathan 2004). Not surprisingly, he noted what a moving occasion this had been for them both. My argument is that if the shaping of a 'European Islam' is being undertaken by Muslim chaplains of this calibre, confidence, and understanding of their faith in relation to the faith of others, then the prospects are very promising. Against a background of media-fuelled anxieties about the supposed threat of Islam in British society that are grounded in ill-informed perceptions of Muslim aspirations, Muslim involvement in chaplaincy is a powerful counter to such ill-informed perceptions. Furthermore, given that chaplaincy is now providing an important avenue for the professional religious employment of Muslim women, the new 'European Islam' is likely to be equally shaped by the 'other half' of the Muslim community.

Muslim involvement in chaplaincy is providing a catalyst for deeper reflection on issues of leadership and pastoral care within the Muslim community more generally. One of the first prison chaplains, Khalil Ahmad Kazi in Batley who was appointed in 1996, has taken the professional skills he has acquired to transform notions of what community and pastoral work by *'ulama* involves (Birt 2006). In 2000, he established the 'Institute of Islamic Scholars' which has:

> created new roles in prison and hospital chaplaincy work, work with local schools and colleges, publishing, community liaison with the police, MPs and policy makers, public lecturing on Islam, interfaith and a support group for drug and alcohol abuse, and has additionally undertaken to reform the supplementary school curriculum to make it relevant to a younger generation. Thus a new professionalism from an experience in chaplaincy has begun to inform the work of some independent academies. (Birt 2006: 699)

This development is surely to be welcomed in the light of recent research by Gabriele Marranci from Aberdeen University which indicates that the support that *ex-offenders* receive is crucially important to help their re-integration back into their families and communities (Marranci 2007).[9] The recent advertisement for the post of 'Muslim Community Chaplain' in the Muslim press (see *The Muslim News*, 30 March 2007) to support ex-offenders of YOI (the Young Offenders Instution) Feltham is indicative that the experiences and skills of Muslim chaplains are as important *outside* prisons as within them.

Some of the most able graduates of the British *dar ul-uloom* are moving into prison and hospital chaplaincy, where they are learning new social and intellectual skills that enable them to engage with greater confidence in the wider society (Lewis 2006). It is worth citing Philip Lewis's comments and reflections about some of these young men at length:

> These are pioneers leaving the comfort zone and security of the relatively closed world of the mosque and Muslim community enclave. Here, one can find examples of a few young men who have moved across three religious and cultural worlds, beginning with schooling in an Urdu-language seminary in Britain, then an Islamic degree at the Arabic-language

---

9   Marranci's findings derive from his study 'Living Islam in prison: the experience of Muslim prisoners in England and Wales in the aftermath of September 11' funded by the British Academy, the Carnegie Trust and the University of Aberdeen.

Azhar *madrasa* in Cairo, followed by postgraduate study at a British university. It is from this small group that some of the most vibrant initiatives are taking place [such as] an innovative drug awareness service developed by a prison imam in cooperation with fellow Muslim health professionals in Batley, and a bold attempt by an imam who is a University of London chaplain to confront radical Islam. These young Imams [and chaplains] embody and enact a vision of Islam as bridging social capital. (Lewis 2006: 280)

Chaplaincy appears to be an important catalyst in these kinds of innovation, and although the total number of Muslim chaplains currently remains quite small, its significance is disproportionate to the actual numbers involved. The example and impact of effective Muslim chaplains could extend well beyond the institutions in which they serve, although they also play an important role within their chaplaincy roles in informing and educating about Islam. The Muslim Chaplain appointed to the Armed Forces in November 2005 stresses that teaching about 'the true face of Islam' and communicating the faith was a 'major part of the role' (Rollins 2007). It is for this and other reasons that more research on Muslim involvement in chaplaincy is warranted.

An Agenda for Future Research

Much of the research that has been conducted on the place of Muslim chaplains in prisons or hospitals has tended to focus so far upon the degree to which they are either excluded or included in local chaplaincy arrangements. The issues that Jim Beckford and I were considering back in the 1990s, and about which he went on to conduct comparative research in more depth in 2000, were principally concerned with issues such as the access that Muslim chaplains had to information, training, people, resources, and so on. I would like to think that our research was perhaps a stimulus for positive change, although there are still serious shortcomings in the facilities and opportunities that Muslim chaplains experience compared to those experienced by chaplains of other faiths (Beckford *et al.* 2005: 232). However, I think that a new set of research priorities has begun to emerge as the significance of Muslim chaplaincy has become apparent. Next year, I will be starting a new research project on Muslim chaplaincy, funded by the Arts and Humanities Research Council and the Economic and Social Research Council, as part of its 'Religion and Society' programme[10]. This project is being conducted in partnership with Markfield Institute of Higher Education in Leicester, and will focus on four main areas of investigation.

People

Firstly, I am interested in the people who practice Muslim chaplaincy. Little research has been done on precisely who decides to become a Muslim chaplain in Britain, and why. Jim Beckford and I established that many 'visiting ministers' had an adventitious route into Muslim chaplaincy (Beckford and Gilliat 1998; Beckford *et al.* 2005), but with the development of the Markfield course, and the possibilities

---

10   My co-investigator is Prof Stephen Pattison at the University of Birmingham.

that are now emerging for Muslim chaplaincy as a career option, I think we need to reflect on the kind of prior training and experience Muslim chaplains bring to their role. It is also important to consider how professional Muslim chaplains are formed a) by the curriculum for their training and b) by the social interactions between students and teachers during training. In other words, how is the identity 'Muslim chaplain' socially constructed, and what sort of educational and theological discourse underpins it?

Practice

Secondly, I am interested in considering what Muslim chaplaincy actually involves. How are Islamic traditions (or indeed other personal, social or religious capitals) deployed by Muslim chaplains? What is said and done, when, where, and how, during Muslim chaplaincy practice? What makes it distinctively Islamic? Which religious texts and/or rituals are utilized as Muslim chaplains conduct their work, and what kind of interpretation of scripture or tradition underpins chaplaincy practice and theology?

Politics

Thirdly, we need to reflect on the politics that govern the people who practice as Muslim chaplains. As my research with Jim Beckford in the 1990s demonstrated, the emergence of Muslim chaplaincy has been, and continues to be, shaped by politics and power dynamics. It has not emerged from a vacuum but has been shaped in a variety of ways by institutional structures and the prevailing political climate. I want to continue looking at the sociological, political, and economic constraints that are shaping the development of Muslim chaplaincy by looking at how Muslim chaplains navigate their way through the politics that can often have a determining impact on their work.

Conclusion

Jim Beckford's work has established the importance of chaplaincy as a distinctive field for research within the social scientific study of religion. He has established that institutional chaplaincy is a prism through which we can better understand a wide range of contemporary social and religious issues, such as the relative power and resources of different faith groups in a multi-faith society, the changing role of religious professionals, and the relationship between faith communities and public institutions. Chaplaincy exposes and illustrates in microcosm, and often in sharp relief, some of the problems of the 'better publicised difficulties surrounding multiculturalism and equal opportunities for ethnic minorities and non-Christian faith communities' (Beckford and Gilliat 1998).

Since the 1990s, other scholars have built upon the work conducted at the University of Warwick between 1994 and 1996, and they have used the findings of *The Church of England and Other Faiths* project as their starting point. As a consequence of this growth in academic activity, chaplaincy is increasingly becoming a distinctive field of study and research in its own right, and will find particular institutional expression in the launch of a new 'Centre for Chaplaincy Studies' at St Michael's College, Cardiff, and Cardiff University in 2008, some fourteen years after Jim Beckford first began his pioneering work in this field.

References

Ansari, H. (2007) 'The Islamic Challenge: Politics and Religion in Western Europe by Jytte Klausen', *Journal of Islamic Studies*, 18 (1): 144–6.

Bajwa, H. (2007) 'Muslim Chaplain Association launched and raring to go', *The Muslim Weekly*, 18th May (no. 182).

Beckford, J. and Gilliat, S. (1996) *The Church of England and Other Faiths in a Multi-Faith Society: report to the Leverhulme Trust*, Warwick: University of Warwick.

—— (1998) *Religion in Prison: Equal Rites in a Multi-Faith Society*, Cambridge: Cambridge University Press.

Beckford, J., Joly, D. and Khosrokhavar, F. (2005) *Muslims in Prison: Challenge and Change in Britain and France*, Basingstoke: Palgrave Macmillan.

Birt, Y. (2006) 'Good Imam, Bad Imam: civic religion and national integration in Britain post 9/11', *The Muslim World*, 96 (October): 687–705.

Bokhari, R. and Gent, B. (2005) 'Editorial', *The Still Small Voice – Newsletter of the Association of Muslim Chaplains*, December: 1.

Burlet, S. and Reid, H. (1998) 'A Gendered Uprising: political representation and minority ethnic communities', *Ethnic and Racial Studies*, 21 (2): 270–87.

Chittick, W. and Murata, S. (2000) *The Vision of Islam*, London: I B Tauris.

Dhalla, M. (1991) 'Doing Time at HM's Pleasure', *The Muslim News*, 21/6/91.

Dudhwala, Y. (2006) 'Building Bridges Between Theology and Pastoral Care', Lisbon, European Network of Health Care Chaplains, http://www.eurochaplains. org/lisbon06.htm#report [Accessed 6 June 2007].

Gilliat-Ray, S. (2000) 'The Sociology of Religious Specialists', in P. Baltes and N. Smelser, (eds), *International Encyclopaedia of the Social and Behavioural Sciences*, Surrey: Elsevier Science Ltd, pp. 13132–6.

—— (2006) 'Educating the *'Ulema*: Centres of Islamic Religious Training in Britain', *Islam and Christian-Muslim Relations*, 17 (1): 55–76.

Haneef, S. (1979) *What Everyone Should know About Islam and Muslims*, Lahore: Kazi Publications.

Klausen, J. (2005) *The Islamic Challenge: politics and religion in Western Europe*, Oxford: Oxford University Press.

Lewis, P. (2006) 'Mosques, 'ulama and Sufis: providers of bridging social capital for British Pakistanis?', *Contemporary South Asia*, 15 (3): 273–87.

Marranci, G. (2007) 'Scotland Must Support Its Muslim Prisoners', *Sunday Herald*, 15th April.

Pathan, S. (2004) 'The International Prison Chaplaincy Association, Lecture by Maulana Sikander Pathan, Muslim Chaplain, HM Prison Service – HMPYOI Feltham', http://www.pkala.net/IPCA/english/reports/Pathan.htm [Accessed 20 November 2007].

Phillips, D. (2006) 'Parallel lives? Challenging Discourses of British Muslim self-segregation', *Environment and Planning D: Society and Space*, 24: 25–40.

Rollins, K. (2007) 'Armed Forces Imam doing duty'. *BBC News*, http://news.bbc.co.uk/2/hi/uk_news/6592031.stm [Accessed 6 June 2007].

Ruthven, M. (1997) *Islam: a Very Short Introduction*, Oxford: Oxford University Press.

Siddiqui, R. (ed.) (2005) '*Khurram Murad – Inter Personal Relations: an Islamic perspective*', Leicester: The Islamic Foundation.

Solomon, E. (2005) 'A Gap Between Policy and Practice', http://www.insidetime.org/Sept_Articles/islamprison.htm [Accessed 6 June 2007].

Spalek, B. and Wilson, D. (2001) 'Not Just "Visitors" to Prisons: the experiences of Imams who work inside the penal system', *The Howard Journal*, 40 (1): 3–13.

Tayob, A. (1999) *Islam in South Africa: Mosques, Imams, and Sermons*, Gainesville: University Press of Florida.

PART III
Religion, Power and Politics

CHAPTER 12

The Religious and the Political[1]

David Martin

The Argument

My argument is simple. Christianity is that particular kind of transcendent vision that looks for 'peace on earth, goodwill toward men'. However, it encounters the social sacred, as articulated by Durkheim, which partly absorbs it, and the resistant secularity of politics, power and violence, as articulated by Machiavelli, which largely deflects it. Mediating between these mighty opposites stands Wisdom, or practical reason, operating as peaceably as may be for the time being. Secularisation takes various forms: the *partial* absorption of Christianity as the sacred legitimation of empire, countered by voluntaristic protest movements operating outside the social space of political necessity, and successive exposures of raw secularity, from Machiavelli to Hobbes, Social Darwinism and the Freudian deconstruction even of love. However, the Enlightenment is yet another partial secularisation, converting the visionary hopes of Christianity into rational potentialities in history, thereby generating the category of secular religion, cherishing unappeasable hopes of political utopia on earth, and/ or a liberation of the self. In both versions it encounters the necessities of politics and of the social sacred embodied in ritual and hierarchy. Liberal Enlightenment is, therefore, a project based on *a mistake about the world*, the *saeculum*. However, the attempt to embrace mere secularity on the Humean empiricist model as a way out of the impasse is itself not viable.

Setting out the Frame

In celebrating a colleague admired both for great scholarly distinction and personal integrity, I want to achieve a fresh angle of vision on the religious and the political by moving the goalposts. I am going to shift the boundaries of what we conventionally mean by secularisation and the transcendent, and I am going to assume the steady persistence of a secular regimen of politics, power and violence associated with our involuntary membership in society as such. Through all the changes and chances of history and culture over millennia this mundane reality can be taken for granted.

However, the regimen of power and violence is only exposed *theoretically* quite late in the history of Christendom by Machiavelli and his various successors, from Hobbes to Sorel and Pareto. Only in the Renaissance is the implicit secular practice

---

1   This chapter is an extended version of my contribution to the British Academy debate on Charles Taylor's work on the occasion of his receiving the 2007 Templeton Prize, 2 May 2007.

converted into an explicit secularisation. Other explicit secularisations follow, such as the Darwinian exposure of the realities of power and violence in Nature, and the extrapolation from the Darwinian model to social relations through Social Darwinism and versions of Nietzsche, and the Freudian exposure of the dynamics of the psyche. Counter-posed to these raw outcrops of the explicitly secular, I trace various incursions of what I call the Christian transcendent, which I see as having a significant association with movements based on the voluntary principle, and therefore operating in social space partly removed from the imperatives of power and violence. These movements, for example Primitive Christianity, monasticism, the Waldensians, the friars, the Anabaptists, some of the Puritans, the Evangelicals and the Pentecostals, have the potential to embody the Christian vision of peace. Whether that vision is realised depends on their social location, for example the Cluniac role in the Crusades, the Dominican involvement in the Inquisition and the Jesuit role in the courts of Counter-Reformation Europe.

In between the various outcrops of the explicitly secular and the incursions of the Christian transcendent, I place the 'social sacred' – or the protecting veil thrown over the lineaments of society, as well as the mediating notion of wisdom or practical reason, holding back both the pressure of the Christian transcendent and the raw reality of the explicitly secular. Wisdom works in the constantly extended interim between the raw present and the forward looking hopes and apocalyptic anxieties of the peaceable kingdom.

The latter part of the argument deals with expressions of the transcendent within the immanent frame characteristic of modernity. These expressions take the form of rival Enlightenment visions, partly derived from the Christian transcendent, and embodied in the nation or the party, or the party in the form of the nation. They also take the form of subjective utopias sought in the self, and inimical to the social realities of institutions, whether political or religious, and to all that such institutions require with respect to authority, hierarchy and ritual. The individualistic vision collides with the imperatives of the collective, and in some of its expressions it even seems to dispense with any framework of meaning and purpose. For example, one in 20 Danes is an explicit atheist, but one in five is implicitly so.

The Christian Transcendent

The Christian transcendent is in tension with the sacred, understood in Durkheimian terms as a manifestation of the majesty of society rather than the judgement and mercy of God. I am referring to the explicitly Christian transcendent because the Islamic transcendent seems more closely related to the Durkheimian sacred. Though in Islam God himself is totally transcendent, his presence is realised in holy lands, holy places and holy temples, rather than in a kingdom 'not of this world'. The Islamic kingdom is of this world and thus inherently political, whereas the Christian kingdom resists incorporation in the political sphere. The difference is crucial, so that Islamic law can form the basis of ordinary society while Christian grace cannot. While it is clear that all over the Christian world the Passion and the Resurrection are acted out in public, especially in Catholic and Orthodox countries, they cannot be acted upon as a basis for ordinary political practice. The action of the Passion cannot be realised politically but belongs to the arena of the Church understood as a divine society set over against the City of Man. That is because it is against the grain, not – as Stanley Hauerwas (2001) maintains – with the grain. You can only think self-offering a collective political tactic, and the power of the Resurrection a political potentiality, if you believe, against the facts, that Christianity is with the grain. The City of Man is at best governed in terms of reciprocity and justice, and for the most part governed by norms of domination, honour, face, prestige, revenge, and struggle for survival. One cannot forgive one's political opponents on the bench opposite, or admit one's own trespasses, without breaking the rules of collective solidarity. Nations do not offer themselves up in love to redeem the international order.

I now need to give some account of the Christian transcendent as it goes against the grain and has some association with voluntary groups operating in social space outside the strict imperatives of politics. I have in mind here the monastic ideal of seeking the peace of God in the solitary place, and the principles of members of the Society of Friends as they tried to establish peaceable relations in Pennsylvania. For the sources of such ideals and principles I go back to Karl Jaspers (1955) on the Axial Age beginning about 1,000 B.C. and to Max Weber (1948) on religious rejections, or transformations, of the world.

The Axial Age, paradigmatically represented by Christianity and Buddhism, replaces the heroic ethic of self-assertion, honour and shame associated with loyalty to the family and the tribe, with an ethic of disinterested self-offering ignoring all particular boundaries. In its Christian version it simultaneously 'puts the body under subjection', questioning the imperatives of sexual reproduction central to Genesis, and affirms the body as the vehicle of God's self-emptying in Christ. The Word became flesh, and divine love became vulnerable in 'the form of a servant'. However, whereas in tribal society time is characteristically experienced as constant recurrence and as seasonal rotation, according to the order of nature, and whereas in Buddhism Nirvana is timeless, Christianity anticipates an advent or epiphany in due time. The Christian transcendent eclipses all the particular locations of holy land, holy place and holy temple, and seeks to replace the regimen of violence always potentially present in the earthly city, with the spiritual temple of the body of Christ made real, realised, in the common language of Pentecost, through the gift of tongues reversing the mutual incomprehensibility of Babel, and in the shared sacrifice of the common meal, known as the Eucharist or Holy Communion.

As time is tilted towards a second advent, suffused by hope and apocalyptic anxiety, so the Christian 'way' is understood as a journey or pilgrimage towards a more 'abiding city', a New Jerusalem 'above', which is 'mother of us all'. Membership in this city is voluntary, because it requires a new birth according to the spirit not the flesh, and a ceremony of admission. This ceremony is a baptismal passage through water to a new life of grace. It is precisely this idea of a journey, in a personal biography and in collective history that some hold is made problematic by modernity. At the same time it is reaffirmed in contemporary life by the increasing popularity of pilgrimage.

What then of the aspiration to peace? Peace is envisaged in the animal kingdom, as well as in society between man and man, and beyond that between man and

God, and inwardly in the heart. The key texts are in Isaiah 11, 1–9, in Micah 4, 1–5 where the prophet anticipates a peaceable kingdom on the mountain of the Lord, in the Sermon on the Mount, and also in the Epistle to the Hebrews 12, 22–4, and in the Epistle to the Ephesians 2, 14–18 where Christ breaks down 'the middle wall of partition' distinguishing Jew from Gentile to inaugurate a 'general assembly' on Mount Zion. The three mountains together symbolise the breaking in of the transcendent, while on the hill of Golgotha the self-offering or sacrificial gift of God secures peace, vertically and horizontally. This is then echoed liturgically. The Eucharist is punctuated by 'Peace be with you: and with thy spirit', by the kiss of peace, and in the closing phases by the prayer 'Grant us thy peace'.

The boundaries between Jew and Gentile are erased, the taboos and ritual acts protecting these boundaries, such as circumcision and food prohibitions, abolished, and ritual itself subordinated to inward sincerity. Peace displaces war, sincerity ritual, the poor the wealthy, the universal the particular, and choice automatic membership. Clearly, so comprehensive a revolution not only encounters resistance or reaction, but socio-logically engenders it, because (for example) even inwardness requires outward and material expression if it is to reproduce itself. In the same way, universality creates the resistant 'other'. The cost of universalism is counted in the resistance of the particular and rival forms of universalism. Faith (or trust) cannot displace law, without either embracing an impossible perfection, fulfilling the law, or an antinomian collapse into moral anarchy, 'sinning the more that grace may abound the more'. Human helplessness and recourse to irresistible grace can be interpreted as licence 'to love God and do as you like'. Once again, this is not simply theology, but the alternative moves or options built into the symbolic socio-logic of Christianity, and frequently realised in Christian history, especially in times of revolutionary crisis (or *kairos*), whether by George Fox or by John of Leyden as he presided over a mixture of moral anarchy and dictatorship.

So far I have repeated my own earlier arguments, though with an emphasis on the key motif of peace in the symbolic socio-logic of Christianity, given my current focus on the coiled up resistance of our social nature as that is built into power, politics and the regimen of violence (Martin 1965). I now need to bring out the theme of choice as realised in voluntary movements with the potential to escape or transcend the necessities of power. I have already suggested some of the incursions of the transcendent in Christian history found in voluntary movements from Primitive Christianity to Pentecostalism. Of course, even a voluntary group needs forms of authority, and has to negotiate disagreements through rules agreed or imposed. The New Testament is hardly a manual of principles of negotiation, and there is much that cannot be settled by waiting on the spirit to bring about consensus. Alternatively, a voluntary group can split up, which is in practice what happens throughout Christian history. Voluntary groups seek to fuse people together in a shared, chosen solidarity, but fusion soon ends in fission.

Once the voluntary group becomes established in power and takes over/is taken over by the state, a fresh power dynamic comes into play. For one thing Christian leaders are now drawn from state-bearing elites, reared on the assumptions of the powerful, and senator and bishop sit adjacent to one another. If social unity is sought through religious unity, sectarian fission must give way to fusion, unity must be imposed and dissidents excommunicated. If Christianity covers the whole of life, comprehensively, rather than being just a ritual practice, the urge to social or imperial unity will create a universal institution, with a universal head, a *Pontifex Maximus*, sitting adjacent to the Emperor, just as bishop sits adjacent to senator. Whereas the distinction between the kingdom of peace and grace and 'the principalities and the powers', created a boundary between Church and world, the boundary now runs through the church-state system. The result is that the space between Christianity and 'the world' is converted into a space between church hierarchies and secular hierarchies, while another space emerges inside the Church between 'secular' clergy and 'religious' virtuosi who pursue Christian ideals in bounded communities, which are in their turn stabilised by a 'rule' administered by authoritative 'fathers-in-God'.

The kingdom of peace will be progressively postponed, while in the interim the secular dynamic of power begins to invade the Church. Power corrupts, and the corruption of the vehicle of hope creates protest movements aiming to restore the pristine gospel: the *virtuosi* emerge, segregating themselves from the wider context of society to create islands of peace. However, these peaceful groups, whether inside or outside the Church, require strong authority since consensus cannot automatically be assumed. The pre-conditions of society as such are *in part* replicated in groups designed to subvert them, else protest itself cannot survive.

The Social Sacred

My basic contrast can be dramatised by comparing the voluntary, mobile, peaceful character of Pentecostalism with Catholicism as a traditional identity still rooted in place, even today. By place I mean the tutelary saints of city and hearth, the crosses erected by highways or in high places, and the territorial organisation of the parish or diocese. I am also referring to the symmetry between ecclesiastical and social hierarchies (notwithstanding the spectacular instances of social mobility via ecclesiastical preferment), and the continuity of tradition from generation to generation secured by automatic paedo-baptism. Paedo-baptism, meaning the baptism of infants, converts a voluntary sacrament into an involuntary rite of passage of reception into a 'natural' community, analogous to circumcision. Catholicism has been the religion of emplacement, mimicking the secular practice of power, given the mingling of personnel in the nurseries of political and ecclesiastical leadership.

However, Catholicism devises normative constraints on the secular practice of power, notably the just war and the just price. It also retains a space between the Christian transcendent and the social sacred, through aspirations to a sanctity not biologically transmitted, through the doctrine of the two swords, ecclesiastical and temporal, and through the assertion of the universal over the local. At the same time the disruptive potency of the transcendent is redirected to support the regime it symbolically undermines, setting up an internal dynamic of legitimation and de-legitimation, above all in iconography. Iconography, as Emile Mâle shows in the Introduction to *The Gothic Image* (1961: 1–26), links the higher order with the lower – as well as overturning the lower in the name of the higher. For example, monks became part of a wealthy 'estate' praying for the rest of society, and receiving gifts from the higher orders to secure a place in Paradise, just as the higher orders demanded service from lower orders in return for the 'service' of protection. The Church earths the lightning of the transcendent, standing between God and man in more senses than one.

For this Durkheimian type of society it is a very serious matter whose insignia dominate the high and holy place, whose emblem flies over the citadel, whose flag is burnt in the public square, whose profane activity pollutes it, whose statue is toppled by whom, whose language is treated as normative, especially for the naming of places, whose icons and holy pictures are defaced or whitewashed out, and whose holy book used as lavatory paper.

So-called 'secular' societies can display sensitivities very like those of conventionally 'religious' societies. When Estonians proposed moving a memorial to Soviet war dead their action was described as 'blasphemous' and a 'desecration'. In Russia at the present time secular and religious expressions co-exist: the cult of Lenin continues in his mausoleum, and Yeltsin's body rested in the recently rebuilt Cathedral of Christ the Saviour in the first state funeral under Orthodox auspices since 1894. So strong is the position of the Orthodox Church today (now reunited at home and abroad) that no party in Russia finds it politic to promote an anti-religious agenda. It was President Putin, the ex-KGB Head, who said Christianity was the bedrock of European civilisation, a sentiment one would not expect to hear even from Gordon Brown or Angela Merkel, both of them children of Christian pastors.

Wisdom, between Raw Survival and the Visionary Gleam

So far we have been dealing with a polar contrast between the voluntary and the involuntary, the unbounded and the located, the potentially peaceful group and an established Church embroiled in the raw dynamic of political power. Beyond that, a Durkheimian understanding of the potency of the social sacred has been contrasted with the tension introduced by the Christian transcendent. I now have to insert the Spirit of Wisdom, Sophia (or practical reason as its secular incarnation) as another middle term between the raw use and abuse of secular power and the tension introduced by the Christian transcendent. Whereas the Spirit can break out in flames in the voluntary sector, or erupt in folk Catholicism when ignited by the supernatural and miraculous, it can also operate as a 'pure and peaceable' mode of governance. Stephen Sykes (2006) has analysed wisdom at work in the person of Gregory the Great and in the maxims that guided him as a monk separated from power and as a politician responsible for justice and the survival and the good of the state. The biblical model here is Solomon, the wise and just ruler of a prosperous nation. In the various writings attributed to him, Solomon concentrated on everyday maxims and proverbs for the proximate future, rather than canvassing an eschatological hope of the 'other kingdom' and the associated anxiety of the apocalypse. For the Solomonic tradition the flow of time is relatively stable, and the office of faith is stoically to withstand its depredations rather than to cherish any ultimate hope of transformation. Were this an essay in political theology rather than sociology I would treat the Solomonic tradition as an instance of government understood as an institution of a good created order. Perhaps I would also say that what are in my view the restrictions placed by the political order on the dynamic of redemption, for example forgiving your political opponents for their mistakes, do not entail some restriction of that dynamic to the Church. After all, my argument implies that ecclesiastical politics exhibit the same features as politics in general.

The Rationality of Religion in the Public Sphere

The role of Wisdom, conceived in the form of Sophia, and allied to practical reason, raises an issue which may appear philosophical, but has important sociological implications. It concerns the rational, or at least the reasonable, articulation of religion in the public sphere. Keith Ward in his *Is Religion Dangerous?* (2006) argues for a reasonable account of faith, and Roger Trigg in *Religion in Public Life* (2007) argues for a rational account. If religion, or rather Christianity (since this is the focus both for Trigg and myself), is a mode of rational thinking, then it appears in the political forum as of right.

But what are the aspects of religion capable of a rational articulation? Presumably they concern the idea of God the Creator (or the transcendent) as argued for in Natural Law, and the status of the human, with all that is taken to imply with regard to abortion, euthanasia, contraception, issues in bio-ethics, like stem-cell research, and normative concepts of gender. Yet it is precisely in these areas that religious interventions strike many observers as problematic. I have already suggested that the drama of redemption and resurrection can be acted *out* in public (for example in Greece) but not acted *upon* in public, but even with regard to God the Creator the European Union was the site of a debate, with the allies of the Pope on the one side, and much of *laïque* Western Europe on the other. Issues of gender notoriously divide parts of Eastern Europe, for example, from secularist voices in Western Europe. These two arenas of contention have both been decided in favour of the secularist view, and the victors are increasingly inclined to press home their advantage, dismissing religion as an essentially private affair. From a secularist viewpoint Europe does not have a soul, and Jacques Delors' quest for 'a soul for Europe is simply a recipe for conflict. Who is in a position to declare which of the traditions that historically have contributed to the formation of modern Europe is normative today: Christianity, monotheism, Enlightened deism or paganism, ancient, romantic or modern?

Christians hold various views about the appropriate contribution of religion in the political forum. The Protestant view varies within a spectrum running from a ceremonially 'established' Church expressing a view as a Church (or ecumenically) but on the model of a voluntary pressure group, to a populist notion of a moral majority and a very different idea of individuals reflecting conscientiously as Christians on such issues as may arise and maybe coming to quite variable conclusions. However, in Germany the Protestant and Catholic Churches have tended to express joint views on questions in the area of eugenics, in part because the Nazi past renders such questions very sensitive. In Britain by contrast, eugenics is a less sensitive area, though still subject to contestation.

The Orthodox view stands at the far end of a spectrum of positions, holding to the traditional Byzantine notion of the *symphonia* between Church and state, but also reluctant to question the state, provided its institutional rights are safeguarded, especially when it comes to religious competition. Thus in Russia the open attitude to religious competition in the early 1990s has become more restrictive, and in Greece the Church, especially under its present (2007) vigorous leadership, has been concerned with restricting religious competition and maintaining religious teaching in the schools, as well as with pan-Orthodox political action (for instance with respect to Serbia) and the essentially Orthodox character of Greek identity over, for example, the issue of religion being specified on state identity cards. In Romania and in Moldova there have been major tensions over which brand of Orthodoxy represents the national identity, and these have roots in historic disputes over appropriate ethnic borders (Hann 2006). The Catholic Church varies in its approach between guarding its specific rights where it is a minority and promoting legislation in accordance with natural law and its role as guardian of civilisation where it is a majority.

What then are the areas of tension with regard to religion in the public sphere? As Charles Taylor has shown, the mainstream Christian Churches of the West, especially their leaders, share most of the values of secular politicians precisely because what Taylor (1989) calls 'the modern moral structure' is the product of an interaction between Christianity and the Enlightenment, notably the human rights agenda, including 'happiness' (or 'felicity' argued for by Thomas Aquinas long before Thomas Jefferson). The areas of contention are likely, therefore, to concern the status, governing conditions, and freedom of activity of religious bodies, above all the socialisation of the next generation through education. Where Church and state have fought over the body and soul of the nation, as in France, education becomes the focus of the struggle, whereas where the struggle has been muted, as in Scandinavia, an agreed minimum of Christian knowledge mutates into generalised understandings of religious traditions. Then there is the issue of proselytism so important to the new religious movements of particular concern to James Beckford. Finally, there are issues clustering around sex, gender and bio-ethics where sectors of the churches have views on the essential constitution of 'the human' strongly opposed to the more or less dominant secular consensus.

Outcrops of Raw Secularity

In one sense the Constantinian establishment of Christianity can be regarded as a secularisation, and if that were followed through all the sacral elements embodied in the legitimation of monarchs like Justinian, Alfred and Charlemagne would be accounted secular. However, that particular shift in criteria is not what interests me here. My present concern is with explicit outcrops of a continuing raw secular practice, running counter to the explicit incursions of the Christian transcendent. The first and great secularisation comes with the Renaissance view of power as articulated by Machiavelli and his successors up to the German military theorists and other European geo-politicians in the nineteenth and twentieth centuries. There is on the one hand a combined Christian and classical tradition of statecraft, combining the classical hero with the saintly administrator, and on the other the dynamic of political survival. What Machiavelli and the Machiavellian tradition exposes is the dynamic of political survival. This exposure scandalised Christian Europe in a way it would not have scandalised more 'secular' civilisations, such as China, unaffected by Christianity, and the sentiments travelling in its wake.

The second great secularisation is associated with Darwin. In one way that was not about raw social power at all, but about raw power and the struggle for survival in the natural world. Nevertheless there was a Christian version of a redeemed cosmos, and a harmonious conception of Nature such as one finds luminously expressed in Haydn's *The Creation* and his setting of James Thompson in *The Seasons* as well as in Handel's setting of Dryden's *Ode to Saint Cecilia*. Nature 'red and raw' did not chime with this view. Moreover, the survival of the fittest soon found expression in Social Darwinism, in debased versions of Schopenhauer's 'life force' and Nietzsche's supra-moral superman, in pagan faiths of blood and soil, and scientific racism. Colin Kidd (2006), in his recent book on the Bible and the forging of race in the Protestant Atlantic world (but not only there), has indicated how Enlightenment racism and scientific racism strained against the Biblical vision of monogenesis in Adam, even though there were plenty of Christian writers capable of subverting that vision, in particular by latching on to the idea in Genesis of the cursed lineage of Ham, and identifying the children of Ham with 'inferior races'.

This is a very complex story, and Darwin himself held firmly to the unity of humankind; but a racism based on the authority of science was very widespread. It was not finally ejected from all respectable science until the years after the Second World War. Just what amalgams were possible can be judged by the combination of Christianity and science represented by a character in Chekhov's short story 'The Duel' (1992: 90–92). The theme could be continued with the deconstruction of love in the myths of Freudian psychoanalysis, and other 'masters of suspicion'. The Christian narrative of the soul on its journey, so central to Puritan introspection and the genesis of the intimate diary, becomes what Philip Rieff (1966), called *The Triumph of the Therapeutic* above all in the United States.

The Dubious Secularity of Enlightenment

But how far was the Enlightenment itself an expression of the secular? Once again, much depends on how you move the goalposts in marking out the boundaries of the religious (or the mythic) and the secular. John Gray in his most recent book, *Black Mass* (2007), argues that the political perversion of religion, in particular the redeployment of the Christian myth of the Apocalypse to promote utopian visions of a world made new, is *the* key to modern history. One of the great themes of the theory of secularisation has envisaged *the* transition from the religious to the political, but in reality there has only been a partial transition for 'the time being', meaning by that our current modernity. In the course of that transition, the power of God held back in the transcendent realm, is translated into human empowerment, unleashing thereby a torrent of exemplary violence. In terms very like those used by the historian Michael Burleigh (2006) and the sociologist, S.N. Eisenstadt (1999),

John Gray, as a political philosopher, instances the terrible history from the Jacobins to the Bolsheviks, as well as the Russian anarchists like Bakunin, and contemporary radical Islamists, American neo-conservatives and neo-liberal Evangelicals.

It is not only the idea of the transition from the religious to the political that needs to be questioned, but also the idea of the transition from the mythic to the scientific. Enlightenment thinking purports to be scientific but it is infiltrated by precisely the myths it pretends to undermine and disprove, in part because such myths are more securely embedded in generic human experience, or rather, I would say, the specific Christian rendering of that experience.

Where Enlightenment thinking most obviously differs from mainstream Christianity is in altering, indeed excising, the Christian coding of the resistance to 'heavens below' through the concept of original sin. The neo-conservative vision of universal democracy imposed by the exercise of American power (for example in Iraq) depends on an optimistic Enlightened translation of Christianity, such as you find in Thomas Jefferson, and with even fewer Christian infusions in Thomas Paine. The horrors of the past, in this account, can be attributed not to a generic human violence, whether biologically or culturally based, or an inherent political dynamic (or, as I suspect, both together), but to specific social formations, above all those that united religious power to political power, Church to state. Strike off the chains imposed on the human by such social formations, insert a 'wall of separation' between Church and state, and there would emerge a new humanity in the image and likeness of American democracy. So much for culture, so much for tradition.

This theme of 'secular religion' has been long-established in the sociology of religion, though John Gray has lent it a new lease of life by the verve with which he presents it, and by a pessimistic and atheist perspective darker and more unrelieved than any found in mainstream Christianity since the bleak and sardonic imaginings of James Hogg in his *Private Memoirs and Confessions of a Justified Sinner* (2004).

At one point in his *Black Mass*, John Gray interprets the Cold War as a conflict between rival versions of the Enlightenment, based respectively in Washington and Moscow. That is clearly correct, and there is no inherent connection between Enlightenment and democracy, any more than there is an inherent connection between Christianity and democracy. It is worth adding that there is an equally plausible connection between Enlightenment and autocracy, particularly the kind of autocracy that pulls down even the flimsy partitions between state and established Church, for example in the St. Petersburg of Peter the Great, and in imperial Berlin and Vienna. This is reform from above, not democracy from below, and it characterised massive swathes of the history of Enlightenment.

The ambiguity that characterises the relation between Christianity, peace and violence is reproduced, and arguably exacerbated, in the Enlightenment, precisely because divine power and judgement has been translated into human power and judgement. Both liberalism and anarchism as movements based on human liberation and autonomy spawn pacific and violent wings. The pacific anarchist tradition of Kropotkin is joined at the hip to the anarchist tradition of violence promoted by Bakunin, just as liberal imperialism in the nineteenth century (and very recently) is joined to liberal pacifism. Both are integrally related to the way the pacifist tradition in Christianity is joined at the hip to the apocalyptic tradition.

The histories of liberal nationalism are replete with mass mobilisations of 'the people' which require ethnic cleansing as a pre-condition of democracy, and not just in Kemalist Turkey in 1922. The origins of nations as 'imagined communities', whether under autocratic aegis (as in Spain in 1492) or created by mass mobilisations, characteristically require the expulsion of the alien. Contemporary politics are infiltrated by the hopes and anxiety of apocalypse, and not just in the various velvet and orange revolutions in the wake of the Communist collapse. There is a persistent pressure for a charismatic leader, who is 'whiter than white', who will purge the corruptions of the old order, and who in turn becomes corrupted. The persistent mythic structure of politics turns on the mystery of innocence corrupted, and on the new order of the world (the *novus ordo seclorum* printed on every American one-dollar bill) subverted by the evil ways of an older, sadder, more resigned world. The 2005 revolution in the Ukraine began in what looked like the passion narrative of an upright leader literally poisoned by the representatives of the old (Soviet) order, and the revolutionary mobilisation in the Madan (or central square) in Kiev was marked by quasi-eucharistic and baptismal celebrations. Within months, the pure new leader was being accused of corruption by his almost equally charismatic second-in-command, until she in turn faced charges of financial irregularities.

The Subjectivisation of the *Eschaton*

One uses a phrase like 'the subjectivisation of the *eschaton*' in heavy quotation marks, and mainly to indicate a connection between what Charles Taylor (1989) calls 'The Turn to the Self' and the immanentisation of the *eschaton* in political religion. Once again, one is dealing with a political translation of Christianity, in particular by way of Luther and pietism, freed from the constraints of the collective and the sacramental. Certainly these constraints have a history of oppression weighing heavily on the minds of subject populations, but the constraints built into collective solidarities are not necessarily oppressive. Sociologically one has a choice of 'oppressions' not a choice between subjective liberation and the oppressions of group solidarity. As will be indicated below, authority, ritual and collective constraints are all pre-conditions of the social, rather than antithetical to authentic sociality. The genuine claims of the individual to autonomy, along with claims to respect through the human rights agenda (once again a fusion of Christian and Enlightened motifs, based on a shared image of our human status) are in tension not only with other claims similarly based, but also with the claims of constitutive social identities. The demand by a Dutch political pressure group for the age of consent to be reduced to the age of four represents a claim based on notions of autonomy and liberation at odds with other claims similarly based, and with any number of constitutive identities, such as a Catholic identity, a Muslim identity or a Jewish identity. Somehow claims are advanced as if all possible items on the agenda of human rights were of the same weight and kind, whereas in practice they are often claims to special treatment by organised interest groups. The political and cultural wars currently opening up in the extended European Union do not arise *solely* because the more recent members of the community are not up to speed with respect to the liberal revolution in the politics of gender.

'The Turn to the Self' assumes two *semi-secular* forms. First it locates the pursuit of fullness, redemption and paradise in the depths of the inner self at the expense of collective redemption; and second, it converts self-offering into self-expression. This gives rise to a tension between an understanding of the self in terms of sincerity, spontaneity and authenticity, and the inherent requirements of social order (cosmic or otherwise), in terms of authority, internalised discipline, ritual and courtesy. Social institutions, including the Church, become identified with oppressive structures and unacceptable demands, including long-term commitments. The spirit wanders at will under the impulse of unappeasable desire. This epiphany of the self is incapable of recognising the structural realities of politics exposed by Machiavelli, and recognised by Christianity under the code name of sin. From this comes the contemporary apathy and scepticism about politics.

The semi-secularisation of Christianity through the rejection of self-offering in favour of self-expression draws its nourishment from resources embedded deep in Christianity, and even in Judaism. The priority of the inner spiritual condition over 'mere' external conformity, taught in the parable of the Pharisee and the Publican, has been taken literally 'to heart', as has the prophetic emphasis on the law written 'on the inward parts' and the reduction of the religious requirement to doing justly, loving mercy and (less inviting) 'walking humbly with thy God'. The opposite of the subjective and individual translation of inward grace is *Halakah*, the objective performance of ritual obligation, without emotion or desire, because that belongs to one's collective social identity. In Adam Seligman's formulation in *Ritual and its Consequences* (2008), the halakhic obligation may be as divorced from meaning as it is from desire, though in Christian rituals the meaning is profoundly embedded in the act, even when the act is so habitual as to be automatic. It can be argued that precisely the attempted reduction of religion to inward states reduces the stakes when it comes to conflicts over doctrine. If the criterion is sincerity rather than truth, one example of sincerity is as good as another, and arguments about truth become surplus to requirements. The eclipse of truth by sincerity is very much a marker of the advanced semi-secular condition, and it leads to pan-relativistic conclusions as inimical to institutional academic disciplines as to institutional religions. If there are no hierarchies of truth, judgement and moral or aesthetic value, no agreed canon of excellence, what becomes of the role of the teacher, let alone of the priest or the imam? No wonder the Roman Catholic Church holds to verities which the contemporary intelligentsia in deconstructivist, relativistic, anti-canonical mode, puts at risk. And the Catholic Church is hardly alone in that: contemporary uses of language are saturated in agreed values about what is 'acceptable', as well as infiltrated with intimations of the sacred and what constitutes a violation.

The issue of the canon lies close to the heart of those putative contemporary secularisations which go beyond the semi-secular to embrace something on the verge of mere secularity. The philosopher Stewart Sutherland (2004: 450) quotes Alasdair MacIntyre on the question of canonicity as saying that 'an encyclopaedia [can] no longer be a set of canonical books for an educated public, since increasingly such publics [have] disintegrated'. I disagree with both MacIntyre and Sutherland, but if that were indeed so, then the university, at one time seen as a replacement for the universal Church, would be going the way of what it purportedly replaced, or (alternatively) the university and the universal Church, the humanist and the Christian, would stand and fall together.

Sutherland argues that the associated privatisation of moral and aesthetic truth, as well as theological truth, undermines a metaphor as fundamental to (say) Plato as to Christianity: the pilgrimage to the 'abiding city' which is to come. Sutherland cites his fellow-Scot, David Hume, here as the Enlightened thinker who most undermined the philosophical pre-conditions for such a metaphor to work existentially, in spite of Kant's attempted restoration. 'Man', to use the phraseology of the Shorter Scottish Catechism, does not have a 'chief end'. He only comes to an end. In Sutherland's formulation, pilgrims have been replaced by tourists who are lovers of sights and sounds, dealers in experience for its own sake, *going* nowhere. In short order the empiricist project leads to a dead end, and the meaningless succession of one damned thing after another on Arnold's 'darkling plain' and the tensions of transcendence introduced in the Axial Age have run their course.

Sutherland's preferred nomad is Shostakovich, who managed to survive the three dangers of exile, execution and deformity of talent and integrity. One is bound to ask: whence come these evaluations of a canonical composer?

There are various possible responses to this. One, expressed by another philosopher, Anthony Kenney, holds that the contemporary world has become all too replete with passionate pilgrims, meaning by that fundamentalists in the U.S.A., Africa and the Middle East, including hitherto secular Turkey. It is a view compatible with the argument of John Gray, even though Gray extends the range of what is meant by fundamentalism.[2]

For a concluding response I turn again to Charles Taylor (2007),[3] who would, I suspect, ask about the philosophical basis and subterranean religious sources that underlie criteria of judgement like 'integrity' and 'deformity of talent'. He would renovate meaning and purpose under the rubric of 'fullness', and perhaps point to a Heideggerian and phenomenological upending of the whole empirical project. In his most recent summa, *A Secular Age*, Taylor has traced the transitions from Christianity to Enlightenment to the modern 'secular age', and has made clear that each stage is a further secularisation of the moral priorities of the previous one. He does not explicitly attempt to do what I have attempted to do here, which is to trace the religious models underlying much of what appears to be secular politics. Instead he has argued that the West has undergone a transition from a condition in which the transcendent is presupposed, to a fragile, precarious condition of contradictions and cross-pressures, where the taken-for-granted, against which it would be necessary to define a critique, assumes the primacy of the immanent. The critique as proposed by Taylor argues for openness to the transcendent rather than dogmatic closure. An analysis such as that offered here is compatible with that view, except that I have

---

2   Spoken contribution by Anthony Kenney to the debate on Charles Taylor's *A Secular Age*, at the British Academy, 2 May 2007 on the occasion of Charles Taylor receiving the 2007 Templeton Prize.

3   My comments focus in particular on chapter 15.

traced the shadow of the transcendent animating the political tradition, with the bare structure of the dynamic of power showing through the disguises of political rhetoric. Back stairs advisers may propose Machiavellian stratagems, but politicians with mass electorates to mobilise continue to rely on the appeal of the *secularis*.

References

Burleigh, M. (2006) *Sacred Causes: Religion and Politics from the European Dictators to Al Qaeda*, London: Harper/Collins.

Chekhov, A. (1992) 'The Duel', in Anton Chekhov, *The Russian Master and Other Stories*, Oxford: Oxford University Press, pp. 90–92.

Eisenstadt, S.N. (1999) *Fundamentalism, Sectarianism and Revolution: The Jacobin Dimension of Modernity*, Cambridge: Cambridge University Press.

Gray, J. (2007) *Black Mass: Apocalyptic Religion and the Death of Utopia*, London: Allen Lane/Penguin.

Hann, C. (ed.) (2006) *The Post-Socialist Religious Question. Faith and Power in Central Asia and East-Central Europe*, Berlin: Lit-Verlag.

Hauerwas, S. (2001) *With the Grain of the Universe: The Church's Witness and Natural Theology*, London: SCM Press.

Hogg, J. (2004) *Private Memoirs and Confessions of a Justified Sinner*, Harmondsworth: Penguin.

Jaspers, K. (1955) *The Origin and Goal of History*, New Haven: Yale University Press.

Kidd, C. (2006) *The Forging of Races: Race and Scripture in the Protestant Atlantic World, 1600–2000*, Cambridge: Cambridge University Press.

Mâle, E. (1961) *The Gothic Image*, London: Fontana.

Martin, D. (1965) *Pacifism: An Historical and Sociological Study*, London: Routledge.

Rieff, P. (1966) *The Triumph of the Therapeutic*, London: Chatto and Windus.

Seligman, A., Weller, R., Puett, M. and Simon, B. (2008) *Ritual and its Consequences: An Essay on the Limits of Sincerity*, Oxford: Oxford University Press.

Sutherland, S. (2004) 'Nomad's Progress', *Proceedings of the British Academy*, 131, London: The British Academy, pp. 443–63.

Sykes, S. (2006) *Power and Christian Theology*, London: Continuum.

Taylor, C. (1989) *Sources of the Self: The Making of the Modern Identity*, Cambridge: Cambridge University Press.

—— (2007) *A Secular Age*, Cambridge Mass. and London: Harvard University Press.

Trigg, R. (2007) *Religion in Public Life: Must Faith be Privatised?* Oxford: Oxford University Press.

Ward, K. (2006) *Is Religion Dangerous?* Oxford: Lion Hudson.

Weber, M. (1948) 'Religious Rejections of the World and their Direction' in H. Gerth and C. Wright Mills (eds) *From Max Weber*, London: Routledge, pp. 323–59.

CHAPTER 13

Religion, Human Power and Powerlessness[1]

Thomas Luckmann

Power and Powerlessness as Elements of the Human Condition

In the year 1146 Otto, Bishop of Freising, expressed the desolate helplessness which human beings experienced in his time:

> Ever since that time we have witnessed disturbances and we cannot but look forward to even greater ones that we shall have to suffer for these and other reasons. An outbreak of violence is expected between our Empire and Hungary …. From Poland comes news of lamentable discord between three brothers, the territorial princes. We hear of continuous battle between powerful lords in Lorraine. In our own country [Bavaria] the confusion of minds has become so abominable that robbery and arson throw everything into disorder not only on the ordinary days of the years but even on days of fasting and penitence, in utter disregard of divine and human law. So heavily are we burdened by the memory of past, the onslaught of present and the fear of future vicissitudes that we are fain to yield to the sentence of death which is our lot from the beginning and we tire of life.[2]

This moving testimony to human impuissance comes from a man descended from the old nobility (he was an uncle of the Emperor of the Holy Roman Empire known as Barbarossa), in high ecclesiastic position, a man clearly much closer to the sources of power than a peasant, monk, townsman or lowly knight of his time. Helplessness, for Otto of Freising, is a constitutive element of the human condition. It is remarkable that he writes of war, robbery and arson, of human helplessness when exposed to human power, human violence, and man-made history. As for helplessness vis-à-vis nature, he seems to take the universal inevitability of drought, floods, earthquakes, and maladies so much for granted that he does not bother to mention them.

Would anyone write even approximately as dejectedly today? There always were prophets of doom and our time is no exception. However, the helplessness in view of overpowering events that marks Otto's words would be highly unusual these days. What is it that has changed in the past eight hundred and some years? Since Bishop Otto's time, mankind has suffered from ills which, if in nothing else, were worse in

---

1   Major parts of this contribution are based on the first of two lectures I gave at the Salburger Hochschulwochen in July 2007.

2   I translated this passage from the German version to be found in the admirable book by Arno Borst (1973) *Lebensformen im Mittelalter*.

their severity than anything that happened before: the Holy Inquisition; the Thirty Years' War; the mass murder of the Indians in the New World; the unspeakable misery of the millions of enslaved negros transported to North and South America; two horrendous World Wars; the Holocaust; Pol Pot's genocide of his own people; and, more recently, the massacres in Srebrenica and elsewhere on our doorstep in Europe; genocide in Rwanda; and something approaching genocide in Darfur. And that is a shortage only of man-made disasters. Nor was there a short list of natural catastrophes: the Black Plague and syphilis; droughts; famines; inundations; and earthquakes. And there is something rather new, at least with regard to its order of magnitude: an amalgam of man-made natural disasters with regard to which even the least restrained ecological prognostications now turn out to have been realistic. In other words, a dearth of natural and man-made disasters cannot explain the difference between the mood expressed in Bishop Otto's chronicle of the world and the prevailing attitudes of our time. The difference, rather, is attributable to several apparently contradictory changes.

Otto and the Christian folk of his epoch were helpless, indeed, but they were consoled by their belief that help, eventually, would come from the omnipotent and benevolent God. In our day, there are few who set such hope in God. The majority of our contemporaries in modern Europe, if not more generally in Western societies, lack the faith from which they could draw such consolation.

In archaic societies the dangerous power of the tribal gods was evident to everyone. Everyone was afraid of it – yet everyone knew that there was a chance for the wrath of supernatural powers to be avoided. Placating the gods and expiating one's trespasses, might with some luck, if one followed the proper procedures, divert their wrath to a scapegoat. The enormous importance of sacrificial offerings (*piacula*) in alleviating the imbalance of power between the extraordinary might of supernatural beings and the helplessness of ordinary humans was documented nearly one hundred and twenty years ago for early Semitic religions by William Robertson Smith (1889). The findings of Robertson Smith have an application well beyond the examples upon which they are founded.[3]

Gods remained powerful and human beings helpless but there was some change. On the one hand, the imbalance of power was radicalized in later monotheistic religions but it was also, to some extent, spiritualized as, for example, in the Christian theology of transubstantiation. The importance of sacrificial rites in coping with this

---

3   More than a hundred years ago the work of Robertson Smith, a great Arabist-Semitologist, successfully combined two different approaches to the study of religion. The history of religious ideas investigated the different ways of the collective experiences, which point beyond everyday life to a realm of transcendence, analyzing the sources indicating when and how such experiences were sacralized. The sociological study of religion describes the institutional and other forms by which such experiences are organized. It should go without saying that the two approaches are complementary. Religious ideas, which are articulated in historical traditions, are not disembodied texts; they cannot be understood without consideration of their *Sitz im Leben* (the social context of their origin), the organizational forms regulating the reception of the texts by particular groups of people. Conversely, a purely formal analysis of religious organizational forms would be an exercise in futility unless it considered what it is that is being organized.

imbalance was preserved in Judaism, Islam and Christendom while the notion of scapegoat took a less literal turn. Thus, in Christian tradition, the idea of Jesus as a substitute expiator for all mankind preceded the notion of his divinity. In the great soteriological religions the basic human experience of powerlessness was made less intolerable by the hope of eventual salvation, a hope that these religions both awakened and promised to fulfil.

How different things are today – or, at any rate, how different are they in our Western societies! The belief of Enlightenment philosophy in the power of reason had spread widely and the rise of modern science, along with the technological achievements associated with it, suppressed, with varying success in town and countryside, in the European North and South, East and West, the elementary human experience of powerlessness.

Nature, so it was thought, was manageable; its power could be harnessed.[4] There seemed to be good evidence in support of this belief. Not all technological invasions of nature ended as catastrophically as Khrushchev's irrigation of the dry steppes of Inner Asia that resulted in the drying up of the Aral Sea, the US Army Corps of Engineers 'management' of the Mississippi River or the dousing of entire human populations with antibiotics irrespective of the danger that viral populations might become resistant. Many advances in medicine and some advances in agriculture may be able to stand the test of time. Earthquakes, slides, fires, drought and starvation, tsunamis and Chernobyl left hardly a dent in the belief in science and in the technological optimism that had spread into Western mentality since the eighteenth century. Many decades ago, the Club of Rome Report fell on deaf ears. The ecological preachers of doom were ridiculed until recently. It is only in recent days, not years, that Al Gore seems to have gained the upper hand over George W. Bush, to express the matter in personal American terms.

While most of our contemporaries in Western societies no longer seek consolation from the great soteriological religions, they had found a substitute hope in the belief that science and technology are all-powerful. Heaven may no longer be promised to the poor but some of the rich, at least, seem to hope that they will be resurrected as long as they can afford their corpse to be frozen by experts, and defrosted at the proper time (after discovery of the aging gene, perhaps).

Such an idea of human omnipotence over nature may seem absurd, even to believers in salvation by science. However, the idea is not limited to nature. The view of human history held by most observers of human affairs today is different from the view that was dominant at the time of Otto of Freising. But does the replacement of older myths by the new assumption that history is the (dubious) accomplishment of mankind necessarily imply that men and women make history just as they wish? The best laid plans…. Can even a devout believer in the progress of reason still cling to the hope that dialogue between people will result in eternal peace and lead to the end

---

4   The medieval fear of nature – when high mountains and deep seas and dark forests had been perceived as especially threatening – receded. It is noteworthy that in the period during which the notion of human power over brute nature gained ground, a romantic view of natural beauty was embraced by artists, writers (Rousseau being one of the chief propagandists) and major segments of the literate citizenry.

of history? The soteriological inflation of dialogue may not have gone out of fashion yet but its lack of realism is likely to doom it to the same fate as the one suffered many decades ago by the equally well-intentioned moral rearmament movement.

My argument is fairly simple. It consists of two assumptions.

The first is that individual experiences of powerlessness are universal.[5] The dominant ideas of an age notwithstanding, elementary experiences of impotence continue to befall the human individual. Even in the protected routines of every day life – assuming that one lives in a society where such routines are protected indeed – many things happen which one would very much prefer not to happen. Not all reasonable projects can be carried out successfully. Furthermore, one feels even more profoundly helpless when confronted with suffering, one's own and that of others, and when one is forced to anticipate death, that of others and eventually one's own. The irresistible power of society matches that of nature. One is subject to the latter directly in social relations and indirectly as laws and institutions regulate one's life.[6] No one who has a body and lives in a society can avoid the experience of impuissance.

My second – and, I should add, equally obvious – assumption is that recurring individual experiences are reported to others. When it is found that others have the same kinds of experience they are subjected to discriminating as well as discriminatory communicative 'treatment'. Some reports are 'censored' and others are 'canonized'. They are articulated in collective memory as patterns of good or bad, true or false experiences, and beyond that, as models for the conduct of life. Socially 'objectivated' patterns of experience and models of action are sedimented in a social stock of knowledge and transmitted to following generations.

The terror of chaos lurking even in apparently safe conditions of everyday life and the accompanying feeling of helplessness is a serious problem for any social order. In different epochs and different societies, social institutions deal with the universally human experiences of impuissance in characteristic ways. According to what for the sake of brevity I shall call the *Zeitgeist* such experiences may become exaggerated at the one extreme and suppressed at the other. Of course such social patterns and models do not entirely replace the original individual experiences of powerlessness but they do mould them significantly.

Traditionally, religious institutions did not play down the experience of helplessness. On the contrary, they sometimes reinforced it by stressing the dichotomy of an all-powerful god and an abjectly powerless individual. However, the dichotomy was overcome by the offer of salvation which an all-powerful god granted to his believers. Since Enlightenment, human beings are not powerless if they use reason to cope with the problems of life. If Reason is the new god the new theology of science offers a substitute for the old offers of salvation.[7] The medieval

---

5   I shall not raise the obvious question whether a sense of power over things and people is not just as universal as its opposite.

6   Next to *extériorité*, Durkheim defined social facts by *contrainte*.

7   One of the few exceptions is to be found in certain religious groupings as, for example, among apocalyptic sects. In Europe, at least, these are at the margins of society. This may explain the exception. The social and economic position of the members of such groups

world of Bishop Otto of Freising was marked by a profound sense of helplessness – and no man, only God could help. Our modern world is – or, until recently, was – characterized by a pervasive sense of the power of Science and Reason over the physical and social world.

Speaking of a dominant worldview invites oversimplification. In very simple archaic society there may be indeed one world view that shapes the view of reality of all people and is taken for granted by everybody, perhaps with a higher degree of reflexiveness by some, and with some slight differences according to age and sex. However, in any more differentiated society, decidedly some groups may hold variant versions of the dominant view. In complex societies, as, for example in the ancient, slavery based empires and, of course, in modern capitalist as well as communist societies, the dominant world view may represent the interests of the dominant class. In consequence, under some – additional – circumstances a view of reality may emerge among other strata that runs counter to the dominant view. If the social structure and stratification is perceived as radically unjust, religious legitimation of highly unequal life-chances may loose their plausibility. Of course even then some intellectual (religious, ideological) ability is required for the formulation of plausible alternatives.[8]

Different versions of the same worldview may vie for dominance and 'counter-cultures' may attempt to destroy the 'mainstream' view of reality. In addition to the class and group based coexistence of competing world views, these may define, one after the other, the view of reality in the life-time of a single individual either by a slow replacement of an earlier by a newer view or by conversion. And, finally, different views of reality may not only follow one in the life-time of individuals but may coexist in the mind of an individual, shaping his or her responses and guiding his or her actions in contradictory ways. This seems to be very often the case with that especially important part of a worldview, the sense of power and helplessness.

Summing up: religious institutions in many ancient societies not only recognized the human sense of being helplessly exposed to a dark this-worldly fate but some of them even accentuated that sense. Coping with the resulting problem of individual and collective disorientation and under certain circumstances even desperation, they offered the promise of this- or other-worldly salvation. The this-worldly optimism of a modern belief in science and technology stands in sharp contrast to the attitudes prevailing in Buddhism and Christianity. It overcomes, with varying success, the

---

(artisans, small merchants and some categories of employees) is threatened by social change. Consequently, there is a comparatively high chance that they will feel powerless, even collectively powerless, quite apart from, and in addition to, the individual sense of impotence in the face of suffering and death. Michael N. Ebertz 'Heilige Reste und ihr Eigensinn' bases these observations on an excellent analysis of the contemporary apocalyptic movement, 'Protestantische und katholische Apokalyptiker' (2000).

8   Even if there is a difference in the level of intellectual power involved, there is a structural similarity between the class ideologies of the nineteenth and twentieth centuries and the rejection of the science and technology based optimism on the part of the modern apocalyptic groups mentioned earlier.

sense of impuissance by offering the hope of this-worldly dominion over nature and society.[9]

In the following remarks I shall turn to one peculiar, not easily suppressed modern aspect of that sense of impuissance, a sense of powerless before the inexorable working of an anonymous social structure. To be sure, the dominant view in modernity is that nature can be tamed by science and technology, and social conflict eliminated by rational discourse. However, this view could not entirely invalidate another, much more pessimistic view of life. That view originates in a peculiarly modern experience of powerlessness in the face of a society whose constraints seem like an alien, anonymous second nature. However, the anonymous economic, political and legal institutions constrain only part, admittedly the larger part, of the typical modern individual's life. In a seeming paradox another aspect of modern experience consists of a sense of autonomy and freedom, of power to manage one's own life, unprecedented in traditional and semi-modern authoritarian – and, *a fortiori*, totalitarian – societies.

Society as Second Nature[10]

The life of an individual was of course always to a large extent predetermined by the society into which he or she was born. The social structure, both in its 'horizontal' institutional organization and its 'vertical' stratification, arranged for the starting point from which an individual's life took off and placed the hurdles which he or she had to clear along the track. However, different societies set the course differently.

At all times, everywhere, human beings had to gather or produce goods and had to find a way to live together. But the rules by which they organized social interaction for these purposes, and the means by which these rules were enforced, varied.

In archaic societies, power, law and economy were, to use Redfield's (1953) term, 'fused' as part of an all-embracing kinship system. The validity of the regulations of interaction was supported by religious values. Furthermore, the regulation of religious interaction such as the definition of some animals and places as taboo or their sacralization, as *piacula*, and so on, did not form a separate domain but were entirely part of tribal life and kin relations. Religious ideas such as myths of origin had an indirect influence but there was no concentrated power of religious institutions, which lacked designated enforcement personnel.

In the feudal system of the European Middle Ages, the economy and the polity were still highly interdependent and its norms had a religious foundation. The relatively high degree of functional specialization of political and economic institutions that had been already reached, regressed after the collapse of the Roman Western Empire.

---

9   It is noteworthy that two variants of 'late' modern society are rather similar as regards the dominance of faith in science and technology. Yet they differ so much in the vitality of organized Christian religion and the corresponding acceptance of its offers of salvation that it is customary to regard America (i.e., the United States) as a religious and Europe as a secularized society. Various scholars have tried to resolve this paradox. My own attempt was presented in Luckmann, 2005.

10   Some of the observations that follow are based on an earlier article (Luckmann 1975).

Interregional economic relations and exchange of specialized products largely came to a standstill. The only exception to regressed social differentiation was the Church, which generally succeeded in retaining its organizational structure and managed to transfer its legitimatory blessings to the emerging political formations of the European Middle Ages.

Institutionally organized, religion was not only the main source of life's meaning and of soteriological hope set against the experience of human impuissance. As an institution it also exercised power, partly directly by the intimidating force of some of its ideas (for example, the fear of hell), partly indirectly by cooptation of secular authorities. Human beings could feel just as powerless vis-à-vis the Church as against other feudal institutions.

The clusters of economic and political institutions developed from the regionally and locally highly interdependent economic and political activities of medieval feudal society to functionally specialized, quasi-autonomous political and economic realms of a supra-regional, national and increasingly global nature. Although there was some interregional economic specialization in the early Middle Ages, the institutional specialization of the economy and the gradual emancipation of economic activities from religious norms set in later. It was favoured by the growth of cities, improvement in the transportation of staples and long-range commerce. The centralization of monarchic power was supported against the feudal nobility by the economic power of the rising bourgeoisie and the introduction of mercantilist economic systems. Feudal arrangements in administration and law were increasingly replaced by a new bureaucratic system. At the same time, the ties between the political realm and the Church began to loosen. The outcome of the earlier controversies concerning the immorality of usury and the eventual resolution of the conflict about the investiture of bishops all point in the same direction: the victory of functionally 'rational' economic and political norms over the religious values that had subordinated the social organization of power and the production and distribution of goods and services to a transcendent universe. The jurisdictional disputes between the post-Constantinian Church and first the dynastic and later the national states were sooner or later resolved in favour of the latter.[11]

These changes did not transform European society at equal speed. Economic and power centres, especially in the West and North, were well ahead of the periphery. The rational bureaucratic transformation of law and administration had already begun in the absolutist monarchies, earliest in France but then also in Prussia and the Habsburg Empire. It was speeded up on the Continent after the French Revolution and the Napoleonic codifications, road-building programs and so on. After the French

---

11 In the long run, the use of the forged 'Constantinian donation' by the Church in its claim to supremacy not only in the supernatural but also in the secular realm failed. The moderate medieval doctrine of the two realms became old-fashioned after Machiavelli's demonstration of the rational realism of 'power politics'. Adam Smith's assumption of the superiority of the 'invisible hand' did for economics what Machiavelli earlier did for politics. Economics and politics were no longer judged morally for what they contributed to the common good. The norms that organized social interaction in these two institutional domains were eventually based on the principle of maximization of functional efficiency within their special jurisdiction.

Revolution the traditional, religiously legitimated monarchies were sooner or later transformed into 'secular' modern nation states, some of which retained constitutional monarchies, as in Great Britain and later, toward the end of the nineteenth century, in Germany and Italy. Still later, in the second decade of the twentieth century, the successor states of the Austro-Hungarian Empire followed the Western example. It is idle to speculate whether this process was inevitable; it certainly was not smooth. Ups and downs of 'progress' and 'reaction' marked the period, as, for example, in the Metternich era after Waterloo and totalitarian states in Italy and Germany after the First World War.

Overall, however, especially after the Second World War, these social changes led to a powerful alliance between parliamentary democracy and industrial capitalism and an increasingly unfettered articulation of functionally rational norms. These increasingly replaced the religious norms, which had previously regulated much of the life of society. The religious legitimation first of economic and eventually also of political institutions lost ground as actual interaction in these institutional domains became 'rationalized'. The trend was supported by the diffusion of the Enlightenment's philosophical critique of Church and religion. Ideological 'disestablishment' of religion in public life was followed sooner or later by some form of legal disestablishment.[12]

Subsequently, these two great institutional domains, the economy and the polity, came to influence life in modern societies in a novel manner. The high degree of functional specialization in separate institutional domains, combined with the bureaucratization of administration and law, led to an unprecedented normative independence in the most important segments of the social structure and, correspondingly, a concentration of power enabling these segments to determine social interaction and crucial aspects of the daily life of individual members of society. On the other hand, religion in its Western social form as a Church lost its institutionally mediated power over the daily lives of the populations of modern societies. The degree to which it also lost its power over the minds of individuals depended to a considerable extent upon the social form of religion in different Western societies. Where it formally retained its post-Constantinian facade as an established Church, a shrinking of its power over the minds of men (and women) followed the factual loss of institutional control over the life of 'its' people. To put it somewhat simplistically, first went the fear of the Inquisition, and then went the fear of hell.[13]

---

12   These range from radical separation in laïcist France and various, at least nominal vestiges of establishment elsewhere on the Continent.

13   Matters went differently where the Christian tradition was essentially represented by Dissent from the established Church(es) and where there was a close connection between religion and social and political life (as observed already by de Tocqueville) at the same time that, at least on the federal level, no established Churches existed. The abandonment of the post-Constantinian model in favor of a denominational one (see Niebuhr 1929) permitted Christianity to adapt much more successfully to the transformation from an institutionally specialized to a privatized social form of religion than the post-Constantinian Churches in Western (and Northern and Southern, and the Catholic and Reformed) parts of Eastern Europe. The Eastern Orthodox Church had pursued a different path throughout the past millennium,

To repeat a general point: The institutions, which together form the social structure, have power; they are defined by the constraint they exercise over social interaction. In the face of such constraint, a certain experience of impotence on the part of the individual is an element of the human condition. However, the general structural type and particular institutional features of an historical society give rise to different forms of that experience. It is an historical social structure that defines the categorical relations of individuals to other individuals, determines a specific interactional frame within which historically specific types of personal identity are formed and provides both motives and constraints for every conduct. In fact, the very chances of survival for an individual organism depend on the kind of society into which he or she was born.

It was already observed, with some simplification, that archaic societies are characterized by a 'primitive fusion' of institutions. Social interactions were categorized almost exclusively by kinship and were thus highly personalized. The meaning of hunting, gathering, and tilling the field was closely connected to kinship ties and to a transcendent universe. The constraints of social structural 'power' were anything but anonymous.

Evidently, matters are quite different in modern societies. The brief account given of functional specialization of institutions, the segmentation of the social structure and the 'emancipation' of social interaction in most areas of life from religious norms indicated that the individual as a person is unimportant for the organization of most social interaction. What is important with regard to the workings of the social structure is an individual's performance as a role-player in different institutional domains.

On the other hand, not all social interaction is closely regulated by social institutions. In archaic societies, where individuals were, so to speak, under close observation almost all of the time, the 'fused' institutions exercised continuous control. In modern societies, the segmentation of functionally specialized institutions into quasi-autonomous domains means that the disciplining power by institutions becomes discontinuous. A space of solitary freedom has emerged in the 'interstices'[14] of the social structure.[15]

---

was subject to a different fate during the communist regime and is now in a somewhat different position than Catholicism and Protestantism elsewhere in Europe.

14   It was Talcott Parsons who introduced this concept.

15   The early beginnings of a 'private sphere' may date back to the transition from the High Middle Ages to Early Modernity. Its full development depends upon the combination of parliamentary democracy and a market economy, which characterizes modern Western societies. In these societies it eventually gained recognition in its individual legal core. It is not entirely solipsistic, however. The family, devoid of political status and largely divorced from economic significance, has become a 'small' institution in the private sphere. The modern social form of religion, too, has basically migrated into this sphere. That is in stark contrast to archaic societies in which family, as part of a larger kinship system, and religion may be somewhat anachronistically said to have been the 'great' institutions of society. Nonetheless, family and religion have been identified as important elements of the 'social capital' of modern societies.

The result is a paradox. It describes human life in modern society in sharply contrasting terms, yet both views are rooted in experiences of real features of modern society.

The close control exercised over the conduct of the individual is anonymous. It is Max Weber's society as a 'second nature', which is subjectively experienced as anonymous, inexorable and inexplicable. The literary symbol of this aspect of life is Franz Kafka's Josef K., lonely and lost in the alienating operation of a bureaucratic machine.

The individual freedom of movement in the private sphere, on the other hand, is the source of a feeling of autonomy, of self-direction, even of power. The many literary images of the self-made man were rarely positive, except where he was seen as a Titan. However, self-direction through self-education was a powerful literary idea already in Goethe's novels *Wilhelm Meisters Lehrjahre* and *Wilhelm Meisters Wanderjahre*. It preceded the 'rebellions' against society that have been fashionably recurring since the Romantic Movement all the way to Hermann Hesse, Jack Kerouac and its final transformation into a hedonistic variety as self-fulfilment, a slogan of modern solipsism.

References

Borst, A. (1973) *Lebensformen im Mittelalter*, Frankfurt/Main: Berlin.

Ebertz, M.N. (2000) 'Heilige Reste und ihr Eigensinn: Protestantische und katholische Apokalyptiker', in M.N. Ebertz and R. Zwick (eds) *Jüngste Tage. Die Gegenwart der Apokalyptik*, Freiburg-Basel-Wien.

Luckmann, T. (1975) 'Rationality of Institutions in Modern Life', *European Journal of Sociology*, I: 3–15.

—— (2005) 'The socio-historical context of religion in Europe and the United States.' Paper presented at the *Yale-Constance Symposium on Nation-Religion*, Constance, July 6–8, 2005.

Niebuhr, R.H. (1929) *The Social Sources of Denominationalism*, New York: Meridian.

Redfield, R. (1953) *The Primitive World and its Transformations*, New York: Ithaca.

Robertson Smith, W. (1927) *Lectures on the Religion of the Semites*, New York, London: D. Appleton & Co.

PART IV
The Spiritual and/or the Religious?

CHAPTER 14

The Church Without and the God Within:
Religiosity and/or Spirituality?[1]

Eileen Barker

Introduction

In his masterful study of social constructionism, *Social Theory and Religion,* James Beckford states that 'One aspect of the sacred that is currently undergoing re-location is the relationship between conceptions of religion and spirituality' (2003: 71). In this chapter, three approaches will be pursued in the search for possible relationships between such conceptions. The first involves proposing two ideal-typical models that locate spirituality in opposition to conservative religiosity on the one hand and to secularism on the other. Secondly, there is a brief overview of some of the meanings that people have attached to spirituality. Finally, a few empirical findings are drawn from a pan-European study of religious and moral pluralism (RAMP). These indicate some of the characteristics that were associated with the respondents' understanding of 'spirituality', thereby suggesting some directions for further investigation.

Locating Spirituality Among Contemporary *Weltanschauung*

Just as processes such as industrialisation, urbanisation, modernisation, rationalisation, bureaucratisation and, to the east of the iron curtain, sovietisation led in their different ways to societal secularisation throughout most of Europe, so have processes such as social and geographical mobility, globalisation, the growth of mass media, the introduction of the Internet and the collapse of state atheism led to increasing multi-culturalism and religious diversity throughout most of the world. Figure 14.1 represents, as an ideal-typical model, something of the range and complex interplay between different types of worldviews or belief systems that have emerged and/or separated themselves from traditional, institutionalised religions – which, it must be stressed, are still responsible for the great majority of religious beliefs and practices to be found in contemporary society. The arrows indicate that there can be developments in many different directions, rather than there being a single direction in which religion is moving; but, in the absence of some kind of

1   An earlier and somewhat longer version of this chapter was originally published in Marinović Jerolimov *et al.* (eds) 2004: 23–47. I would like to thanks Sally Stares for her invaluable help with the statistics. I would also like to express my gratitude to the Economic and Social Research Council for funding the British part of the RAMP research.

political or military coercion, the overall trend in Europe (and, indeed, elsewhere) would appear to be towards increased diversification.

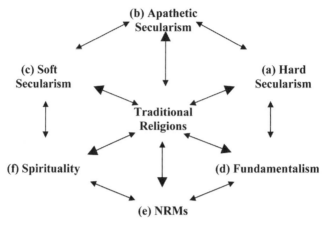

Figure 14.1

The top half of the model extends from (a) hard secularism (manifest as atheism), through (b) an apathetic secularism that is due more to disinterest in religious matters than to any strong antagonism, to (c) a soft, part-time secularism which might, when pressed, encompass a belief in some sort of god or special force and is quite likely to call on the traditional religions at times of crisis and for *rites de passages*. The lower part of Figure 14.1 represents (d) the appearance of strong conservative revivals and fundamentalist innovations (not necessarily an oxymoron), and (f) at the other extreme, the emergence of beliefs and practices of a more spiritual orientation. Between the two poles are (e) numerous new groups or movements that are more or less conservative or spiritual in nature.

Types of Conservative Religiosity and Contemporary Spirituality

The model depicted in Table 14.1 delineates two ideal-typical caricatures consisting of clusters of theological and social beliefs or orientations that allow us to locate, for comparative purposes, a particular movement or group of individuals nearer or further from one or other of the ideal-typical poles which are labelled respectively spirituality and religiosity.[2] The null hypothesis is that groups or individuals who exhibit one or more of the characteristics belonging to the spirituality cluster are more likely to exhibit other spiritual characteristics than characteristics associated in the model with the traditional religion cluster. If, for example, an unchurched individual believes that the source of the Divine is within himself and that when

---

2   Being ideal types in the Weberian (1949) sense of the word, these models are analytical tools intended to be used to facilitate comparison. Actual groups and individuals will not fit neatly into any one type; they will, rather, exhibit a cluster of characteristics that may be *relatively* closer to one type than to another. In other words, the types are more or less useful, not more or less true.

he dies his soul will be reincarnated, then the model invites us to predict that he would be less likely to believe in Satan and original sin than another individual if she attends church and believes in a personal God who revealed Himself through the Old Testament. The possibility of falsifying such a prediction through empirical testing is, of course, part and parcel of the scientific enterprise (Popper 1963: ch.1).

Table 14.1   An ideal-typical distinction between Scriptural religiosity and spirituality, indicating hypothesised oppositions in theological and social orientations.

	Religiosity (of The Book)	*Spirituality*
The Divine	Transcendent and Particular	Immanent and cosmic
Source	Without	Within
Origins	Creation	Creating
Source of Knowledge	Scripture/revelation	Experience/mysticism
Authority	Dogma/Priesthood/Tradition	Personal experience
Theodicy	Evil/sin/Satan	Lack of attunement, balance &/or awareness
Life after death	Salvation/resurrection/ damnation	Reincarnation/transmigration/ Mokṣa
Time	Temporal/historical	Eternal/a-historical
Change	Lineal: past/present/future	Cyclical: then/now/then
Perspective	Analytical	Holistic/syncretistic
Anthropology	Man in God's image	Humans as part of Nature
Distinctions	Dichotomous: Them/us	Complementarity: Us (them=them/us)
Sex/gender	Male/(female)	Feminine~(masculine)
Relations	Controlling	Relating ('sharing')
Social Identity	Group (membership of tradition)	The inner 'me'/the 'true self'
Control	External authority	Internal responsibility
Organisational unit	Institution/family	Individual/network
Place of worship	Synagogue; church; mosque	Informal building; temple; shrine; open air
Communication	Vertical hierarchy	Horizontal networking
Goal	Grace; redemption; atonement	Self-knowledge; enlightenment
Eventual aspiration	Salvation	Liberation; nirvana
Attitude to nature	Dominion	Co-operative harmony
Understanding situation	Historical narrative	Myth
Healing/medicine	Allopathic (conventional)	Ayurvedic (alternative/ complementary)
Civilization	Western	Eastern
Thinking	Left brain	Right brain

For a movement or individual near the religiosity pole, the Divine is seen as a transcendent, personal God, separate from the believer, although possibly also dwelling within him or her. There is belief in a creation myth and an eschatological faith in an eventual end time. The world is likely to be divided into dichotomous distinctions (them and us; before and after; good and bad; male and female; godly and satanic). Truth and morality tend to be absolute and are known through God's revelation in the Bible or through some specially chosen prophets. Human beings are considered inherently sinful and in need of God's grace to receive salvation. Following death, the body is resurrected into heaven (or damned to hell, possibly after a period in purgatory).

For the spiritually oriented type, 'the god within' is an integral part of the human individual, who will, in turn, be conceptualised as an integral part of nature and/or of the cosmos. Time tends to be perceived as basically cyclical, tied to the seasons and the natural cycle of birth, growth, death and rebirth. Truth and morality are likely to be seen as relative to the context rather than as absolute, universal laws or commandments. Concepts such as sin and guilt are alien; yin and yang complementarity and balance are stressed with, perhaps, a greater (rebalancing) emphasis on the feminine and on an awareness of environmental issues. A fundamental value is placed on personal experience and personal responsibility.

But, to repeat, these are methodological caricatures. The two clusters of characteristics are unlikely to be found unambiguously together in reality. It is perfectly possible for actual groups and/or individuals to be closer to one pole on some characteristics and to the other pole on others.

Conceptions of Spirituality and/or Religion

The concept of spirituality is, of course, by no means new; it has long been in common usage and is familiar to any English speaker. However, even the most cursory survey of the literature reveals a vast array of different meanings being promoted or assumed. Logically, there are five different kinds of relationships that could exist between the concepts of religiosity and spirituality. First, the two concepts could be completely interchangeable. Secondly, spirituality could be seen as one or more (possibly very different) sub-divisions of religiosity, examples could be the Spiritual Baptists (Shouters), religions involving spirit possession (Lewis 1988), or Spiritualism (Nelson 1969). A variant of this would be when spirituality is seen as the very core of religiosity, lying, perhaps, in the mysticism experienced by the 'truly religious', such as Meister Eckhardt, Hildegard of Bingen, or Julian of Norwich – or, more recently, Thomas Merton, Bede Griffith, Mother Theresa or the Dalai Lama. Spirituality in this sense may be pursued by a variety of means such as the exercises of Ignatius of Loyola, the practices of Sufism, the devotions of the Indian siddha, or diverse forms of meditation, chanting or yoga, including practices associated with contemporary New Age and/or Human Potential groups.

Conversely, a third conception is that religiosity is a subsection of spirituality. This is the position taken by some New Agers or Human Potential practitioners who see spirituality as embracing all aspects of life. There are, however, other New Agers who want to distance themselves from religion, which is seen as institutionalised and, thus, dead. They (like some conservative religionists who are highly suspicious of New Age ideas and associate them with the idea of spirituality) would prefer to adopt the fourth position, conceptualising religion and spirituality as entirely discrete phenomena. Finally, the two concepts can overlap, sharing some characteristics but not others. The overlap may be almost complete, or it may be almost non-existent – as, for example, when the President of the Shri Ram Chandra Mission, Shri Parthasarathi Rajagopalachari (1992: 104), declares '… spirituality represents everything that religion is not. The only thing we can say they have in common is the idea of God'.

In a study of Americans who were largely, though not entirely, selected from Christian churches, Zinnbauer and Pargament (1997: 555) found religiosity was perceived as identical to spirituality by 3 per cent of their respondents, as encompassing it by 10 per cent, encompassed by it by 39 per cent, overlapping it by (42 per cent, and separate from it by 7 per cent. Three quarters (74 per cent) of their respondents identified themselves as both-religious-and-spiritual, 4 per cent as religious-but-not-spiritual, 3 per cent as neither-religious-nor-spiritual and 19 per cent as spiritual-but-not-religious. In other words, a total of 93 per cent identified themselves as spiritual, compared to 78 per cent identifying themselves as religious. When they compared the spiritual-and-religious with the spiritual-not-religious, the former were, unsurprisingly, more likely to attend church, to follow some sort of religious orthodoxy, and to exhibit right-wing authoritarian tendencies, while the latter were more likely be involved with New Age beliefs and practices (Zinnbauer and Pargament 1997: 559).

Those who identified themselves as spiritual-not-religious in Zinnbauer and Pargament's study were similar in many ways to the 'highly active seekers' identified by Wade Clark Roof (1993) from among America's baby-boomers. Later studies of the post-war generation in the West, led Roof and others to characterise late- or post-modern spirituality as (1) placing an emphasis on individual choice, (2) mixing codes, (3) drawing on both New Age and Eastern religions *and* conservative, evangelical (often charismatic or Pentecostal) religions, (4) placing a high premium on religious experience and growth, and (5) displaying an anti-institutional and anti-hierarchical stance (Roof *et al.* 1995: 247–52).

Sometimes the distinction between spirituality and religiosity is used to fill an apparent overlap between the religious and the secular, particularly those segments of the population that are labelled 'the unchurched' (Hunt 2003) or 'believers not belongers' (Davie 1994). The modern (or, perhaps more cogently, the post-modern) understanding of spirituality as the kind of new-age manifestation outlined in Table 14.1 is frequently associated with the USA (and California in particular), but although it is sometimes assumed that the emergence of unchurched spirituality is a comparatively new phenomenon, it has a long history in different societies throughout the world.[3] Turning the clock back two millennia, for example, we learn that the Gnostic Gospels were 'spiritual' in a number of ways not unlike those of

---

3   It has been estimated that in the late 1600s less than one third of all adult Americans belonged to a church; then, by the start of the Revolutionary War, only about 17 per cent of

some contemporary movements: they embraced mystical experiences, promoted the importance of the feminine and distinguished the false from the true church not in its relationship to the clergy but through the quality of personal relationships and 'spiritual fellowship with those united in communion' (Apocalypse of Peter, quoted in Pagels 1982: 118). Not altogether surprisingly, this account of Jesus' teachings was suppressed by some of the early Christian leaders because it lacked the dogmatic boundaries and hierarchical structures that were deemed necessary to hold the Church together. There have, nonetheless, been numerous themes running throughout Christianity from the days of the Early Church to contemporary spiritualities such as the Charismatic movement, Liberation theology or the ecumenism of Taizé, all of which can be conceptualised as spirituality in the sense that they embrace 'some kind of vision of the human spirit and of what will assist it to achieve full potential' (Sheldrake 2007: 2).

From a slightly different standpoint, Robert Fuller (2001: 13) argues that, although the early colonists might have been very religious according to some criteria, this was not in the commonly accepted sense of the word. He provides a fascinating account of the history of alternative spiritual practices throughout American history, charting the interplay of such phenomena as the occult, witchcraft, divination, astrology, intermingled with alchemy, Hermeticism, Rosicrucianism, Swedenborgianism, Metaphysical religion, a variety of alternative medicines and world views, and psychological spirituality, ending up with what he terms 'the new eclecticism'.

Today there are numerous books, particularly those on the New Age and modern Paganism, that provide descriptions of how individuals and small groups use the concept of spirituality (see, for example, Anthony *et al.* 1987; Bowman 1999; Crowley 1998; Ellwood 1994; Fox 1991; Griffin 1999; Hanegraaff 1999; Heelas and Woodhead 2005; Pennick 1997; Wuthnow 2001), but few studies have tried to test how a random sample of an entire population might understand the concept. There have, however, been some.

In a telephone survey conducted in 1999 with a randomly selected national sample of 100 adults aged 18 and over, respondents were asked what the word spirituality meant to them. The most frequent responses referred to 'Belief in God and/or seeking to grow closer to God', followed by 'Belief in a higher power, something beyond oneself/sense of awe and mystery in the universe', then 'Inner peace/state of mind' (Gallup and Jones 2000: 184–5). It is worth noting that almost a third defined spirituality with no reference to God or a higher authority (ibid: 49). When asked whether they thought of 'spirituality' more in a personal and individual sense, or more in terms of organised religion and church doctrine, 72 per cent of the respondents said the former, and 21 per cent the latter (ibid: 185).

In a survey of what they called 'the congregational domain' (participants in Christian churches) in the English town of Kendal, Heelas and Woodhead (2005: 74) found 57 per cent considered 'spirituality' to be 'obeying God's will'. When they asked members of Kendal's 'holistic milieu' (participants in alternative and/ or New Age activities) what they thought best described their core beliefs about

---

Americans were churched. By 1980, however, church adherence was about 62 per cent (Finke and Stark, 1992: 15).

spirituality, Heelas and Woodhead (ibid: 98) found 21 per cent choosing the response 'Spirituality is being a decent and caring person'; 20 per cent choosing 'Spirituality is love', and 10 per cent 'Spirituality is healing oneself and others'.

None of these studies was available at the time I was invited to join a team of social scientists interested in exploring European religious and moral pluralism (RAMP) in greater depth than had been possible with the European Values Surveys (with which several of them were connected). Having become familiar with unchurched seekers and New Age practitioners in my qualitative research, I was eager to include questions that would enable us to explore the distribution and content of spirituality. My suggestions were, however, met with scepticism. We were Europeans, not Americans, and almost all my colleagues were scholars who focused primarily on large-scale surveys rather than in-depth interviews or observation. They said they did not really understand what I was getting at, and that not only would our respondents have no idea what we meant if we were to ask them about spirituality, but we would have no idea what they meant if they responded to such questions. It was gently suggested that perhaps I had spent too much time talking to 'weirdoes' in California. I, on my part, wondered whether perhaps they had spent too much time sitting in front of their VDUs. Eventually, however, they agreed to include one question on spirituality, and I had to content myself with adding some of the other questions in which I was interested to the end of the British questionnaire.

The English version of the question (number 39) that was included was formulated as: '*Whether or not you think of yourself as a religious person, would you say that you have a spiritual life – something that goes beyond just an intellectual or emotional life?*' This was situated in a section with questions about subjects such as belief in God, salvation, what happens after death, membership of a faith community, and attendance at a place of worship.[4] Question 37 had asked: '*Whether or not you go to church or a place of worship, to what extent would you say that you are a religious person?*'

The RAMP Results[5]

As it turned out, both my colleagues and I had been right. They had been right in saying that the concept of spirituality had not been satisfactorily operationalised and we did not really know what it had meant to the respondents. Indeed, the question on spirituality had been translated in a slightly different way into the different languages, and even within any particular country it was clear that it had meant something different to different respondents. But I had been right in suspecting there was something out there that we needed to investigate.[6]

---

4   Question 38 concerned the extent to which religious beliefs influenced the respondents' daily life and how they made important decisions.

5   Although five more countries were involved in the creation of the questionnaire, only 11 were successful in gaining funds. The British questionnaire, which lasted just over an hour, involved a representative sample of 1466 respondents aged 18 or over.

6   Interestingly, it transpired that question 39 had not met with the mass rejection which had been predicted by some of the RAMP team. Overall, 92 per cent of the respondents were

Table 14.2   Cross tabulation of self-assessments of religiosity and spirituality (percentages)

| | | | Q39 Do you have a spiritual life? | | Total |
			No	Yes	
Q37 Do you consider yourself a religious person?	Not religious		74	26	100
			70	25	
		Total	35	12	48
	Am religious		29	71	100
			30	75	
		Total	15	37	52
Total			50	50	100
			100	100	
		Total	50	50	100

N=7,393. Due to rounding, numbers do not always add up.

The respondents were asked to indicate the extent to which they considered themselves to be religious and to have a spiritual life on a 7–point Likert scale. In Table 14.2, responses 1–3 and 5–7 have been collapsed into, respectively, 'am not religious/spiritual' and 'am religious/spiritual'. If respondents entered the neutral value of 4 in one or both of their answers, they were removed from this calculation. Of the remaining respondents, just over half (52 per cent) considered themselves religious, and exactly half (50 per cent) considered they had some sort of spiritual life. A quarter (26 per cent) of the non-religious and 71 per cent of the religious considered themselves spiritual. Had the question about spirituality not been asked, more than one in ten (12 per cent) of all these respondents – a quarter (26 per cent) of all those who denied being religious – might have been classified as secular when in fact they considered themselves spiritual. Of course, we may not know what they meant by 'spiritual', but it is doubtful that many of them would have taken it to mean secular.[7]

---

willing to answer. Respondents in Roman Catholic countries (which included two central European countries) tended to be most confused by the term, while Britons and the Dutch apparently had few problems.

7   When Marler and Hadaway (2002: 292) compared five American studies that asked about religiosity and spirituality, all of these had an even higher percentage of respondents claiming to be spiritual-but-not-religious than the percentage that emerged from the RAMP survey. This could be because: (a) the respondents were American rather than European; (b) not all the American samples were randomly selected from the population as a whole; (c) slightly different questions were asked; and/or (d) slightly different answers were open to the respondents, RAMP having offered a neutral option.

Despite the fact that it means eliminating around a third of the respondents, for the purposes of brevity and clarity, most of the following discussion will focus on the four groups of respondents who fell clearly into one of the following four categories: neither-religious-nor-spiritual ('neither'); religious-but-not-spiritual ('only-religious'); spiritual-but-not-religious ('only-spiritual'); and both-spiritual-and-religious ('both').[8]

Country

Roughly the same proportion of Belgians, Danes, Finns, Britons, Hungarians, and Dutch – but a far larger proportion of Swedes and Norwegians, a considerably lower proportion of Italians and Portuguese, and almost no Poles – fell in the 'only-spiritual' category. However, the total proportion who agreed to being spiritual ('both' *and* 'only-spiritual') was remarkably consistent between the countries. In other words, it was the extent to which they called themselves religious (with or without spirituality) that varied more dramatically (by 62 percentage points compared to a variation of 27 points for spirituality).

Sex

Although, as might be expected, there was a significant difference between the sexes when asked if they considered themselves religious (44 per cent males; 60 per cent females) or spiritual (42 per cent males; 57 per cent females), perhaps more unpredictably, there was almost no difference between males and females who considered themselves 'only-religious' (14 and 16 per cent respectively) or 'only-spiritual' (12 and 13 per cent).

Age

As can be seen from the right-hand figures in Table 14.3, the older they were, the more likely respondents were to call themselves spiritual and (to an even greater extent) religious. As many as 41 per cent of young people (but only 26 per cent of over-64s) said they were 'neither', while 28 per cent of under-25s (but 49 per cent of over-64s) claimed to be 'both'. Respondents under 25 were only marginally more likely to call themselves spiritual than religious, but there were more than twice as many under-25s as over-64s calling themselves 'only-spiritual'. A breakdown by country indicates that this was a general pattern (albeit with a few wobbles), with a

---

8   The neutral responses were included when a comparison was made between each individual's answers to see whether s/he claimed to be *equally*, *more* or *less* spiritual than religious. Although over a third (38 per cent) considered they were more religious than spiritual, nearly a third (32 per cent) considered themselves equally spiritual and religious and only slightly less (30 per cent) saw themselves as being more spiritual than religious. Curiously, in those instances when spirituality was rated more strongly than spirituality, it was probable that the ratings for both were high; but when religiosity was rated stronger, it was more likely that both scored low. Overall frequencies indicated that spirituality received a slightly more emphatic yes or no, while religion received more moderate affirmations and denials.

higher percentage of 'only-spiritual' the younger the respondent. This was especially evident among the Scandinavians, with over a third of Swedish under-25s (compared to a fifth of over-64s), and a quarter of Danish under-25s (compared to less than a tenth of over-64s) claiming to be 'only-spiritual'.[9]

In other words, while the additional use of the conception of 'spirituality' does not compensate for the drop in religiosity amongst the younger generations, when used as an *alternative* to religiosity it exposes the existence of a statistically and socially significant way of being something other than either 'religious' or secular.

Table 14.3   Age by religiosity/spirituality

	Neither religious nor spiritual (a)	Only- Religious (b)	Only- Spiritual (c)	Both religious and spiritual (d)	Total	All religious (b+d)	All spiritual (c+d)
Under 25	41	14	17	28	100	42	45
25–34	41	14	13	31	100	45	45
35–44	39	13	13	35	100	48	48
45–54	35	14	13	38	100	52	51
55–64	28	18	9	44	100	63	54
Over 64	26	17	8	49	100	66	57

N=7378

It might of course be that such patterns are related to changing age rather than any changes in society as a whole, and that we would have got similar results 50 years ago and can expect to have a similar age distribution in the mid-twenty-first century. There was, however, no evidence that the older respondents had been less religious when they were younger. An alternative possibility is that young people are not doing or believing something fundamentally different from their elders, but are merely using a different concept – spirituality – which has been popularised within youth culture. More research needs to be conducted into both these possibilities, especially in Europe.

Beliefs

Moving from the ascribed variables of sex and age to questions that could provide some clues as to what clusters of beliefs might be correlated with the different combinations of self-assessed religiosity and spirituality, a pattern emerges which clearly supports the suspicion that the conception of leading a spiritual life can mean at least two very different things to different respondents. Perhaps unexpectedly, those who reported that they were 'both' would appear to be *more* traditionally religious according to the ideal-typical model set out in Table 14.1 than 'only-religious' respondents, while those who were 'only-spiritual' were likely to be *less*

---

9   There were too few 'only-spiritual' respondents in any cohort for there to be any significant pattern among either the Portuguese or the Polish respondents.

traditionally religious than 'only-religious' (though, unsurprisingly, more religious than 'neither'). This is clearly demonstrated in Table 14.4, with respondents claiming to be 'both religious and spiritual' being considerably more likely than the 'only-religious' to favour a personal God, while for the 'only-spiritual' respondents the most popular option was the 'God within', followed by 'an impersonal spirit or life force', then not knowing what to believe, with 15 per cent not believing in any kind of God.

Table 14.4   Concepts of God: Q32 'Which of these statements comes nearest to your own belief?' (percentages)

	Neither religious nor spiritual	Religious not spiritual	Spiritual not religious	Both religious and spiritual	All
I believe in a God with whom I can have a personal relationship	7	45	9	62	33
I believe in an impersonal spirit or life force	15	14	28	11	15
I believe that God is something within each person, rather than something out there	28	37	35	26	29
I don't believe in any kind of God, spirit or life force	29	1	15	0	12
I really don't know what to believe	22	4	13	1	10
Total	100	100	100	100	100

N=7,313 (*Percentages do not always add up to 100 due to rounding.*)

Table 14.5   Life after death: Q.33 'What do you think happens to us after death?' (percentages)

	Neither	Only-Religious	Only-Spiritual	Both
Nothing – death is the end	43	17	24	8
There is something, but I don't know what	23	38	32	36
We go either to heaven or to hell	2	15	4	24
We all go to heaven	1	5	1	6
We are reincarnated – that is, after our physical death we are born in this world over and over again	3	5	12	8
We merge into some kind of eternal bliss after this life	1	4	3	8
Other	2	1	4	3
I don't know whether there is anything or not	26	15	22	8
Total	100	100	100	100

N=7,314 (*Percentages do not always add up to 100 due to rounding.*)

Similarly, Table 14.5 shows that while 'both' respondents were the most likely to believe in the possibility of going to heaven (30 per cent, compared to 20 per cent 'only-religious'), the 'only-spiritual' respondents were the most likely to opt for reincarnation (12 per cent),[10] although many more (32 per cent) chose the 'something, but don't know what' option.

The same pattern appeared with responses to questions added to the British survey as shown in Table 14.6.

Table 14.6   Religious/Spiritual percentage agreeing with statements

	Neither	Only-Religious	Only-Spiritual	Both
I believe in the power of prayer	9	60	24	77
Jesus will return to the earth some day	6	37	8	52
One can see the work of Satan, who is sometimes known as Lucifer, at work in the world today	11	33	16	50

In other words, so far as conventional Christian beliefs were concerned, respondents who said they had a spiritual life and combined it with religiosity could be mapped close to the religiosity pole of the ideal types depicted in Table 14.1, but respondents claiming to have a spiritual life while denying that they were religious would be mapped nearer the spirituality pole – and those calling themselves religious but not spiritual would be somewhere in the middle.

Principle Components from the British Data[11]

Patterns for other beliefs and practices were less easy to detect, however. Clearly the variety of different meanings and characteristics related to leading a spiritual life were not going to emerge through cross tabulation alone, so, using the extra data obtained from the British survey, which had a further 41 statements added to the end of the questionnaire, factor analysis and principle component analyses were used to probe a bit further into the variety of profiles correlated with those who felt they had some sort of spiritual life. A three-component solution offered a relatively clear summary of the patterns of correlations, albeit one explaining only just over a quarter (27 per cent) of the variance in the data. I have labeled these components (a) traditional religiosity; (b) unorthodox authoritarianism; and (c) liberal spirituality.

---

10   That this was less than half the result obtained by the European Values Survey – 24 per cent of British respondents in 1990 (Ashford and Timms 1992) – can be explained by the fact that EVS respondents could say (as many did) that they believed *both* in reincarnation and in resurrection, while RAMP respondents were asked to choose *between* reincarnation and other possibilities. (For an interesting discussion about the ways reincarnation is conceptualised in Britain, see Walter and Waterhouse 2001).

11   Further details of the analyses, including the correlations between each item and each component are available in Marinović Jerolimov 2004: 42–4.

Component 1: Traditional religiosity

The component that emerged most clearly accounts for 14 per cent of the variance. Correlating the component score with questions 37 and 39, it was found to be positively related both to religiosity (Pearson's correlation coefficient = 0.76) and to spirituality (0.50). Items with high loadings on this component indicated a strong acceptance of orthodox Christian dogma (around 70 per cent of Britons call themselves Christians of one sort or another), and the importance of religious practices. A conviction that both God and Satan are active in the world and that prayer can make a difference also loaded highly on this component, as did support for mainstream religious leadership and the belief that it should play a central role in the society as well as in individuals' lives.

Component 2: Unorthodox authoritarianism

The second component accounts for 6 per cent of the variance. There was no correlation (at the 0.05 level of significance) between this component score and either religiosity or spirituality. Mainstream religious beliefs did not load highly on this component; instead the dimension reflected a number of non-orthodox beliefs that could be described as superstitions and possibly science fiction. A generally negative reaction towards religious people and some quite strong ethnocentric, racist, and anti-minority-religion sentiments figured in this component,

Component 3: Liberal spirituality

The third component also accounts for 6 per cent of the variance. Its component score was uncorrelated with religiosity, but positively correlated with spirituality (correlation = 0.36), and it was the component that most clearly resembled the model of spirituality characterized in Table 14.1. Items with high loadings reflected unorthodox rather than traditional Scriptural beliefs, but these tended to be related to 'other worlds' and alternative perspectives rather than specific superstitions. Tolerance for minority beliefs and practices was reflected in high loadings for the relevant survey items, and statements in support of multi-culturalism also loaded relatively highly. The racist and ethnocentric attitudes found in component 2 had negative loadings in this component.

Concluding Remarks

One thing that emerges quite clearly from the RAMP and other data is that the term 'spiritual' means different things to different people, some seeing it as complementary to religiosity, others in opposition to it, and yet others understanding the two concepts as having more complicated relationships, with one encompassing or overlapping with the other. Surveys alone are not, however, a sharp enough instrument to be able to identify and disentangle these diverse conceptualisations as they exist in contemporary society.

What is evident is both that secularisation has not yet triumphed and that claims that secularisation should be reinterpreted as a uni-dimensional shift from religiosity to spirituality are not viable – there is far more than that going on. Space permitted only three components to be described in this chapter, but further manipulations of the data suggest several clues about different ways of 'constructing the sacred'. Some variations of the spirituality caricatured in Table 14.1 are certainly to be found in contemporary Europe but, in both theory and practice, it is an amorphous, rather than systematic or well-developed package – the beliefs and practices of this type by their very nature eschew both dogma and boundaries but celebrate individual choices and emphases which, at their non-extreme extreme represent a multiplicity of countless self-constructed 'Sheilaisms'.[12] Yet, at the same time, there *are* clusters of beliefs and practice that cohere together – even if they cannot yet be recognisably captured by any unambiguous label.

The exact label is not, of course, important – it is people's beliefs and practices that we want to explore. But, although qualitative research can employ other tools, language is a fundamentally important medium through which beliefs and practices are constructed and transmitted. And, just as the sociology of religion had to learn that merely asking whether our respondents believe in God does not distinguish between many different kinds of beliefs in many different conceptions of gods, so we now have to develop yet more sophisticated and sensitive tools for distinguishing between different ways of being religious and/or spiritual that may owe as much to (socially inspired) individual constructions as to institutionalised traditions.

This chapter describes an unfinished journey. But it represents one attempt to explore that aspect of the sacred – 'the relationship between conceptions of religion and spirituality' – which, as Beckford pointed out, is 'currently undergoing relocation'.

References

Anthony, D., Ecker, B. and Wilber, K. (eds) (1987) *Spiritual Choices: The Problem of Recognising Authentic Paths to Inner Transformation*, New York: Paragon.

Ashford, S. and Timms, N. (1992) *What Europe Thinks: A Study of Western European Values*, Aldershot: Dartmouth.

Barker, E. (2004) 'The Church without and the God within: religiosity and/or spirituality?' in D. Marinović Jerolimov, S. Zrinščak and I. Borowik (eds) *Religion and Patterns of Social Transformation*, Zagreb: IDIZ (Institute for Social Research in Zagreb), pp. 23–47.

Beckford, J.A. (2003) *Social Theory and Religion*, Cambridge: Cambridge University Press.

Bellah, R.N., Madsen, R., Sullivan, W.M., Swidler, A. and Tipton, S.M. (1985) *Habits of the Heart: Individualism and Commitment in American Life*, Berkeley: University of California Press.

---

12   Sheilaism is a term that owes its origin to a young nurse named Sheila Larson who described her faith as 'Sheilaism. Just my own little voice.' (Bellah *et al.* 1985: 221)

Bowman, M. (1999) 'Healing in the spiritual marketplace', *Social Compass* 46 (2): 181–90.

Crowley, V. (1998) *Principles of Jungian Spirituality*, London: Thorsons.

Davie, G. (1994) *Religion in Britain since 1945: Believing without Belonging*, Oxford: Blackwell.

Ellwood, R.S. (1994) *The Sixties Spiritual Awakening: American Religion Moving from Modern to Postmodern*. New Brunswick, NJ: Rutgers University Press.

Finke, R. and Stark, R. (1992) *The Churching of America 1776–1990: Winners and Losers in our Religious Economy*, New Brunswick, NJ: Rutgers University Press.

Fox, M. (1991) *Creation Spirituality: Liberating Peoples of the Earth*, New York: HarperCollins Publishers.

Fuller, R.C. (2001) *Spiritual but not Religious: Understanding Unchurched America*, Oxford: Oxford University Press.

Gallup, G. and Jones, T. (2000) *The Next American Spirituality: Finding God in the Twenty-First Century*, Colorado Springs: Victor (Cook Communications).

Griffin, W. (ed.) (1999) *Daughters of the Goddess: Studies of Healing and Identity in Goddess Spirituality*, New York: AltaMira.

Hanegraaff, W.J. (1999) 'New Age spiritualities as secular religion', *Social Compass* 46 (2): 145–60.

Heelas, P., Woodhead, L. *et al.* (2005) *The Spiritual Revolution: Why Religion is Giving Way to Spirituality*, Oxford: Blackwell.

Hunt, K. (2003) 'Understanding the spirituality of people who do not go to church', in G. Davie, P. Heelas and L. Woodhead (eds) *Predicting Religion: Christian, Secular and Alternative Futures,* Aldershot: Ashgate, pp. 159–69.

Lewis, I.M. (1988 [1971]) *Ecstatic Religion: A Study of Shamanism and Spirit Possession*, London: Routledge.

Marler, P.L. and Hadaway, C.K. (2002) '"Being religious" or "being spiritual" in America: a zero-sum proposition', *Journal for the Scientific Study of Religion* 41 (2): 289–300.

Nelson, G.K. (1969) *Spiritualism and Society*, London: Routledge & Kegan Paul.

Pagels, E. (1982 [1979]) *The Gnostic Gospels*, Harmondsworth: Penguin.

Pennick, N. (1997) *The Sacred World of the Celts: An Illustrated Guide to Celtic Spirituality and Mythology*, Rochester: VT.

Popper, K.R. (1963) *Conjectures and Refutations: The Growth of Scientific Knowledge*, London: Routledge & Kegan Paul.

Rajagopalachari, P. (1992) *Religion and Spirituality*, Pacific Grove, CA: Shri Ram Chandra Mission.

Roof, W.C. (1993) *A Generation of Seekers: The Spiritual Journeys of the Baby Boom Generation*, San Francisco: HarperCollins.

Roof, W.C., Carroll, J.W. and Roozen, D.A. (1995) 'Conclusion: the post-war generation – carriers of a new spirituality', in W.C. Roof, J.W. Carroll and D.A. Roozen (eds) *The Post-War Generation & Establishment Religion: Cross-Cultural Perspectives*, Boulder CO: Westview, pp. 243–55.

Sheldrake, P. (2007) *A Brief History of Spirituality*, Oxford: Blackwell.

Solomon, R.C. (2002) *Spirituality for the Skeptic: The Thoughtful Love of Life*, Oxford: Oxford University Press.

Walter, T. and Waterhouse, H. (2001) 'Lives-long learning: the effects of reincarnation belief on everyday life in Britain', *Nova Religio* 5 (1): 85–101.

Weber, M. (1949) *The Methodology of the Social Sciences*, New York: Free Press.

Wuthnow, R. (2001) *Creative Spirituality*, Berkeley: University of California Press.

Zinnbauer, B.J. and Pargament, K.I. (*et al.*) (1997) 'Religiousness and spirituality: unfuzzying the fuzzy', *Journal for the Scientific Study of Religion* 36 (4): 549–564.

CHAPTER 15

Contemporary Religions and the Public Arena:
Centring on the Situation in Japan

Susumu Shimazono

Personalized Religions and New Spirituality Movements and Culture

James Beckford is well-known in Japan for his studies on New Religious Movements (NRMs) and cult controversies. I have greatly benefited from his work on religion and post-modernity (Beckford 1984; Beckford 1992; Beckford 1996). He has also presented an important paper examining the relationship between New Social Movements (NSMs) and spirituality in the sociology of religion (Beckford 1989). His point of attention is important for this author and will have great significance for the sociology of religion in the future. Inspired by his work, this author has been examining the religious situation in industrialized countries, in Japan in particular, using the concept of "New Spirituality Movements and Culture" (NSMC) (Shimazono 1993; Shimazono 1999; Shimazono 2005). This paper will try to examine the resacralization trend in contemporary Japanese society by further elaborating the above concept.

Already in the 1960s, Thomas Luckmann discussed the emergence of new religious trends replacing organizational religions (Luckmann 1967). Luckmann considers that humans always need a comprehensive value system; in other words, they need a worldview to relate their own self to the world. Since the time of the Middle Ages, comprehensive value systems have been monopolized by specific organizational systems such as churches. However, in contemporary society, the monopoly on worldviews held by systematic religions can no longer survive. Instead, a time has come when individuals are building their own worldviews at the personal level. Luckmann names these worldviews with a strong individualistic nature as "invisible religions." He sees that, as secularization theorists have said, organized religions may seem to decline, but, in their place, personally oriented religious beliefs without organizational forms are coming to the fore.

As Luckmann predicted, new religious trends have become explicit in recent years. These trends took the shape of various movements and cultures and are often called "New Age" in the West and the "Spiritual World" in Japan, a phenomenon which, as mentioned above, the author names the New Spirituality Movements and Culture (NSMC) (Shimazono 1993; Shimazono 1999).

Many people in the NSMC see themselves as participants in this new trend in order to reform the world and bring about a greater evolution of human beings. This feature permits the NSMC to be called a "movement" in that it has a goal to achieve in the future, and that it arouses people's zeal to take action. There are, however, many participants in the NSMC who do not want to take part in joint actions. They are more interested in "changing themselves" and are not enthusiastic about joining in activities with others, or taking on positions of responsibility for their colleagues and others. Instead, many share the notion that the accumulation of transformations in individuals' consciousness will automatically lead to the reform of human consciousness as a whole. This individualistic orientation, lacking in any enthusiasm for joint action, is more appropriately seen as a new form of consumerism-like "culture", rather than a "movement." As the phenomenon basically has aspects of both "movement" and "culture", it can be most accurately perceived as being a "New Spirituality Movements and Culture".

What characterizes the NSMC both conceptually and in practice? Those who are involved in this trend are of the opinion that they are presenting a new worldview, or a new movement or culture that has overcome the defects of traditional religions and of modern science and rationalism. They consider that the dominant culture of today has been developed on the basis of traditional religions and modern science, and that it is faced with a difficult stalemate. Because of this, they are looking for alternative ways of living. This tendency suggests a special expression of consciousness transition from modern to post-modern civilization which is widely spread throughout the contemporary world. There are, of course, people who consider that the sources of their thoughts are to be found in the distant past. Even in this case, however, it is important to note that the process of historical change whereby ancient thoughts have returned to the fore with new meanings came about after the arrival of modern rationalism.

It is considered that such changes occur as individual persons go through changes in spirituality (mentality), consciousness, psychology or physique. In this sense, participants in the NSMC are aiming at "self-transformation." Their interest is directed towards gods and spiritual beings around themselves: the higher self, oversoul, qi, cosmic energy, aliens, universal consciousness and so on. Even more importantly, beside this interest in such super-ordinate dimensions, are changes that the participants in the NSMC experience in their souls, minds, consciousness or bodies. The NSMC participants exhibit a strong interest in a transcendental state of consciousness as a strong transformational experience. In order to experience such changes, various kinds of practices are adopted, including meditation, breathing methods, visualization, and body work. These practices stem from the practices of Native Americans, shamanism, tribal and folk religions of the world, and/or from those practices developed through religious or mystical traditions in India, China or Japan; alternatively, they may have been devised by adapting ideas from new forms of psychology and psychotherapy.

Individual experiences of transformation can be spiritual in nature, but they may also be little more than casual experiences occurring in one's daily life. For example, among alternative health improvement methods and psychological therapies, there are some practices which are included in those adopted by the NSMC. Many people learn to practice yoga or qigong just for their health. Some people accept a therapy based on Jungian psychology purely as a means of treating neurosis. There are, on the other hand, people who find deep spiritual or ideological meanings in such practices and thoughts. And there is a wide range of people between the two polar positions. It can be seen that this variety indicates differences in the degree of influence exerted by the NSMC.

A similar thing can be said of contemporary mass culture or amusement culture. Subjects sympathetic to the NSMC abound in movies, videos, comics, science fictions, and video games. Magazines featuring occult and fortune telling, and New Age music also share much with the NSMC. These media are not tools intended to propagate the movements and culture, but they do serve to cultivate the ground to attract people to the movements and the culture. Just as a folk culture of worshipping saints has provided a basis for the Catholic churches, popular health and therapy cultures and the magico-religious popular culture can be seen as offering a foundation for the New Spiritual Movements and Culture.

This phenomenon has developed while being closely linked with the globalization processes of the contemporary world, particularly new communication methods promoted by the progress of the communication media. People involved in the NSMC obtain necessary information from their personal living quarters through books, images and sounds reproduced from various devices such as recorded tapes, broadcast, or telephones without taking part in group life or having any direct person-to-person contact. When they are asked to take part in a gathering, lecture course, workshop and so on, an emphasis is placed on individual practices rather than group practices. Except for the small number of people who are living off propagating knowledge and practices, the majority of participants do not consider that they belong to any particular organizations or religious bodies; they are, rather, individually obtaining information as an "audience" or "client" (Stark and Bainbridge 1985). It is common for such participants to see the NSMC taking the form of a "loose network."

Information and culture are rapidly disseminated throughout the globe by means of a wide variety of media. National and local cultures are in some senses firmly maintained, but they are often mixed on the global scene. A certain kind of culture or information spreads across the borders in a short period of time. The NSMC can be understood as part of a new global information and culture. Often the sources of information and culture and the areas accepting them can be distinguished. Needless to say, the United States is extremely important as a source in the case of the NSMC. Europe, Japan and India are producing and transmitting information and culture of this kind to a certain extent. In the future, China will grow to be a large source of information and culture. In this sense, the NSMC is a global phenomenon and at the same time, a multifaceted phenomenon with multiple centres.

Rooted in the nature of this phenomenon, there are close interrelations between being individualistic, and being global, multi-centred and multifaceted. Except for a small number of leaders and people interested in management, individuals have multiple connections with information and cultural resources that are globally spread, but are not in any exclusive relationship with a particular system of discourse or doctrine, rituals or community. Here lies a difference from traditional religions, which have been supported by the clergy and the group of intellectuals who maintain the systematized discourse on one hand, and by the community of followers on the other hand. Because of the social structure of this cultural transmission, it is justifiable for participants to say that the NSMC is not a religion.

If the definition of religion is expanded, the phenomenon could be considered to be a religion. But it is not at all groundless for participants not to consider their NSMC to be a "religion". Considering that many participants understand their activities in relation to their own identity not as "religious" but as "spiritual" activities, it is appropriate to call the phenomenon the NSMC, while incorporating emic elements. These movements and culture appear to be phenomena coinciding with the tendency of personalization of religions and with the withdrawal of religions from the public arena. However, a closer examination will prove that there are complicated relations between the NSMC and the public arena. In the following section, the present status of religions will be reviewed from a viewpoint of the position of religiosity in the public arena. By so doing, a clue for explaining the entangled relations between the NSMC and the public arena can be found.

Re-sacralization in Various Institutional Spheres

We can observe the changes that occurred from traditional religions to New Religions, and from New Religions to the NSMC from both the perspective of the transformation in institutionalized religions, and that of the religious commitment of the individual. Within these trends, changes in religions from community participation to individual participation can be found. When looking at these trends in isolation, the secularization and privatization of religions are both conspicuous.

However another process must be examined in parallel. That is a tendency whereby various institutions that are deemed to consist of secular principles are, in fact, incorporating religious elements. This trend has occurred because the assumptions of modern liberalism and rationalism could no longer be sustained, and instead, concepts and practices containing religious assumptions came to be introduced or recognized in these institutions. In such cases, religious elements were supplied from both traditional religions and the NSMC. In traditional religions in Japan, Shinto nationalist elements are more important than elements from other religious organizations. This trend can be understood as the re-sacralization of social spheres in which secularization would have seemed to have prevailed, or as a phenomenon occurring in the social sector and problem areas in which secularization has hardly developed (for Europe and America, see Casanova 1994). In what follows, it will be mainly a number of tendencies in Japan that will be examined.

Medical Services

In the process of modernization, great trust was placed in scientific rationality. The human body was reduced to mechanical parts, and an emphasis was given to understanding the functions of various organs and body tissues. It has been assumed that impaired physical functions can be recovered by medical instruments and skills, and that human health can be maintained and improved. On the basis of the self-evident power of modern scientific technology, the modern medical care system has been developed with biological science and hospitals as its major pillars and has achieved great results. The hospital has been a part of the realm of secularism. However, frustration is mounting against modern medical care. Is not modern medicine treating humans as objects? It is endeavoring to separate humans from nature, human emotions from the body, divide the body into parts, and to control them using cold, systematized knowledge. Even at scenes of psychiatric care, any truly human interaction between doctors and patients is lacking.

For people dying in a hospital and their families, their deaths are treated too clinically, without giving consideration to meaning and emotional factors. There is an increasing demand for intelligence and sensibility to nurture and to cherish life rather than the cold rationalism of modern science. Can a tender intelligence and sensibility exist without spirituality? At present, approaches to bring healing effects are in great demand. Although people expect the existing religious groups to meet their demand, they expect to receive a greater healing effect from the traditions of animism and mysticism which have been carried over in an unorganized manner. Originally, traditional medicine and alternative medicine could not be separated from religions and spirituality. Modern medicine may take a partial step toward re-sacralization.

Nursing Care, Welfare Services and Therapies

The concept of a welfare state whereby the burdens of nursing care and welfare services are entrusted to the government is retreating. Nursing care and welfare services covered by public funds may be increasingly reduced. Then, of those people in need of care, by whom and how will they be taken care? And with what motivation do caregivers give their services? Whether they are family members or volunteers, it is not only a utilitarian motivation that supports "love" and a sense of "duty." Even if they say, "I am doing this for myself," they may be feeling a link with something beyond themselves; with, for example, "spirit", "cosmic energy" or the "source of life." "Mental care" is often called for today. This is because interaction among people in the hope of "healing" each other is needed. It is often understood as an attempt to achieve self-realization through the work of something beyond oneself. Transpersonal psychology is meant to provide this kind of mental care. In Japan in the past, people took care of parents and family members as a matter of course. This was because people felt their ties to the souls of ancestors and the family, and because filial piety towards parents was considered to be a holy duty. Today, when the "secular morality" that once was widely spread is feeble, what motivates people to extend care and help? It may be natural that religious motivations are involved.

Education

The education system in Japan after World War II was reorganized on the principle of secularism by repealing the Imperial Rescript on Education and excluding State Shinto. However, the same controversies have occurred, repeatedly questioning whether an educational system based on secularism is satisfactory or not. Skeptical voices will rise. What should moral education be based on? It is not recommendable to teach a specific value system to children, but it is not enough either to teach them by just putting together fragmented knowledge and lessons. Is it not necessary to teach about religions which have played very important roles as the basis of morality throughout history? There are countries in which religions are taught in public schools. The demand for religious education and/or education on religions is mounting in France and the United States, both of which were models for Japan's postwar educational system. In the United States, there is a tendency among parents to start home schooling or to enroll their children in private schools because the public schools do not give religious education. There is also a tendency to provide character building education as an alternative to the present content-intensive school curriculum. Examples are the Steiner School movement and holistic education or death education (named life and death education in Japan). These are supported to some extent by the spiritual consciousness of the "transcendental" dimension.

The social services mentioned above are sometimes provided by public institutions, or when private institutions provide these kinds of services, they often require public support. In these service sectors, a tendency towards re-sacralization can be observed – or at least a tendency to accept something sacred or transcendental as being unavoidable can be seen. Religious discourses, vocabularies and motivations are making inroads into public institutions through medical care, nursing care, welfare services, therapies, and education. In cases where they have already set in, they are unlikely to be reversed; rather, it appears that they will be expanded further.

Ethical Consensus and Negotiation

Deliberations over the appropriateness of organ transplants from brain-dead donors became active in Japan through the 1980s. The major questions were how agreement can be ethically obtained, and how safety can be ensured in applying advanced scientific technology to the manipulation of life. The problem was not limited to organ transplant operations; in the late 1990s, problems arising from cloning technology had to be addressed, leading to the drafting of a Bill to prohibit cloning a human being. Behind the cloning problem, there are various ethical problems involved with human reproductive technology and human genome analysis. Further, there are controversies over genetically modified food and other kinds of life-manipulation.

In an effort to obtain public acceptance for bio-ethics and environmental ethics concerning medicine and food caused by the advancement of industries and scientific technologies, referral to religious discourses cannot be avoided. In western countries, the issue of induced abortions continues to remain the major focus of formal involvement by religious organizations. In Japan, the relations between animistic religious sentiments and the concept of brain death have been discussed, and many religious organizations and religious leaders have expressed their reluctance to consider brain death as human death. Their view has exerted a significant influence on public opinion. Among ecological oppositions against environmental destruction, religious and spiritual considerations are frequently included, as typically shown by the spiritual environmentalists or "Deep Ecology" proponents. Public debates in which religious interests occupy an important position concerning scientific and technological development and economic growth can be expected to increase in the future.

National Rituals

In the 1980s in Japan, there were heated discussions over whether the conduct of the Great Thanksgiving Festival after the enthronement of the present Emperor, and the funerals of the late emperor and other Imperial Family members in the Shinto tradition, were contrary to the present Constitution, which stipulates that there should be a separation between politics and religions. Discussions have been continuing for a longer period over how to console the souls of people who died "for the sake of the state" in modern wars, and how the state should involve itself in this. Oppositions to the state's involvement by conducting the Great Thanksgiving Festival and enshrining the deceased soldiers in Yasukuni Shrine are based on the Constitution, or derive from apprehension about the revival of State Shinto and militarism. However, there are also people who accept religiously oriented rituals as state rituals by quoting examples from practices in other countries and referring to the "Japanese tradition". Considering that the Emperor conducts many Shinto rituals in the Palace while being the symbol of the nation, it is not altogether evident that State Shinto has been totally abolished. Moreover, the ideology of "national polity" may still be active. For example, the words of the national anthem contain Shinto elements. There was an objection to holding the funeral of the late Princess Diana totally in the Christian style in Britain. In many countries, the official position of religions can become a focus of controversy in relation to conducting state rituals. In Japan, the issue has become a greater political issue than in other countries, and is likely to remain an important factor leading to political tension.

Religious System

Many issues have emerged over the relationship between politics and religions, and freedom of belief. It was assumed that these problems would be solved with the principles of a modern state. However, it has proved to be difficult to reach an agreement on what is the basis of criteria for a modern understanding of politics and religion, and on ways to apply such criteria. Just by listing problems around the religious system in recent years, it is understood that a number of problems covering a wide range of issues have been raised. They include: how can an organization be identified as a religious organization? Is it desirable to give preferential taxation status to religious organizations? Is it right to subsidize private schools and hospitals run by religious organizations? To what extent can the state exert influence on religious organizations through the granting of preferential tax treatment? How can religious organizations be dealt with when they have committed crimes? To what extent can political commitment by a religious organization be acceptable? Is it not violating freedom of belief for corporations to impose certain religious practices on their employees? To what extent can religious rituals conducted by local governments be acceptable?

As illustrated by the lawsuit brought by the Christian wife of a deceased Christian Self-Defense Force serviceman objecting to his enshrinement in Yasukuni Shrine, these problems are related to the problems that surround state rituals. Government subsidies and other commitments have been offered to specific religious organizations. Admitting this fact, it should be examined how far these practices can be accepted. There will be increasing opportunities for confrontation if different demands from religious and secular organizations with different interests are presented for discussions. The question of the status of religious organizations, and freedom of belief, are questions of public significance with religious implications.

Re-sacralization and Change in Awareness

The above mentioned social issues or problem areas are realms in which religious factors are involved in public arenas. With the process of globalization, people have become more conscious about their own country by comparing it with other countries, and are becoming more aware of the characteristics of the systems of their own country. At the same time, they have come to question what had been accepted as a national consensus, and an age has begun in which public opinion is becoming increasingly diversified and conflicts between and among the various positions are becoming more apparent. What had been accepted as a national consensus was largely dependent on the self-evident fact of being a nation state and a generally accepted secularism. A secular nationalism shared by the nation over and beyond political positions made conflicting viewpoints and points of disagreement between different religious groups inconspicuous. In Japan, freedom of belief and the separation of government and religion provided for in the Constitution were believed to lay a solid foundation for unity. The dominant concept in people's minds was that "religions" would remain active within a certain private domain without intruding into the public arena.

However, after the 1980s, the sense of a clear-cut boundary between the secular and the religious became blurred. In many areas in which every problem seemed to be solvable by secular principles, people have come to consider religious intervention to be unavoidable. People have become aware of the existing religious involvement in the public arena, and, at the same time, they have become less opposed to the need for avoiding religious involvement. The potentiality of re-sacralization at the institutional level, or, at least, the probability that this matter will become a point for argument has been increased.

It will require further in-depth research to clarify the extent of the influence of institutional sacralization and an expanded religious involvement in the public arena on the changes occurring in the consciousness of individual Japanese. Even so, some general observations may be made by examining trends in the discourses of religious groups and other ideological debates. From the author's observations, the following two points are noted.

First, religious elements are gaining strength in the nationalistic consciousness of the Japanese (Shimazono 1997). It was in the late 1980s that references were actively made to animism and Jomon culture in what has been termed Theories on the Japanese or Japanese Culture (Shimazono 1995). While containing ecological consciousness, scholars and popular writers have expressed their views that the religious and spiritual tradition of Japan would make a positive contribution to the human civilization of the future. Following the mid-1990s, optimistic views about the future perspective of humans based on animism and ecology diminished, influenced by the Great Hanshin Awaji Earthquake, the Aum Shinrikyo incidents and the economic setback. Instead, the focus of public opinion appeared to turn to modern history and the value of the state. One example is the "Liberalist Historic View" urged by nationalist scholars and writers that drew great public attention. Instead of self-sufficiency supported by affluence, people's interests seem to be directed to more serious struggles over political power relations in the process of globalization. Even so, the explosive hit of an animated film "Princess Mononoke" dealing with animism, released in 1997, suggests that nationalism with religious implications has a strong appeal for contemporary Japanese individuals.

Secondly, the needs for religious elements are increasingly considered important among professionals in certain social realms. Concern for "healing" was already apparent in the 1980s. In the beginning, it was based on the interest of individuals as consumers, but, in the 1990s, the concern for healing permeated into institutional realms. There are increasing numbers of people engaged in the fields of medicine, nursing care, welfare, education and so on who are consciously pursuing "healing" and spirituality. It was during the 1990s that there was an increase in the number of academic societies and conferences concerned with transpersonal psychology, Jungian psychology, holistic medicine and alternative medicine with the support of many teaching professionals who were pursuing spirituality besides teaching in schools. Opportunities to receive religious or spiritual training have increased both in public institutions and private institutions with high social recognition. At the same time, cases of practising care with spiritual elements at the actual sites of service provision are also increasing. In the field of art, an interest in spirituality has become more conspicuous.

Provided that the above observations are correct, it is predicted that religions in a broad sense will occupy an important position in the public arena in Japan in the 21st century. Religious influences on at least some aspects of the daily life of individuals will become stronger. This may seem contradictory to the trends of secularization and privatization that were described at the beginning of this chapter.

In fact, however, there is no contradiction. First, what appear to be the processes of secularization and privatization can be seen to include a transition of the locations of religious elements. In place of a communal religious orientation tied to kinship and a neighborhood community, individual religious orientations are spread through the individuals obtaining knowledge through the various information media in order to cultivate themselves. This process has not exerted influence merely on individuals, but has also been significantly related to the rise in religious interest in the medical and educational systems. As typically shown in the NSMC, there might have been some public elements contained in apparently personal religious orientations.

Secondly, it can be said that there was a transition from a period in which secularism and privatization were dominant to one in which re-sacralization has been prominent. It may be correct to see this shift as occurring in a wider area of the world since the 1960s, when high expectations, led by the advancement of scientific technology, were placed on the progress of society. In the post-1970s, skeptical views of the dominance of modern rationalism or the concept of a nation state became prevalent. This should be examined in comparison with the phenomenon called the expansion of fundamentalism (Kepel 1991; Marty and Appleby 1991; Ruthven 2004). As a matter of fact, phenomena in the United States, the Islamic countries, and India are often considered in this context. The author considers that this transition has also occurred in regions where so-called fundamentalism is not so much noticed, such as Europe, Southeast Asia and East Asia, and, certainly, Japan (Shimazono 2004).

Becoming aware of religious (and/or spiritual) aspects in the public arena, and the development of dialogue between people of different religious orientations, and between the religious and the non-religious, will become an unavoidable issue in the world of the 21st century. The importance of listening to voices that are religious (in a broad sense) in the public arena alongside other, different voices should be much more widely recognized in the sociology of religion of the future.

References

Beckford, J. (1984) 'Holistic Imagery and Ethics in New Religious and Healing Movements', *Social Compass*, 31, 2–3): 259–72.

—— (1989) *Religion and Advanced Industrial Society*, London: Unwin Hyman.

—— (1992) 'Religion, Modernity and Post-modernity', in B. Wilson (ed.) *Religion: Contemporary Issues*, London: Bellew.

—— (1996) 'Postmodernity, High Modernity and New Modernity: Three Concepts in Search of Religion', in K. Flanagan (ed.) *Postmodernity, Sociology and Religion*, London: Macmillan.

Casanova, J. (1994) *Public Religions in the Modern World*, Chicago: The University of Chicago Press.

Heelas, P. (1996) *The New Age Movement*, Oxford: Blackwell.

Heelas, P. (ed.) (1998) *Religion, Modernity and Postmodernity*, Oxford: Blackwell.

Ikado, F. (1972) *Sezoku Shakai no Shukyo (Religions in the Secular Society)*, United Church of Christ in Japan Press.

Kepel, G. (1991) *La Revanche de Dieu: Chrétiens, juifs et musulmans à la reconquête du monde*, Paris: Editions du Seuil.

Luckmann, T. (1967) *The Invisible Religion: The Problem of Religion in Modern Society*, New York: Macmillan.

Marty, M.E. and Scott Appleby, R. (eds) (1991) *Fundamentalisms Observed*, Chicago: The University of Chicago Press.

Melton, J.G. (1990) *New Age Encyclopedia*, Detroit: Gale Research.

Ruthven, M. (2004) *Fundamentalism: The Search for Meaning*, Oxford University Press.

Shimazono S. (1993) 'New Age and New Spiritual Movements: The Role of Spiritual Intellectuals', *SYZYGY: Journal of Alternative Religion and Culture*, 2, 1–2, Winter/Spring 1993: 9–22.

—— (1995) 'Theories on the Japanese and Religions', *Tokyo University Annual Report on Religious Studies* 13: 1–16.

—— (1997) 'Secularism and Nationalism in Contemporary Japan', in Nakano, T., Iida T., Yamanaka, H., (eds) *Shukyo to Nationalism*, Sekaishso-sha, pp. 217–35.

—— (1999) '"New Age Movement" or "New Spirituality Movements and Culture"', *Social Compass*, 46, 2: 121–33.

—— (2004) 'Individualization of Society and Spiritualization of Individuals: Resacralization in the Second Modernity or Post-modernity', *Sociological Review (Shakaigaku Hyoron)*, 54, 4: 431–48.

—— (2005) *From Salvation to Spirituality*, Trans Pacific Press.

Stark, R. and Bainbridge, W.S. (eds) (1985) *The Future of Religion: Secularization, Revival and Cult Formation*, Berkeley: University of California Press.

Wilson, B. (1966) *Religion in Secular Society: A Sociological Comment*, Harmondsworth: Penguin Books.

York, M. (1995) *The Emerging Network: A Sociology of the New Age and Neo-Pagan Movements*, Lanham, Maryland: Rowman & Littlefield.

CHAPTER 16

Toward a Sociology of Spirituality:
Individual Religion in Social/Historical Context[1]

Meredith B. McGuire

Most people probably presume that 'spirituality' refers only to the private aspect of religion. One point of this essay, however, is that a sociological analysis of what I am calling 'spirituality' reveals important features of *both the private and the public aspects* of religion in a modern society. How people attend to the spiritual, in a given historical and societal context, tells us much about the larger society in which those spiritualities are practiced. Sociology can better understand the linkages between the individual and society by carefully analyzing how individuals make sense of their social worlds and act accordingly.

Specifically, I propose that our field needs to give attention – much more carefully researched and analytically precise attention – to the personal beliefs and practices by which individual spiritual lives are shaped and transformed, expressed and experienced, over time. In some respects, this task is merely an extension of Weber's mandate – to try to understand the subjective meanings of social action. In other respects, however, it is a corrective to sociology's long history of an overly institutional conception of religion at the level of the individual.

Spirituality, as I am trying to focus the concept, is *not* a new or peculiarly modern (much less 'post-modern') phenomenon. It is merely a way of conceptualizing individual involvement in religion that allows for the considerable diversity of meanings and ritual practices which ordinary people use in their everyday lives. Spirituality can refer to the important qualitative differences in religion-as-lived among people who are officially of the same institutional religion, perhaps even the same congregation. If we want to understand how individual religion in Europe or the Americas today compares to that of earlier centuries, we should not speak of *'levels'* of people's religiosity, but rather we should try to discern changes (and continuities) in the qualitative *patterns* of individuals' religion.

We cannot compare quantifiable levels of spirituality, individually or collectively. For instance, we cannot measure whether people in the 1950s were more 'spiritual' than in the 1990s. We can try to describe and compare patterns of individual religion. These patterns are highly relevant to sociology's larger theoretical questions about the location and influence of religion in modernity.

1   The first version of this essay was presented at the Nordic Sociology of Religion conference, Oslo, Norway, July, 2000. A slightly shorter version was published as McGuire (2000). Reprinted by permission. The author thanks Jim Spickard and Janaki Spickard-Keeler for their help in polishing the manuscript.

My current research aims to historicize the discussion of spirituality. I ask, for instance: How are the patterns of spirituality in the USA or Europe different – different from each other and different compared to 100, 300, or 700 years ago? If the sociology of religion could get beyond its conceptual limitations – especially those inherited from Protestant, European, and male images of individual religiosity – perhaps we would discover that religion-as-lived has much less of a public-private split than we previously assumed.

I build upon Thomas Luckmann's theoretical contributions to rethinking individual patterns of belief and practice in modern societies. Already in the 1960s, Luckmann was noticing the 'supermarket' of diverse spiritual alternatives and what seemed to be a peculiarly modern pattern of bricolage of personal meaning systems (1967). In the 1970s, Luckmann offered trenchant critiques of the methodological use of institutionally defined 'religiosity' as a way of tapping individual belief and practice in modern societies (1973). And at the end of the 1980s, he was suggesting that our interpretation of late modernity needed closer attention to the level of individuals' religion, where – rather than disappearing or waning – religion may actually be expanding. According to Luckmann, in the meaning systems prevalent in late modernity, it is not religion that is shrinking, but rather what is shrinking is the scope of the transcendent, especially the transcendent of official religions' meta-narratives (1990).

Although I build upon Luckmann's (and to a lesser extent, Berger's) analyses for my own approach, I find their conceptualization of the individual's religion to be far too cognitive. Even Luckmann's broad conceptual approach to religion is too focused on meaning systems as ways of thinking about the world. To grasp the individual's religion, we need to be able to take into account, not just symbols and cognitive frameworks, but also individual emotions, embodiment and experience. The individual's religion encompasses not just how a person views his or her world, but also how the individual literally experiences and acts upon that world. Thus, different spiritualities imply different approaches to human agency.

'Spiritual, not Religious'

Nearly two decades ago, in my study of non-medical healing (McGuire 1988), I interviewed one man who said: 'I'm probably not very religious, but I consider myself a deeply spiritual person.' I had no trouble understanding the second part of that statement since, already in the interview, he had described some of the spiritual practices he observed with considerable discipline as part of his participation in healing. He spent several evenings a week in healing practices, utilizing Buddhist meditation and the practice of Tai Chi as part of his personal spiritual work, as well as a variety of Eastern-inspired and New Age healing approaches in his work as a psychotherapist. But I was startled at his statement that he was not very religious, because I also knew that he was a fairly active member of the Methodist church and an ordained clergyman. This experience illustrates both the relevance of examining contemporary spirituality and the difficulties of operationalizing the key concepts.

On one hand, this appears to be a peculiarly modern phenomenon. Here was an active, committed member of one religion who combines elements of numerous other religions borrowed from distant cultural traditions. Here was an educated professional whose religious life includes an eclectic array of body rituals and practices that appear to be irrational. The very notion of being 'spiritual-but-not-religious', likewise, seems as though it could happen only in a modern, complex society. For example, it is hard to imagine that a sixteenth century miller, appearing before a court of the Inquisition, would explain his individual religion as 'spiritual, but not very religious'.[2] Before the early modern period, this distinction probably made no sense in people's ways of thinking about individual religion.

On the other hand, perhaps we are mistaken in our expectation of cognitive consistency between individuals' religion, as institutionally framed, and their actual, lived religion. It may only be intellectuals who care about rational coherence in religion ways of thinking, perceiving, and acting. In a forty-year career of interviewing people about their individual religion, I have the impression that only a small and unrepresentative proportion struggle to achieve tight consistency among their wide-ranging beliefs, perceptions, experiences, values, practices, and actions. For example, one nurse, who was head of a paediatric unit at the most prestigious hospital in the area, used a kind of symbolic magic in her private healing efforts. After working personally with someone needing healing, she would offer them a piece of blessed cloth to use at home when they did their healing visualizations in private. While telling me that the cloth had to be cotton or some other natural fibre (and not a polyester blend), she became a little embarrassed about the apparent irrationality of her practice. So she added, 'I know, it sounds weird, but it works – and it works better with cotton – and that's what matters'.

The apparent disintegration of what Luckmann calls the 'great transcendences' may have had an impact mainly on the individual religions of those who expect those great transcendences to order, with consistency and unity, their personal experiences of transcendence. But there may have been, all along, a disjuncture for the vast majority of believers. For the rest, perhaps, the 'centre' never did hold.

Rhetorics of Spirituality

A few years after my study on healing was published, I urged Clark Roof to go beyond his 'Baby Boomer' survey, to actually interview respondents about their spiritual lives. He, too, subsequently discovered that a sizeable proportion responded that they considered themselves to be 'spiritual, but not religious' (and Roof categorizes these as 'spiritual seekers'). At the same time, a large proportion self-identified as both religious and spiritual (Roof subdivides this category into 'mainstream believers'

---

2   Inquisition records, meticulously transcribed, have been an interesting source for historiographers who try to 'capture' the quality of early modern individual religion. Since the Inquisition itself was part of the period's boundary-setting processes, the interactions between inquisitors and ordinary people are particularly instructive. See especially Ginzburg (1983); Tedeschi (1991). See also, Martin (1987; 1993).

and 'Born-again Christians').[3] Roof bases his 'map' of individual religion on the finding that people (or, at least his post-World War II generation, American sample) describe their personal religious identities in terms of inner experience and/or outer institutional framework.

He interprets these patterns as reflecting American culture and character. The USA, according to Roof, epitomizes a 'Quest Culture', a marketplace of religious and spiritual commodities, and societal values of flexibility, pragmatism, and individual freedom of choice. Unfortunately, Roof's interpretation is too historically and culturally narrow to be readily applicable outside the United States (unless we posit that consuming American films and pop music and ingesting McDonald's burgers have inevitably doomed Europe and the rest of the world to follow the same cultural path as the USA).

Roof operationalizes 'spirituality' in terms of interviewees' self-identification (although respondents did not necessarily use the term 'spiritual'). Generally, they considered themselves 'spiritual' when they identified with the experiential aspects of religion. They considered themselves 'not religious' when they rejected church-delineated beliefs and practices as norms for their individual religious life. Roof makes a crucial mistake, however, by uncritically accepting this self-identification of spirituality and religiosity as the basis for his sociological interpretation. He fails to distinguish the rhetoric and ideological uses of the term 'spirituality' from the empirical and analytic referents.

It *is* noteworthy that, in late modernity, a considerable number of people choose a rhetoric of spirituality. Those claiming 'the spiritual' for their own religious life, in contrast to 'religious' (attributed to others) are, indeed, telling us something. But they are telling us more about the *ideological valence* of the terms 'spirituality' and 'religiosity' than they are about their specific spiritual practices and experiences.

I suggest three interpretations of the contemporary rhetoric of spirituality.

First, it reflects an advanced stage of official religions' loss of cultural dominance. Whereas nineteenth century rhetorics may have existed as ideological tools to distinguish the individual practices for being Catholic from those for being Protestant or Jew, only the adamant secularists ideologically distinguished themselves from official religion and religiosity. In the United States, there were numerous nineteenth century movements (such as the various Metaphysical churches, nature religions, and mystical sects) comparable to today's 'spirituality' movements, but they used the rhetoric of religion for the sake of *cultural legitimacy*. The contemporary rhetoric of spirituality, by contrast, claims a legitimacy superior to religion by alluding to the personal depth and moral uprightness that being spiritual implies, but without the restrictive or superficial boundaries imposed by official religions.

Second, the contemporary rhetoric of spirituality reflects the extremes of privatization of individuals' religion in the context of advanced pluralism. One observer notes that contemporary claims to spirituality have an 'imagined ontological referent that remains unspecified, because people do not want to be limited to anything

---

3   Roof's four-fold typology also includes 'religious, but not spiritual' (characterizing fundamentalists and other dogmatic traditionalists), and 'not religious, not spiritual' (a residual category of secularists) (Roof 1999).

specific; so they agree not to talk about their spiritual lives in detail'.[4] There is some truth to this interpretation, for some contemporary rhetorical uses of spirituality, because the 'imagined ontological referent' must substitute for the authority which former patterns of spirituality imputed to tradition. Thus, this interpretation likens spirituality to ethnicity and nationality, which also premise a sense of commonality upon an imagined linguo-genetic origin (Anderson 1993).

But there are other reasons why people might agree not to talk about the core referent of the concept. One reason is an avoidance of judging another's spiritual practices, given an ideological commitment to pluralism. When people decide not to rely on an overarching institutional authority to distinguish 'true' from 'false' spiritualities, their pluralistic tolerance is enhanced by agreeing not to talk about specificities. For example, one local Episcopalian congregation achieved considerable spiritual vitality by encouraging, in small group settings, a wide range of options as diverse as 12–step, Taize, and so-called 'Celtic' spiritualities, while tacitly agreeing not to make comparisons or note inconsistencies among them (Spickard 1996). Spirituality, in the abstract, was a congregational ideal. In its specifics, it could become divisive, so peace was made possible by avoiding comparisons.

Another reason for not specifying the referent of spirituality involves sub-cultural norms of privacy. For example, a researcher who interviewed members of a Presbyterian women's Bible study group found that all the women strongly valued the group's mutual support of their individual spirituality. These women had seriously pursued spiritual practices, and most of them described to the researcher profound and often mystical experiences. However, in their years of meeting each week, none had shared with other members any specific mention of their personal spiritual experiences. They all cared a lot about their individual spiritual lives, but middle-class (and Presbyterian) norms of propriety prevented them from talking about the specifics (Davie 1995a and 1995b).

Third, some rhetorical uses of spirituality are devices for creating and symbolizing social-class distinction. Accordingly, the individual spiritual lives of the elite are labelled 'spirituality' and, thus, desirable. The spiritual lives of non-elite persons are rhetorically denigrated as 'superstition', 'magic', 'hysterical emotionality', 'ritualistic' or 'superficial religiosity'. Several historians have noted that, in early modern times, both the Protestant and Catholic Reformations produced rhetorics of religiosity that similarly distinguished the emerging elites from non-elites. Popular religion was actively suppressed and denigrated as 'magic', 'emotional', 'orgiastic', 'impure' and 'improper'. Upper-class and aspiring middle-class religiosity was valorised as 'proper', 'sober' and 'upright'.[5]

Sociologists need to be alert to such ideological uses of self-identification as 'spiritual'. Rather than accept the rhetoric of spirituality uncritically, we need to ask: What does it mean, for our understanding of a thoroughly modern, rationalized, and

---

4   James Spickard, personal communication.

5   See Burke (1978) and Connolly (1982). Connolly's study is especially interesting, because he shows that both Catholic and Protestant clergy were battling to suppress Irish popular religious practices, and that their objections were not theological but about issues of propriety, sobriety, and civil obedience.

institutionally differentiated society, such as the USA, that the quality of spirituality can be claimed as a basis of elite distinction?

Historicizing the Sociology of Religion and Spirituality

Drawing boundaries is a concrete political and historical process. Definitional boundaries are the outcomes of *contested meanings*. In this case, definitions represent boundaries around what is to be considered 'properly religious', or what is considered valid individual 'spiritual' practices or experiences. For Europe and the Americas, the entire Reformation period – comprising a series of both Protestant and Catholic reforms – illustrates the uses of *power* in changing the definitional boundaries of acceptable Christian belief and practice.

Unfortunately, since its nineteenth century foundations, sociology has uncritically accepted many of the resulting boundaries as definitive of institutional and individual religion. Historians have shown that late medieval definitions of religion privileged *practice* (such as participating in calendric rituals), which involved bodies and emotions in individual religious experience and expression. By contrast, the religious reformations of early modern times were aimed at controlling practices, while privileging *belief* (such as the rejection of heresy or preaching based on Biblical exegesis).[6] Sociology of religion – especially in the USA, but also in Europe – has focused its analysis of individual religion almost exclusively on religious beliefs and values. We have not paid enough attention to emotions, rituals, body practices, and religious experience.

We have mistakenly defined individual religiosity in terms of church (or parallel organizational) affiliation and participation. Sociology's reliance on overly institutional definitions of individual religion has, thus, resulted in discounting much of women's religious practice, which has historically been in the context of domestic ritual. An observant Orthodox Jewish male's individual practice of his religion would 'count' as 'religious', because it involves, for example, participating in synagogue rituals or studying and discussing scripture with other men at the synagogue school. His wife's individual religion is less likely to be considered 'religious' because it is not easily differentiated from other domestic activities. When is preparing a kosher meal or baking the Sabbath loaf a personally meaningful religious practice, and when is it just 'cooking'?

Similarly, overly institutional conceptions of individual religion discount the many popular religious expressions – especially those of ethnic minorities whose cultural patterns of religiosity are not welcomed in official religions. For example, would the Cuban-American who practices Santería to get a job or be healed of alcoholism register as 'religious' on our sociological measures? Another example: the spirituality involved in a twenty-first century Mexican-American woman's decoration of the home altar and family graves for the El Día de los Muertos (the

---

6   See Muir (1997). Note, however, that sociology's historical basis is limited to Western Christianity. Eastern (Orthodox) Christianity has continued, to this day, its emphasis on religious *practice*, rather than belief, and has continued to comfortably encompass popular religion. See Dubisch (1990) and Kokosalakis (1987).

Day of the Dead) celebration in San Antonio, Texas, tells us more about the vitality of her individual religion than any standard measure of her frequency of church attendance, Bible reading, prayers, or reception of Communion.

It is precisely these defined-out characteristics of religious practice and experience that a sociology of spirituality must analyze. Some features of their spirituality described by middle-class respondents in my researches and others' include: holism, autonomy, eclecticism, tolerance, this-worldly activism and pragmatism, appreciation of materiality, and blurring of boundaries between sacred and profane. The parallels between these characteristics of contemporary spiritualities and the characteristics of popular religion – contemporary, as well as pre-modern – are remarkable.

Parallels: Then and Now

Developing patterns suggest some links between public religion and private religion. Luckmann argues that, as social differentiation at the public level becomes greater and more complex, it becomes increasingly difficult to 'maintain the social universality' of a particular religious worldview at the private or individual level. Accordingly, even as the scope of these particular transcendent worldviews shrinks, religion may expand in a florescence of diversity of individual religious options or intensity of individual religious experience (Luckmann 1990: 132). Indeed, these same processes make it now possible to see the religious diversity that actually existed in the past, unacknowledged or even suppressed.[7]

There was enormous diversity in pre-modern spiritual practice, experience and expression. Only a grossly over-simplified reading of European history could conclude – as Stark and Iannaccone (1994) have done – that medieval Europe had a monopolized religious market, artificially constraining the options for individual religious consumption. Having only one food store in town is hardly a monopoly if the people of the town grow most of their own food.

In pre-modern Europe, localism and diverse popular religious practices produced a huge array of 'home-grown' religious options. There were sacred sites scattered throughout the local landscape (such as the St. Olav's spring in Luster County, Norway), and popular pilgrimages journeyed to more distant places of sacred power (such as the St. Olav pilgrimage across the mountains to Trondheim). People practiced rituals for blessing, protecting, healing, divining and prospering. Popular religion proffered ways of dealing with powerful emotions (for instance, 'wake-house' celebrations linked sexuality and death, grieving and exuberant laughter, singing and dancing). Popular religious elements so thoroughly overlapped official religion that no one felt the need to choose one *or* the other; diverse popular religious practices were simply different ways of being Christian. The Reformations did not make people 'more' religious than before. Rather, they urged people to become differently religious.

Several historians have depicted pre-Reformation popular Christianity as, not stagnant and monopolized by a single central authority, but rather as vibrant and very

---

7   José Casanova, personal communication.

much 'of the people' (Duffy 1992; Schmitt 1983). The religious practices of ordinary people in late medieval and early modern Europe were highly eclectic and diverse. For instance, an Irish farm family could call on numerous 'patron' saints (most of which were not recognized, much less canonized by the church in Rome) who had a special relationship with their community or locale. One saint might be known for help in childbirth, another for successful fishing, another for healing throat problems, another for protecting the crops, and so on. The farm wife would practice devotions to a different set of folk saints from those of her husband; she could pick and choose from a repertoire of religious practices, knowledge of which was learned in the socialization of women. Hers was a cultic pattern of commitment to the specific practices she used, because it was possible to be a committed Christian and still practice the cults of diverse saints, chosen eclectically (rather than authoritatively prescribed).[8]

How is the eclecticism of a pre-modern Irish farm family different from the contemporary eclecticism of someone who belongs to the Methodist church, while simultaneously practicing yoga, Zen meditation, and Native American purification rituals and New Age healing rituals? This is not merely a rhetorical question. We must confront the similarities of the enormous diversity and eclecticism of pre-modern and late modern religious practice; at the same time, we must understand how these practices are qualitatively different.

Class, gender (see Bynum 1986; Rublack 1996), localism (see Christian 1981) and cultural accretions account for enormous diversity of individual spiritual practice before the boundaries of religion and religiosity were redrawn. For example, the spirituality expressed in the fifteenth century by the elite and exclusively male Irish pilgrimage to Saint Patrick's Purgatory on Lough Derg was demonstrably different from the spirituality expressed in the same period by a rural shopkeeper and his wife 'making rounds' (a devotional ritual journey at a holy site) among the standing stones of Glencolumbkille in remote Donegal, or at the holy well on Scattery Island, or participating in the folk pilgrimage to Croagh Patrick (a ritual journey originally part of Lughnasa – a pre-Christian religious festival – but, later, a significant Christian devotion) (see French 1994; Connolly 1982; Carroll 1995; Nolan and Nolan 1989). Historians who started from church-defined conceptual boundaries have pejoratively dubbed cultural accretions (such as Christianizing a pagan holy site) as 'syncretism' (see Shaw and Stewart 1994; Stewart 1995), implying that it is possible to discern a pure Christian practice from one tainted by non-Christian influence. From an anthropological perspective, however, *all* cultures are syncretic and the existence of any truly pure tradition – whether linguistic, ethnic, national or religious – is highly improbable.

I find four key elements shared by both contemporary and earlier forms of popular spirituality.

---

8   For a clarification of this age of 'cult' and 'cultic modes of adherence', see McGuire (2001: 144–57).

Religious eclecticism

The first key element is religious eclecticism. Modern societies' norms of religious pluralism mean, not only that individuals have many options for their religious affiliation, but also that they can draw upon diverse spiritual traditions for their personal spirituality. For example, one woman (a full-time volunteer worker in a US Catholic peace-and-justice centre) said:

> I think it would be easier to change the color of my eyes or to get a new genetic code than it would be to stop being a Roman Catholic .... [but] I really set aside exclusive Roman Catholicism. ... I remained a religious woman and I have never stopped thinking of myself as a religious woman, ever, not for a moment. But I began to weave in understandings of a variety of different religious and ... spiritual traditions, and ... ways of behaving in the world – concrete actions. So the traditions that I looked most closely at were Native [American] traditions, the Jewish tradition (and I – because of intermarrying in my family – have a number of men and women who came out of a Jewish faith tradition) and Zen Buddhism and Tibetan Buddhism. (Quoted in McGuire and Spickard 2003: 143)

This quotation illustrates a widespread sense of spiritual autonomy, documented among a sizeable proportion of Americans (Hammond 1993; McGuire 2001; McNamara 1992; Roof 1993).

Many active church members feel free to choose components of their individual faith and practice, combining elements of their official religious tradition with other culturally available elements, such as Asian and Native American religions, New Age spirituality, popular religious practice, popular psychology, spirituality attuned to the feminist or ecology movements, aesthetic expressions, and ethnic sensibilities. Not unlike medieval popular religion, this eclecticism is often creative, using religious elements in ways unforeseen and uncontrolled by their traditions. For example, last summer one of my department colleagues and her sister made the pilgrimage to Santiago de Compostella in Spain. While they did it for personal spiritual growth, neither woman considers herself religious, much less Catholic. Similarly, modern youth (who neither know anything about Catholic liturgy nor understand Latin) can meditate to the strains of Gregorian chant, such as the popular recordings of the Anonymous Four, a quartet of women who sing chants written by the twelfth century mystic, Hildegard of Bingen. Many of these contemporary admirers consider Hildegard to be a proto-feminist. These examples illustrate some qualitative differences between the pre-modern and late modern religious eclecticism. Such patterns are worth studying in more detail.

Exactly *how* do people select, combine, and creatively transform elements of their individual religion? For example, interviewing San Antonio Latinas in their homes, my research assistant and I asked about their home altars in order to explore their personal spiritual practices. *Altares*, a part of Mexican-American popular religious expression, have been completely overlooked by previous researchers who focused on church-oriented religiosity. Latino Catholics typically appear to be less religious than 'Anglo' Catholics, because indices of religiosity have measured only behaviours such as Mass attendance and reception of Sacraments. But we need to examine all aspects of people's spirituality. There is every indication that, for both traditional Mexican-American women and for the thoroughly 'modern', educated women in our study, their spirituality is far more closely linked with spiritual practices and experiences in the context of home and family than with the ritual practices in the context of church, priest and public Sacraments. While they might tell a social survey interviewer 'the Mass is most important' (because they have learned that is what they ought to say), in practice, contemplation at their home altar may be central (Díaz-Stevens 1996).[9]

While our middle-class Latina respondents chose different elements for their home *altares* than would working-class women, they were as serious – and far more conscious – about the altar's place in their daily personal spiritual practice. Exemplifying the eclecticism of contemporary patterns of spirituality was one teacher (aged 38) who was working out of her home as an author and part-time consultant to a school district:

> She was raised Catholic and considers herself to be Catholic still, although she attends Mass only about every other month, usually to please her mother whom she visits several times a year. At the same time, however, she considers herself a very spiritual person, and she sets aside at least an hour daily for meditation –the first priority for her morning as soon as the children leave for nursery school. Her home altar held several traditional items, including a family heirloom cross brought from Mexico generations ago, pictures of several deceased or distant loved ones, 18 candles of all sizes, small bouquet of wildflowers, and an amulet (*milagro*) attached to the frame of one grandmother's photo (she explained it reminded her to work for the healing of her grandmother's arthritis). There were numerous and prominent non-traditional items as well: amethyst crystals used in healing meditations, oriental incense and Tibetan prayer bell, a large colorful triptych of Frida Kahlo, and a modern representation of the Virgin of Guadalupe as a young Chicana in running shoes, with her blue cape flowing behind her and her athlete's thighs flexed, as she runs vigorously along a road with the snake held confidently in her hand. (McGuire 1997: 4)

This description may convey the complexity of trying to identify and locate spirituality in contemporary America. Some aspects of her spirituality were clearly identified with Christian tradition, some represented her identification with her Mexican heritage, some symbolized her feminism, but none of these traditions or cultural heritages was used in a tradition-bound or deterministic way. Rather, in contemporary spirituality, traditional practices become cultural resources – along with cultural resources drawn from other spheres of life such as art – which individuals select and employ with relative autonomy (Beckford 1989).

---

9 I agree heartily with Michael Carroll (1996) that the 'theory of religion' developed by Rodney Stark and his associates reflects precisely this kind of androcentric and euro-American-centric bias; all of the indicators of religious participation, commitment or piety used by Stark are measures of official religion. Popular religious expression or domestic religious practices, characteristic particularly of women's lives simply do not register in such analyses.

Materiality

The second unifying factor is materiality. Another significant characteristic of contemporary patterns of spirituality is that they are markedly this-worldly, linked with materiality. One powerful linkage is their *attention to the human body*. Of course, since one of my studies focused on health and healing, I have heard literally hundreds of narratives describing spiritual meanings of health and illness, body rituals for healing and holiness, and a vast array of body symbols. Exemplifying this attention to the body, one man (aged 41), a member of a Buddhist-inspired meditation centre, explained:

> ... we all are given this body only for the purpose of transcending into another plane of awareness which does not require body and would not really function with one – you wouldn't want a body. ... You want to eventually transcend this bodily existence, because it is very limited ... but, in order to do that, *you must first have a body.* (Quoted in McGuire 1995: 25)

He proceeded to link this 'having' a body with attentiveness to one's body through meditation, body ritual (such as Tai Chi, yoga poses and breathing exercises), and being spiritually conscious about eating and other everyday body experiences. The goal of this attentiveness to body is deeper levels of consciousness, balance and harmony. According to such groups' beliefs, the physical performance of these body practices is an action which, itself, accomplishes what it represents. Body practices make body metaphor a reality (McGuire 1996).

Because of this attention to the body, some – but not all – contemporary patterns of spirituality involve noticeably *sensual* ways of being spiritual. For example, one meditation circle deliberately chose which sensual elements to stimulate their meditation each night. They often chose a colour in which parts of the room were draped, echoed in the colour of candles lit in the centre of the circle; sometimes they passed around crystals or other symbolic objects to hold and feel during meditation. They evoked the sense of smell with incense or an herbal oil diffuser; sounds, too, were chosen (for example, playing an audiotape of the ocean or forest bird calls, sounding Oriental prayer bells, chanting and silence were deliberate parts of their meditation). Not only senses, but also space and time were deliberately transformed with ritual and symbolic meanings. Participants moved their bodies into ritually created 'sacred' space; they participated in new calendric rituals; they learned ritual meanings to the timing of their breaths, the length of meditation, the position of their hands to concentrate healing energy where it was needed.

Another evidence of the linkage of materiality and spirituality is seen in the valorization of *mundane domestic materiality*, such as the processes of growing, cooking and eating food. For some – admittedly, a minority of respondents in these studies – these were important spiritual practices. One woman (aged 30), who devoted many hours a week to growing special foods for her family, said that this food's contribution to the family's health and well-being was not only because it was organic and full of nutrients, but more importantly because it literally conveyed emotional and spiritual, as well as physical, nurturance because of how it was grown and prepared. Two couples, who incorporated Buddhist meditative practices into their Christian spirituality, described their cooking and eating as 'mindful', and as 'being fully present'. One father, however, laughingly reminded me that they have had to work to preserve that spiritual practice now that they are parents of a 14-month-old baby. The mother added that, while cooking still has a spiritual quality, she hasn't found any way to make changing diapers or soothing a colicky baby into a mindful practice!

Pragmatic concerns

The third element that contemporary spirituality shares with its earlier counterparts is a focus on pragmatic concerns. Although most respondents have also spoken of abstract or even ethereal matters, on a day-to-day basis their spirituality is always linked with pragmatic and very human needs: dealing with a difficult teenager, getting a job, finding money to repair an old but necessary appliance, healing arthritic hips, recovering from a divorce, learning how to cope with stress. For this reason, many respondents were willing to try a number of approaches, and keep or discard them according to whether they 'work'. Nevertheless, their various spiritual approaches also affected how they understood the definition of 'work'. For example, one woman described successfully using the laying-on-of-hands to 'heal' her hopelessly scrambled checkbook. A young man said that, although he had not gotten the job that had been his object, he considered his chanting to have 'worked' when the couple in the next apartment gave him their washing machine the week before his old one broke.

In order for healing or other pragmatic goals to be realized, however, many respondents believed they needed to pray or meditate to discern what they really needed. One healing group emphasized that, in order to heal an illness, one must discover why it occurred, take responsibility for it, and learn and grow in the areas of one's life to which the illness 'points' or symbolically refers. Only then could the healing rituals work. For example, one woman (aged 37) explained:

> I hurt myself very badly skiing, and I was going through a situation in my life where I felt I could shoulder no more. And it was my shoulder that I tore up. It was very ironic the fact that it was my left shoulder. The left side is the female side .... I was having a lot of indecision about the female role in my life and I felt 'I can't take this any more!' It was like, 'I can't shoulder any more of this responsibility'. (Quoted in McGuire 1988: 149)

Thus, in her description of how her healing worked, this woman paid proportionately less attention to the emotional, spiritual and physical exercises she used after this realization until she was well. She was convinced her healing worked, because the new understanding of her problems 'fitted' and because she rapidly became better after she reached that understanding.

This pragmatic approach, thus, is one factor guiding the spiritual eclecticism of many contemporary seekers. In this respect, it is similar to pre-modern popular religion, where confidence in the effectiveness of a given faith healer, a particular pilgrimage, a holy well, a special devotional prayer, or petitions through a certain saint is always contingent. Popular religiosity requires no permanent commitment to a single way for meeting pragmatic needs; when one approach fails, others may be more effective.

Blurred boundaries between the sacred and profane

The fourth similarity between earlier forms of popular religiosity and these contemporary patterns is the blurred lines between sacred and profane spheres. Historically, the creation and protection of sacred/profane boundaries resulted in specific requirements of religious ritual purity, such as the need for Confession before Communion or the requirement of ritual purification ('churching') of women after childbirth before returning to participation in the Sacraments. Unlike official religions, however, popular religion blurs boundaries between sacred and profane.

To understand contemporary religious expressions – including popular religious expressions – we should begin by questioning whether the tidy dichotomy between sacred and profane (upon which the distinction of official religion is based) is an accurate or useful conception of religious life (Parker 1996). One study of religious beliefs and practices in pre-industrial Germany suggests, on the contrary, that the sacred is experienced from *within* the profane, within the very human context of the historical, cultural, and socially shared situation of believers (Scribner 1984: 17–18).

This generalization finds corroboration in an anthropological analysis of 'Los Pastores', a popular religious drama performed in the Mexican barrios of San Antonio, Texas, since 1913. As performed in the backyards and homes, this devotional ritual, its fulfillment of *promesas* and its surrounding festivities, especially the meal, is constitutive of communal sociability (Flores 1994). It is precisely because *el Niño Dios* (the Christchild) is experienced in the context of the profane – a neighbour's yard, where only last week the neighbourhood teenagers were fixing their low-rider cars – that it can speak profoundly to people's lives. Unlike official religion's segregation of 'sacred' space, time and ritual practices, in popular religious expression, *everyday* life is imbued with meaning through mundane human social practices, such as household calendric rituals or meaning-laden postures and gestures (see Bourdieu 1977; Hart 1992; Scribner 1984).

A similar blurring of lines between 'sacred' and 'profane' exists among some – but not all – contemporary spirituality groups. It is, in part, due to the fact that their symbolism and ritual have been consciously chosen and created, rather than received. There is relatively little mystification possible when the objects used in a ritual or set apart for their symbolism have been – in the recent memory of all present – drawn from ordinary household or garden objects. This experiencing the 'sacred' from within the 'profane' is also embraced and valued in much contemporary spirituality. While many respondents spoke of seeking occasional spiritual retreats from their mundane lives, most also described a goal of daily spiritual practice that meshed with the reality of their everyday, practical lives of work, family, domestic chores and ordinary interpersonal relationships.

Some Concluding Interpretations

My use of the term 'spirituality' is, in some respects, unfortunate. The concept has been taken over in recent years by the mass media and advertising campaigns, such that one can buy a huge range of goods and services to enhance one's spirituality. Thus, one use of rhetorics of spirituality is marketing commodities. Analyzing this commodification of spirituality is one worthwhile task for a sociology of spirituality, but the banality of the concept has made it extremely difficult to use analytically.

By 'spirituality' I wish to convey a sense of an individual *condition-in-process*, suggesting experience – unfinished, developing, and open.[10] I began using the term a number of years ago to distinguish my approach to individuals' religion from the dominant approach in the field. In contrast to 'religiosity', 'spirituality' might be used to refer to patterns of spiritual practices and experiences that comprise individual 'religion-as-lived' (Hall 1997). 'Religiosity' could still be useful for describing individual religion in terms of such characteristics as formal membership or identification, rates of participation in religious services, frequency of prayer and scripture reading, assent to church-prescribed creeds and moral prescriptions, and so on. It is extremely difficult, however, to operationalize such a notion of religiosity to apply to all Christian church-defined beliefs and practices, much less to all religions. Implicit in most sociological definitions of 'religiosity' is a heavy bias toward only certain Protestant patterns of religiosity (for instance, a devout, practicing Quaker would appear less 'religious' than an equally devout, practicing Southern Baptist). Thus, most twentieth century studies of individual religion have been ethnocentric, androcentric and Eurocentric.[11]

If we take a less biased perspective on both pre-modern and contemporary spirituality, we see some fascinating signs of religious vitality. While co-existing alongside traditional patterns of spirituality, contemporary patterns – at least among middle-class North Americans – appear to be characterized by emphasis on holism, tolerance and individual autonomy, and this-worldly orientation. Perhaps because spiritual practice is separated from its earlier institutional location, it has allowed a new 'space' for a spiritually based social activism, a linking of spirituality and materiality, addressing pragmatic concerns of everyday life, and celebrating the sacred from within the profane.

In what ways is this different from patterns of spirituality not controlled or promulgated by church-type institutions in earlier times? For example, is the mysticism or the popular religiosity of these late modern movements qualitatively different from those in late medieval or early modern times?

My hunch is that earlier patterns of spirituality – among uneducated laypersons, as well as among the religious of the middle and upper classes – were far more holistic, eclectic, and this-worldly than we have believed. Even among solid church-goers of

---

10   Compare Martin Marty's (1995) contrast of 'isms' and 'ities'.

11   This bias is a fatal flaw in the work of Rodney Stark and others who try to apply rational-choice economic models to the interpretation of religion in modern societies, because they utilize an ethnocentric operational definition to interpret (poorly understood) history. See Carroll (1966); Parker (1996); Parker (1998).

the eighteenth and nineteenth centuries, individual spiritual practices may have been far more diverse than we realize. Late modernity may be distinctive, however, in both institutional and individual *reflexivity*. Structural features of modern societies not only enable, but indeed compel members to construct personal narratives, to reflect on and consciously choose elements of their self-identity (Giddens 1991). Spiritual traditions, in this context, serve as cultural resources from which individuals may draw for their own bricolage of practices (Beckford 1989).

Despite all the emphasis on individualism and autonomy, however, many respondents in these studies emphasized communal support and experiencing the sacred in communal contexts. What does it mean when, in the face of modern rationality and the legacy of Cartesian dualism, we hear people describing spiritual lives of profound interconnectedness and experiential intersubjectivity? My hunch is that these small groups where people find, not only social support, but indeed experiential confirmation and communion in their spiritual journeys, are important locations of spirituality in modern societies. Partly because we do not yet have the language or conceptual apparatus for refining our understanding of spirituality (McGuire 1996), sociologists must – for now – end in a trail of unanswered questions. It is, however, a promising path for future research. We need to develop more theoretically sophisticated and methodologically precise research to refine any sociology of spirituality. Survey and other quantitative approaches are not well-suited to the task (as Luckmann pointed out 25 years ago), but much qualitative research is far too unsystematic and imprecise and shallow.

We need to develop a better way of conceptualizing individual religion, in all its complexity. We should tap, not merely individual beliefs, opinions, attitudes, values and knowledge, but also individual practices, religious experience, emotional involvement, physical involvement, senses (such as sense of time and space), and so on. We must try to understand more deeply how personal religious experience and expression is linked with collective experience and expression – especially in the late modern context where people participate in multiple and often contradictory communities or impersonal collectivities. Thus framed, a sociology of spirituality can contribute to our understanding of religion – public and private – and social change in the twenty-first century.

References

Anderson, B. (1993) *Imagined Communities*, London: Verso.

Beckford, J. (1989) *Religion and Advanced Industrial Society*, London: Unwin Hyman.

Bourdieu, P. (1977) *Outline of a Theory of Practice*, New York: Cambridge University Press.

Burke, P. (1978) *Popular Culture in Early Modern Europe*, London: Temple Smith.

Bynum, C.W. (1986) '" ... And woman his humanity": Female imagery in the religious writing of the later Middle Ages', in C.W. Bynum, S. Harrell, and P. Richman (eds) *Gender and Religion: On the Complexity of Symbols*, Boston: Beacon, pp. 257–88.

Carroll, M.P. (1966) 'Stark Realities and Eurocentric/Androcentric Bias in the Sociology of Religion', *Sociology of Religion*, 57, 3: 225–39.

—— (1995) 'Rethinking Popular Catholicism in Pre-famine Ireland', *Journal for the Scientific Study of Religion*, 34, 3: 354–65.

Christian, W. (1981) *Local Religion in Sixteenth Century Spain*, Princeton: Princeton University Press.

Connolly, S.J. (1982) *Priests and People in Pre-famine Ireland, 1780–1845*, Dublin: Gill and Macmillan.

—— (1995a) *Women in the Presence: Constructing Community and Seeking Spirituality in Mainline Protestantism*, Philadelphia: University of Pennsylvania.

Davie, J.S. (1995b) 'Speaking without Tongues: Women's Communicative Styles in Contemporary Mainline Protestantism', presented to the Society for the Scientific Study of Religion.

Díaz-Stevens, A.M. (1996) 'Latino Popular Religiosity and Communitarian Spirituality', presented to PARAL (Program for the Analysis of Religion among Latinos).

Dubisch, J. (1990) 'Pilgrimage and popular religion at a Greek holy shrine', in E. Badone (ed.) *Religious Orthodoxy and Popular Faith in European Society*, Princeton: Princeton University Press, pp. 113–39.

Duffy, E. (1992) *The Stripping of the Altars: Traditional Religion in England, 1400–1580*, New Haven, CT: Yale University Press.

Flores, R.R. (1994) 'Para el Niño Dios: Sociability and commemorative sentiment in popular religious practice', in A.M. Stevens-Arroyo and A.M. Díaz-Stevens (eds) *An Enduring Flame: Studies on Latino Popular Religiosity*, New York: PARAL, City University of New York, pp. 171–90.

French, D.R. (1994) 'Ritual, Gender and Power Strategies: Male Pilgrimage to Saint Patrick's Purgatory', *Religion*, 24: 103–15.

Giddens, A. (1991) *Modern and Self-Identity: Self and Society in the Late Modern Age*, Stanford, Ca: Stanford University Press.

Ginzburg, C. (1983) *The Night Battles: Witchcraft and Agrarian Cults in the Sixteenth and Seventeenth Centuries* (translated by J. and A. Tedeschi), Baltimore: The Johns Hopkins University Press.

Hall, D. (ed.) (1997) *Lived Religion in America*, Princeton: Princeton University Press.

Hammond, P.E. (1993) *Religion and Personal Autonomy: The Third Disestablishment in America*, Columbia, S.C.: University of South Carolina Press.

Hart, L.K. (1992) *Time, Religion and Social Experience in Rural Greece*, Lanham, Md.: Rowman & Littlefield.

Kokosalakis, N. (1987) 'The political significance of popular religion in Greece', *Archives des Sciences Sociales des Religions*, 64: 37–52.

Luckmann, T. (1967) *The Invisible Religion: The Problem of Religion in Modern Society*, New York: Macmillan.

—— (1973) 'Comments on the Laeyendecker et al. research proposal', in *The Contemporary Metamorphosis of Religion: Acts of the 12th Conference Internationale de Sociologie Religieuse*, Lille, France: CISR, pp. 55–68.

—— (1990) 'Shrinking transcendence, expanding religion?', *Sociological Analysis*, 50, 2: 127–38.

Martin, J. (1987) 'Popular culture and the shaping of popular heresy in Renaissance Venice', in S. Haliczer (ed.) *Inquisition and Society in Early Modern Europe*, Totowa, NJ: Barnes & Noble Books, pp. 113–28.

—— (1993) 'Theories of Practice: Inquisition and the discovery of religion', unpublished paper presented to Trinity University Humanities Symposium.

Marty, M. (1995) 'Materialism and spirituality in American religion', in R. Wuthrow (ed.) *Rethinking Materialism*, Grand Rapids, MI: Wm. B. Eerdmans Publ., pp. 237–53.

McGuire, M.B. with the assistance of Kantor, D. (1988) *Ritual Healing in Suburban America*, New Brunswick, NJ: Rutgers University Press.

—— (1995) Alternative therapies: The meaning of bodies in knowledge and practice', in H. Johannessen, S.G. Olesen, and J.O. Andersen, eds. *Studies in Alternative Therapy 2: Body and Nature*, Odense: Odense University Press, pp. 15–32.

—— (1996) 'Religion and healing the Mind/Body/Self', *Social Compass: International Review of Sociology of Religion*, 43, 1: 101–16.

—— (1997) Mapping contemporary American spirituality: a sociological perspective,' *Christian Spirituality Bulletin: Journal of the Society for the Study of Christian Spirituality*, 5, 1: 1–8.

—— (2000) 'Toward a Sociology of Spirituality: Individual Religion in Social/ Historical Context', in *Tidsskrift for Kirke, Religion, og Samfunn* (now entitled *Nordic Journal of Religion and Society*),13: 99–111.

—— (2001) *Religion: The Social Context*, Belmont, CA: Wadsworth.

McGuire, M.B. and Spickard, J.V. (2003) 'Narratives of Commitment: Social Activism and Radical Catholic Identity', *Temenos: Studies in Comparative Religion*, 37–38: 131–50.

McNamara, P. (1992) *Conscience First, Tradition Second: A Study of Young American Catholics,* Albany: State University of New York Press.

Muir, E. (1997) *Ritual in Early Modern Europe*, Cambridge: Cambridge University Press.

Nolan, M.L. and Nolan, S. (1989) *Christian Pilgrimage in Modern Western Europe*, Chapel Hill: University of North Carolina.

Parker, C. (1996) *Popular Religion and Modernization in Latin America: A Different Logic*, Maryknoll, NY: Orbis.

—— (1998) 'Modern popular religion: A complex object for study of Sociology', *International Sociology*, 13, 2: 195–212.

Roof, W.C. (1993) *A Generation of Seekers*, San Francisco: Harper San Francisco.

—— (1999) *Spiritual Marketplace: Baby Boomers and the Remaking of American Religion*, Princeton: Princeton University Press.

Rublack, U. (1996) 'Female spirituality and the infant Jesus in late medieval Dominican convents', in B. Scribner and T. Johnson (eds) *Popular Religion in Germany and Central Europe, 1400–1800*, New York: St. Martin's Press, pp. 16–37.

Schmitt, J.C. (1983) *The Holy Greyhound: Guinefort, Healer of Children since the Thirteenth Century*, Cambridge: Cambridge University Press.

Scribner, B. (1984) 'Cosmic order and daily life: Sacred and secular in pre-industrial German society', in K. von Greyers (ed.) *Religion and Society in Early Modern Europe, 1500–1800*, London: Allen & Unwin, pp. 17–32

Shaw, R. and Stewart, C. (eds) (1994) *Syncretism/Anti-syncretism: The Politics of Religious Synthesis*, London: Routledge.

Spickard, J.V. (1996) 'Life on two levels', a report on an Episcopal congregation in San Antonio, Texas, prepared for the 'Spiritually Vital Episcopal Congregations' Project, Nancy Ammerman, principal investigator.

Stark R. and Iannaccone, L. (1994) 'A supply-side reinterpretation of the 'secularization' of Europe', *Journal for the Scientific Study of Religion*, 33: 230–52.

Stewart, C. (1995) 'Relocating syncretism in social science discourse', in G. Aijmer (ed.) *Syncretism and the Commerce of Symbols*, Goteborg, Sweden: Goteborg University/IASSA, pp. 13–37.

Tedeschi, J. (1991) *The Prosecution of Heresy: Collected Studies on the Inquisition in Early Modern Italy*, Binghamton, NY: Center for Medieval and Renaissance Studies.

Appendix
A list of James A. Beckford's
most important works

Single-Authored Publications by James A. Beckford

(1972) A sociological study of Jehovah's Witnesses in Britain, University of Reading. PhD

(1972) 'The embryonic stage of a religious sect's development: the Jehovah's Witnesses', *A Sociological Yearbook of Religion in Britain*, 5: 11–32.

(1973a) 'A Korean evangelistic movement in the West', *The Contemporary Metamorphosis of Religion?* The Hague: Conférence internationale de la Sociologie des Religions: 319–35.

(1973b) *Religious Organization*, The Hague: Mouton.

(1975a) 'Organization, ideology and recruitment: the structure of the Watchtower movement', *Sociological Review*, 23, 4: 893–909.

(1975b) *The Trumpet of Prophecy: A Sociological Study of Jehovah's Witnesses*, Oxford: Blackwell.

(1976a) 'New wine in new bottles: a departure from the church-sect conceptual tradition', *Social Compass*, 23, 1: 71–85.

(1976b) 'Structural dependence in religious organizations: from "skid road" to Watch Tower', *Journal for the Scientific Study of Religion*, 15, 2: 169–75.

(1977a) 'The explanation of religious movements', *International Social Science Journal*, 29, 2: 235–49.

(1977b) 'The Watchtower movement world-wide', *Social Compass*, 24, 1: 5–31.

(1978a) 'Accounting for conversion', *British Journal of Sociology*, 29, 2: 249–62.

(1978b) 'Cults and cures', *Japanese Journal of Religious Studies*, 5, 4: 225–57.

(1978c) 'Sociological stereotypes of the religious sect', *Sociological Review*, 26, 1: 109–23.

(1978d) 'Through the looking-glass and out the other side: withdrawal from the Rev. Moons Unification Church', *Archives de Sciences Sociales des Religions*, 45, 1: 95–116.

(1979) 'Politics and the anti-cult movement', *Annual Review of the Social Sciences of Religion*, 3: 169–90.

(1981a) *Coming out of a cult*, Conference of the International Society for the Sociology of Religion, Lausanne.

(1981b) 'Cults, controversy and control: a comparative analysis of the problems posed by new religious movements in the Federal Republic of Germany and France', *Sociological Analysis*, 42, 3: 249–64.

(1981c) 'Functionalism and ethics in sociology: the relationship between "ought" and "function"', *Annual Review of the Social Sciences of Religion*, 5: 106–35.

(1981d) 'A typology of family responses to a new religious movement', *Marriage and Family Review*, 4, 3–4: 41–55.

(1982a) *The articulation of a classical sociological problematic with a modern social problem: religious movements and modes of social insertion*, Annual meeting of the Society for the Scientific Study of Religion, Providence, RI.

(1982b) 'Beyond the pale: cults, culture and conflict', in E. Barker (ed.) *New Religious Movements: A Perspective for Understanding Society*, New York: Edwin Mellen Press, pp. 284–301

(1983a) '"Brainwashing" and "deprogramming" in Britain: the social sources of anti-cult sentiment', in D.G. Bromley and J.T. Richardson (eds) *The Brainwashing and Deprogramming Controversy*, New York: Edwin Mellen Press, pp. 122–38.

(1983a) 'The cult problem in five countries: the social construction of religious controversy' in E. Barker (ed.) *Of Gods and Men: New Religious Movements in the West*, Macon, GA: Mercer University Press, pp. 195–214.

(1983b) 'The public response to new religious movements in Britain', *Social Compass*, 30, 1: 49–62.

(1983c) 'The restoration of "power" to the sociology of religion', *Sociological Analysis*, 44, 1: 11–31.

(1983d) 'Some questions about the relationship between scholars and the new religious movements', *Sociological Analysis*, 44, 3: 189–96.

(1983e) *The state and control of new religious movements*, 17th International Conference for the Sociology of Religion, London, CISR.

(1983f) 'Talking of apostasy, or telling tales and "telling" tales', in N. Gilbert and P. Abell (eds) *Accounts and Action*, Aldershot: Gower, pp. 77–97.

(1984a) 'Holistic imagery and ethics in new religious and healing movements', *Social Compass*, 31, 2–3: 259–272.

(1984b) 'Religious organization: a survey of some recent publications', *Les Archives de Sciences Sociales des Religions*, 57, 1: 83–102.

(1985a) *Cult Controversies: The Societal Response to New Religious Movements*, London, Tavistock.

(1985b) 'The insulation and isolation of the sociology of religion', *Sociological Analysis*, 46, 4: 347–54.

(1985c) 'Religious organization', in P.E. Hammond (ed.) *The Sacred in a Secular Age*, Berkeley, CA: University of California Press, pp. 125–38.

(1985d) 'The world images of new religious and healing movements' in R.K. Jones (ed.) *Sickness and Sectarianism*, Aldershot: Gower, pp. 72–93.

(ed.) (1986a) *New Religious Movements and Rapid Social Change*, London: Sage.

(1986b) *The role of the state and government in the management of controversial new religious movements*, Religion and the State: the struggle for legitimacy and power, Council on religion and international affairs, New York.

(1989a) 'Politics and religion in England and Wales', *Daedalus*, 120, 3: 179–201.

(1989b) *Religion and Advanced Industrial Society*, London: Unwin-Hyman.

(ed.) (1990a) *Nuove forme del sacro: Movimenti religiosi e mutamento sociale*, Bologna: Il Mulino.

(1990b) 'The sociology of religion 1945–1989', *Social Compass*, 37, 1: 45–64.

(1990c) 'The sociology of religion and social problems', *Sociological Analysis*, 51: 1–14.

(1991a) 'Great Britain: voluntarism and sectional interests', in R. Wuthnow (ed.) *Between States and Markets: The Voluntary Sector in Comparative Perspective*, Princeton, NJ: Princeton University Press, pp. 30–63.

(1991b) *Religione e società industriale avanzata*. Rome: Borla.

(1992a) 'Religion, Modernity and Postmodernity', in B.R. Wilson (ed.) *Religion: Contemporary Issues*, London: Bellew, pp. 11–23.

(1992b) 'Religione e società nel Regno Unito', *La religione degli Europei*. aa.vv. Torino, Edizione della Fondazione Giovanni Agnelli, pp. 217–89.

(1992c) 'Tendenze e prospettive', *La religione degli Europei*, aa.vv. Torino, Edizione della Fondazione Giovanni Agnelli, pp. 485–502.

(1993) 'States, governments and the management of controversial new religious movements', in E. Barker, J.A. Beckford and K. Dobbelaere (eds) *Secularization, Rationalism and Sectarianism*, Oxford: Clarendon Press, pp. 125–43.

(1994a) 'Final reflections', in J. Fulton and P. Gee (eds) *Religion in Contemporary Europe*, Lewiston, NY: Edwin Mellen Press, pp. 160–68.

(1994b) 'The mass media and new religious movements', *ISKCON Communications Journal*, 4: 17–24.

(1994c) 'The media and new religious movements', in J.R. Lewis (ed.) *From the Ashes: Making Sense of Waco*, Lenham, MD: Rowman & Littlefield, pp. 143–8.

(1995) 'Cults, conflicts and journalists', in R. Towler (ed.) *New Religions and the New Europe*, Aarhus: Aarhus University Press, pp. 99–111.

(1996a) 'Postmodernity, high modernity and new modernity: three concepts in search of religion', in K. Flanagan and P. Jupp (eds) *Postmodernity, Sociology and Religion*, London: Macmillan, pp. 30–47.

(1996b) *Report on controversial religious groups in the UK*, Coventry: University of Warwick, Department of Sociology, pp. 1–24.

(1997) 'The transmission of religion in prison', *Recherches sociologiques*, 28, 3: 101–12.

(1998a) '"Cult" controversies in three European countries', *Journal of Oriental Studies*, 8: 174–84.

(1998b) 'Ethnic and religious diversity among prisoners: the politics of prison chaplaincy', *Social Compass*, 45, 2: 265–77.

(1998c) 'Re-enchantment and modernisation: the recent writings of Alain Touraine', *European Journal of Sociology*, 1, 2: 194–203.

(1998d) 'Secularization and social solidarity: a social constructionist view', in R. Laermans, B.R. Wilson and J. Billiet (eds) *Secularization and Social Integration*, Leuven: Leuven University Press, pp. 141–58.

(1998e) 'Three paradoxes in the relations between religion and politics in an English city', *Review of Religious Research*, 39, 4: 363–78.

(1999a) 'The management of religious diversity in England and Wales with special reference to prison chaplaincy', *MOST Journal on Multicultural Societies*, 1, 2: 10 pp.

(1999b) 'The mass media and new religious movements', in B.R. Wilson and J. Cresswell (eds) *New Religious Movements: Challenge and Response*, London: Routledge, pp. 103–19.

(1999c) 'The politics of defining religion in secular society: from a taken-for-granted institution to a contested resource', in J.G. Platvoet and A.L. Molendijk (eds) *The Pragmatics of Defining Religion: Contexts, Concepts and Conflicts*, Leiden: E.J. Brill, pp. 23–40.

(1999d) 'Rational choice theory and prison chaplaincy: the chaplain's dilemma', *British Journal of Sociology*, 50, 4: 671–85.

(1999e) 'Social justice and religion in prison: the case of England and Wales', *Social Justice Research*, 12, 4: 315–22.

(2000a) 'Religious movements and globalization', in R. Cohen and S. Rai (eds) *Global Social Movements*, London: Athlone Press, pp. 165–83.

(2000b) '"Start together and finish together": shifts in the premises and paradigms underlying the scientific study of religion', *Journal for the Scientific Study of Religion*, 39, 4: 481–95.

(2000c) 'When the battle's lost and won', in M.S. Archer and J.Q. Tritter (eds) *Rational Choice Theory: Resisting Colonization*, London: Routledge, pp. 219–33.

(2001a) 'Choosing rationality', *Research in the Social Scientific Study of Religion*, 12: 1–22.

(2001b) 'The continuum between 'cults' and 'normal' religion', in P. Côté (ed.) *Chercheurs de Dieux dans l'Espace Public*, Ottawa: Les Presses de l'Université d'Ottawa, pp. 11–20.

(2001c) 'Developments in the sociology of religion', in R.G. Burgess and A. Murcott (eds) *Developments in Sociology*, London: Prentice-Hall, pp. 143–63.

(2001d) 'Doing time: space, time, religious diversity and the sacred in prisons', *International Review of Sociology*, 11, 3: 371–82.

(2001e) '"Dystopia" and the reaction to new religious movements in France' – Unpublished paper presented at the annual meeting of the Society for the Scientific Study of Religion, Columbus, OH October

(2001f) 'Perspectives sociologiques sur les relations entre modernité et globalisation religieuse', in J.-P. Bastian, F. Champion and K. Rousselet (eds) *La Globalisation du Religieux*, Paris: L'Harmattan, pp. 273–82.

(2001g) 'Social movements as free-floating religious phenomena', in R.K. Fenn (ed.) *The Blackwell Companion to Sociology of Religion*, Oxford: Blackwell, pp. 229–48.

(2001h) 'The tension between an Established Church and equal opportunities in religion: the case of prison chaplaincy', in P.D. Nesbitt (ed.) *Religion and Social Policy*, Walnut Creek, CA: Alta Mira Press, pp. 29–53.

(2002) 'Banal discrimination: equality of respect for beliefs and worldviews in the UK', in D.H. Davis and G. Besier (eds) *International Perspectives on Freedom and Equality of Religious Belief*, Waco, Texas: J.M. Dawson Institute of Church-State Studies, pp. 25–41.

(2003a) 'Sans l'état pas de transmission de la religion? Le cas de l'Angleterre', *Archives de Sciences Sociales des Religions*, 121: 57–67.

(2003b) *Social Theory and Religion*, Cambridge: Cambridge University Press.

(2004a) 'Contemporary configurations of religion', in O.G. Winsnes (ed.) *Contemporary Religion and Church*, Oslo: Tapir Akademisk Forlag, pp. 9–26.

(2004b) "Laïcité', 'dystopia', and the reaction to new religious movements in France', in J.T. Richardson (ed.) *Regulating Religion. Case Studies from around the Globe*, New York: Kluwer/Plenum, pp. 27–40.

(2004c) 'New religious movements and globalization', in P. Lucas and T. Robbins (eds) *New Religious Movements in the 21st Century*, New York: Routledge, pp. 253–63.

(2004d) 'Religion and postmodernity', *Sociology Review*, 14, 2: 2–4.

(2004e) 'Social justice and minority religions in prison: the case of England and Wales' in J.T. Richardson (ed.) *Regulating Religion. Case Studies from around the Globe*, New York: Kluwer/Plenum, pp. 237–45.

(2005a) 'La politique du gouvernement travailliste en matière d'enseignement religieux', in J.-P. Willaime and S. Mathieu (eds) *Des Maîtres et des Dieux*, Paris: Belin, pp. 113–20.

(2005b) 'Muslims in the prisons of Britain and France', *Journal of Contemporary European Studies*, 13, 3: 287–97.

(2006a) 'Le communità religiose e lo stato britannico', *Democrazia e Diritto*, 44, 2: 124–40.

(2006b) 'A minimalist sociology of religion', in J. A. Beckford and J. Walliss (eds) *Theorising Religion. Classical and Contemporary Debates*, Aldershot: Ashgate, pp. 183–97

(2006c) 'The sociology of religion in the Nordic region as seen from the other side of the North Sea', *Nordic Journal of Religion and Society*, 19, 1: 1–11.

(2007) 'Prison chaplaincy in England and Wales – from Anglican brokerage to a multi-faith approach', in M. Koenig and P. De Guchteneire (eds) *Democracy and Human Rights in Multicultural Societies*, Paris and Aldershot: UNESCO and Ashgate, pp. 267–82.

Co-authored and co-edited publications

Beckford, J.A. and J.T. Richardson (1983) 'A bibliography of social scientific studies of new religious movements', *Social Compass*, 30, 1: 111–35.

Hampshire, A.P. and J.A. Beckford (1983) 'Religious sects and the concept of deviance: the Moonies and the Mormons', *British Journal of Sociology*, 34, 2: 208–29.

Beckford, J.A. and M. Levasseur (1986) 'New religious movements in Western Europe', in J.A. Beckford (ed.) *New Religious Movements and Rapid Social Change*, Sage, pp. 29–54.

Beckford, J.A. and M.A. Cole (1988) 'British and American responses to new religious movements', *Bulletin of the John Rylands University Library of Manchester*, 70, 3: 209–25.

Beckford, J.A. and T. Luckmann (eds) (1989) 'The Changing Face of Religion', *Sage Studies in International Sociology*, London: Sage.

Barker, E., J.A. Beckford and K. Dobbelaere (eds) (1993a) *Secularization, Rationalism and Sectarianism*, Oxford: Clarendon Press.

Robbins, T. and J.A. Beckford (1993b) 'Religious movements and church-state issues', in D.G. Bromley and J.K. Hadden (eds) *The Handbook on Cults and Sects in America (Part A)*, Greenwich, CT: JAI Press, pp. 199–218.

Beckford, J.A. and A. Suzara (1994) 'A new religious and healing movement in the Philippines', *Religion*, 24, 2: 117–42.

Beckford, J.A. and S. Gilliat (1995) 'The Church of England and other faith communities in a multi-faith society', *World Faith Encounter*, 10: 59–64.

—— (1996) *The Church of England and other faiths in a multi-faith society*, University of Warwick.

—— (1998) *Religion in Prison. Equal Rites in a Multi-Faith Society*, Cambridge: Cambridge University Press.

Ball, W. and J.A. Beckford (1997) 'Religion, education and city politics: A case study of community mobilization', in N. Jewson and S. MacGregor (eds) *Transforming Cities: Contested Governance and New Spatial Divisions*, London: Routledge, pp. 193–204.

Hedges, E. and J.A. Beckford (1999) 'Holism, healing and the New Age', in S. Sutcliffe and M. Bowman (eds) *Beyond the New Age: Alternative Spirituality in Britain*, Edinburgh: Edinburgh University Press, pp. 169–87.

Beckford, J.A. and S. Gilliat-Ray (1999) 'Prison chaplaincy', in S. Horner and M. Stacey (eds) *Incarceration Humane and Inhumane. Human Values and Health Care in British Prisons*, London: The Nuffield Trust, pp. 49–64.

Beckford, J.A. and J.T. Richardson (eds) (2003) *Challenging Religion: Essays in Honour of Eileen Barker*, London: Routledge.

Beckford, J.A., D. Joly, and F. Khosrokhavar (2005) *Muslims in Prison: Challenge and Change in Britain and France*, Basingstoke: Palgrave.

Beckford, J.A., D. Joly and F. Khosrokhavar (2005) *Les musulmans en prison en Grande Bretagne et en France*, Louvain: Presses Universitaires de Louvain.

Beckford, J.A. and J. Walliss (eds) (2006) *Theorising Religion. Classical and Contemporary Debates*, Aldershot: Ashgate.

Joly, D. and J.A. Beckford (2006) '"Race' relations and discrimination in prison: the case of Muslims in France and Britain', *Journal of Immigrant & Refugee Studies*, 4, 2: 1–30.

Beckford, J.A. and N.J. Demerath III (eds) (2007) *The SAGE Handbook of the Sociology of Religion*, London: Sage.

Beckford, J.A. and D. Joly (2007) 'Societal framework in Britain and France: Muslims in prison' in C. Bertossi (ed.) *European Anti-Discrimination and the Politics of Citizenship. Britain and France*, Basingstoke: Palgrave Macmillan, pp. 171–92.

Beckford, J.A. and J.T. Richardson (2007) 'Religion and Regulation' in J.A. Beckford and N.J. Demerath III (eds) *The SAGE Handbook of the Sociology of Religion*, London: Sage Publications, pp. 396–418.

Index